Przemysław Skulski

Colour illustrations by
Andrzej M. Olejniczak

Reggiane RE 2001, RE 2005 and Beyond

STRATUS

Published in Poland in 2024
by STRATUS s.j.
ul. Żeromskiego 6A,
27-600 Sandomierz, Poland
e-mail: office@mmpbooks.biz
as
MMPBooks,

http://www.mmpbooks.biz

ISBN
978-83-67227-63-6

Editor in chief
Roger Wallsgrove

Editorial Team
Robert Pęczkowski
Artur Juszczak

Colour Plates
Andrzej M. Olejniczak

Scale Plans
Dariusz Karnas

DTP
Stratus sp.j.

Printed by
Wydawnictwo
Diecezjalne i Drukarnia
w Sandomierzu
www.wds.pl

PRINTED IN POLAND

Table of Contents

Introduction ... 3
Reggiane RE 2001 *Ariete* I ... 4
Mass Production ... 13
Versions, Prototypes, and Projects ... 17
RE 2001 (*Caccia Diurni*) ... 17
RE 2001 *Cinematografico and Fotografico* ... 17
RE 2001 CN (*Caccia Notturna*) ... 17
RE 2001 CB (*Caccia Bombardiere*) ... 19
RE 2001 GV ... 19
RE 2001 OR ... 20
RE 2001bis ... 21
RE 2001 *Delta* ... 21
RE 2001 *Ligneo* ... 26
RE 2001 G ... 26
RE 2001 H ... 26
RE 2001 DB 605 ... 26
RE 2001 *Scorta* ... 26
Reggiane RE 2001 in Combat ... 33
The Regia Aeronautica ... 33
Aeronautica Cobelligerante Italiana and *Aeronautica Militare* ... 57
Aviazione Nationale Repubblicana ... 58
Luftwaffe ... 60
Camouflage and markings ... 61
RE 2005 *Sagittario* ... 78
Mass Production ... 85
Projects ... 88
RE 2005 *Bifusoliera* ... 88
RE 2005 *Lignea* ... 88
RE 2005 *Navale* ... 88
RE 2205 – Combat Deployment ... 89
Regia Aeronautica ... 89
Aeronautica Cobelligerante Italiana and Aeronautica Militare ... 95
USAAF ... 95
Aeronautica Nazionale Repubblicana ... 95
Luftwaffe ... 96
Camouflage and Markins ... 98
Reggiane's Development Projects ... 106
RE 2004 ... 106
RE 2006 ... 106
Jet-Powered Reggiane ... 107
Post-War Developments by Longhi ... 107
RE 2001 (day fighter) Technical Description ... 108
RE 2005 *Serie 0* Technical Description ... 138
RE 2001 Recovery ... 160
RE 2001 (M.M.08071) Restoration ... 166
RE 2005 museum photos ... 173

Acknowledgements

The author would like to thank the following persons and institutions for their assistance in their work on the book: George Papadimitriou, Saverio Radogna, Fabrizio Sanetti *(Museo Storico Dell'Aeronautica Militare* Italiana).

The author would like to thank the following persons and institutions for providing photographs: George Papadimitriou, CMPR Ravenna, Gruppo Amici Velivoli Storici, Instituto LUCE, *Museo Storico Dell'Aeronautica Militare Italiana*, *Stato Maggiore Aeronautica*.

Introduction

In the first part of the publication dedicated to Reggiane aircraft, there was a discussion of the RE 2000 and RE 2002 fighters, as well as the RE 2003 reconnaissance aircraft. What these machines had in common was that they were powered by radial engines. The second part of the Reggiane aircraft monograph is devoted to the RE 2001 and RE 2005 fighter aircraft, which were powered by inline engines. The publication also pays attention to unrealized projects such as RE 2004 and RE 2006, as well as plans for building jet-powered aircraft.

During the prototype research of the RE 2000 *Falco* fighter aircraft, the designers at Reggiane began considering the possibility of using the German Daimler-Benz DB 601A-1 inline engine as propulsion (produced in Italy under license as Alfa Romeo R.A. 1000 R.C. 41-I "Monsone"). Besides offering more power, the German power unit also provided more favorable aerodynamics for the airframe, which could enhance the fighter's performance. Another argument in its favor was that it was a proven design, guaranteeing reliability under operational conditions. The combination of the German engine with the Italian airframe led to the creation of the RE 2001 *Ariete I*. Although the Reggiane fighter was well-liked by pilots, it didn't mean it met the demands of the battlefield. During combat operations, it turned out that the RE 2001's performance at high altitudes was significantly inferior to that of enemy fighters. This forced Italian pilots to engage in battles at medium and low altitudes. A major flaw was also its weak armament, insufficient in confrontations with Allied bombers and fighters. However, the RE 2001's versatility was a notable advantage. The aircraft was developed into versions including a night fighter, fighter-bomber, torpedo bomber, and reconnaissance model.

In 1941, work began at the Reggiane factory on a developmental version of the RE 2001, powered by the FIAT R.A. 1050 R.C. 58-I "Tifone" engine (the Italian licensed production of the German Daimler-Benz DB 605A). This led to the creation of the Reggiane RE 2005, considered by some historians and aviation enthusiasts as the best, and certainly the most elegant, Italian fighter of the World War II era. Indeed, the aircraft, named *Sagittario* (Archer), boasted a refined silhouette. It was also a plane equipped with sufficiently powerful armament to pose a serious threat to Allied aviation. However, its performance was inferior compared to other Italian designs like the Macchi C.205V *Veltro* and the FIAT G.55 *Centauro*. During operation, issues emerged with the landing gear, and high-speed dives caused vibrations in the rear part of the fuselage.

Indeed, perhaps the most significant problem with the Reggiane fighters was that, under wartime conditions, the Italian aviation industry was unable to produce either the *Ariete I* or the *Sagittario* in the quantities needed by the Italian air force. Consequently, both designs couldn't significantly influence the course of the battles. A fundamental factor contributing to the limited production of these aircraft was problems with the inline engines. Power units designed in Italy proved unreliable, making the acquisition of licenses for the production of German Daimler-Benz engines a necessity. However, even in such circumstances, the supply of engines was insufficient.

Subsequent designs worked on at the Reggiane factories reached the stage of unflown prototypes (RE 2006) or conceptual works (RE 2004). Ideas for using mixed propulsion, known as motorjet, on Reggiane fighters (RE 2005 SF/R and RE 2006 SF/R) also never came to fruition. Even more mysterious are the jet projects of Reggiane. To this day, it remains unclear whether the RE 2007 project actually existed. In contrast, the Caproni-Reggiane Ca 2008 refers to a project developed in the post-war period.

The end of World War II marked the cessation of Reggiane's association with aviation. The 1950s and 1960s were a tumultuous period of restructuring for the company. After being forcibly dissolved, the company "rebirthed," focusing on the production of railway rolling stock and equipment for the agricultural-food industry. However, the real renaissance of the company began with the construction of port cranes, which gained international acclaim. In the last thirty years, the company has undergone several ownership transformations, also changing its production profile (currently specializing in the production of cranes and container handling trucks).

Reggiane RE 2001 *Ariete I*

During the prototype testing of the RE 2000 *Falco* fighter aircraft, a proposal emerged to employ the German Daimler-Benz DB 601A-1 inline engine, boasting a maximum output of 1175 HP, for its propulsion. This engine, surpassing the radial engine in power, brought the dual benefits of enhanced reliability and improved aerodynamics to the aircraft, potentially elevating its performance.

The design plans for the RE 2000 fighter with the DB 601A-1 engine began in July 1939. In the autumn, construction of a wooden mock-up of the aircraft began, into which an original German engine was installed. It was assumed that the future propulsion of the aircraft would be a licensed version of this power unit produced in Italy under the name Alfa Romeo R.A. 1000 R.C. 41-Ia 'Monsone'.

At the beginning of 1940, construction commenced on a prototype aircraft designated as RE 2001. This aircraft was assigned the military number M.M.409. It was not a new aircraft per se, but one of the RE 2000 *Falco* prototypes, retrofitted with a new engine. The prototype's development was completed in June 1940, and it took its maiden flight on 14 July. The aircraft achieved a top speed of 568 km/h at an altitude of 5,500 metres. Due to ongoing issues with the prototype's integral fuel tanks, the Ministry of Aviation mandated a redesign of the wing to incorporate self-sealing fuel tanks of a conventional design. The modification involved replacing the RE 2000's five-spar wing with a three-spar structure. This wing comprised a fuselage-mounted central section housing the self-sealing fuel tanks and the main landing gear bays. The central wing section contained two fuel tanks – a front one with a capacity of 264 litres and a rear one with 200 litres. Complementing these was an 80-litre reserve fuel tank located in the fuselage, behind the cockpit. External consoles, housing the engine's coolant radiators, were attached to the central section. Another change was the cockpit canopy – instead of the rearward-sliding limousine style used in the RE 2000, the new aircraft featured a two-part canopy, hinged to open to the right.

Wooden mock-up of RE 2001 at Reggiane facilities.

Assembly of the first prototype of RE 2001 (M.M.409).

The armament was identical to that of the RE 2000: two 12.7 mm Breda-SAFAT machine guns located in the fuselage, above the engine, with an ammunition supply of 350 rounds per barrel.

In December 1940, research commenced on the second prototype, bearing the number M.M.408. Compared to its predecessor, only minor modifications were introduced – the layout of ventilation openings in the engine cover was altered, the shape of the "hump" behind the cockpit was modified (removing the small windows), and an additional hatch was added to the fuselage. On 14 March 1941, the aircraft was completely destroyed during a forced landing following a propeller pitch mechanism failure. The accident claimed the life of the renowned Italian aviator, Pietro Scapinelli, who had won the Bleriot Cup in 1933 and was also a test pilot for the Reggiane company.

Preparation for the flight of the first prototype RE 2001 (M.M.409). During its first flight, the aircraft had its canopy removed.

Modified first prototype of RE 2001 (M.M.409). The photos show that the prototypes had different wheel rims (like the RE 2000 Falco) compared to the serial machines.

Details of the cockpit canopy of the first prototype RE 2001 (M.M.409).

Ground crew servicing the first prototype RE 2001. Visible is the method of opening the cockpit canopy and the open armament compartment cover in the fuselage.

Second prototype of Reggiane RE 2001 (M.M.408). Notable is the modified "hump" behind the cockpit.

Pietro Scapinelli (on the right), winner of the Bleriot Cup in 1933, next to the MC.72 aircraft. Later, he became a test pilot for Reggiane.

Wreckage of the second prototype RE 2001 (M.M.408), which crashed on 14 March 1941, in which Pietro Scapinelli died.

Prototype RE 2001bis (M.M.409/538) with radiators built into the wings. The aircraft had only 12.7 mm Breda-SAFAT machine guns in the fuselage. The front part of the fuselage was painted yellow.

Reggiane RE 2001 Serie 0 *(M.M.08074).*

Reggiane RE 2001 Serie 0 *(M.M.08077) during tests at Centro Sperimentale Aeronautica in Guidonia.*

Reggiane RE 2001 Serie 0 *(M.M.08075) during tests at Centro Sperimentale Aeronautica, Guidonia, in the spring of 1941. The front of the aircraft, including the propeller spinner, is yellow – a quick identification marking used by the Italians from spring to autumn 1941.*

Prototype RE 2001 G (M.M.9921) at Reggiane facilities in 1943. Note is the extended leg of the tail wheel.

Prototype RE 2001 G (M.M.9921) with a mock-up of an aerial torpedo.

Reggiane RE 2001 (M.M.90754) adapted for carrying a bomb filled with liquid oxygen, Furbara range, April 1943. In the background, an RE 2002 with a torpedo.

Mass Production

In February 1941, the Reggiane company received an order for 10 RE 2001 *Serie 0* aircraft (M.M.8071–M.M.8080), which were pre-production models. These aircraft were constructed between May and September 1941. They were based on the second prototype M.M.408, but with further modifications. The most significant change was the installation of two 7.7 mm Breda-SAFAT machine guns in the wings, each with an ammunition supply of 600 rounds. The planes were also fitted with an antenna mast behind the cockpit, the retractable tail skid was replaced with a fixed one, and a modified windscreen was installed. Most of the *Serie 0* aircraft were equipped with the original German DB 601A-1 engines. Interestingly, there has been some ambiguity in clearly determining the aircraft's name. Publications mention two names: *Falco II* and *Ariete I*. However, based on official documents from the Reggiane company, it seems that the latter is the correct designation. The name *Falco II*, in some sources, is attributed to the prototype RE 2001bis.

At the Reggiane facilities, there were concerns that the situation with the RE 2000 *Falco*, which received only a small order from the Italian air force, might repeat itself. Therefore, from the beginning, there was an effort to offer the new aircraft to foreign customers. Sweden expressed interest in the RE 2001, intending to purchase 100 aircraft and acquire the engines directly from the Daimler-Benz factories in Germany. However, due to the high demand for fighters from the *Regia Aeronautica*, the contract was ultimately not signed. The Italian air force was the only recipient of the serially produced RE 2001.

The RE 2001 aircraft were built in several production series (as indicated in the table). Within some series, aircraft of different versions were produced – day fighters, night fighters, and fighter-bombers. Some unrealistic orders were cancelled, and others were revised. As a result, there are discrepancies between various sources (Govi, Gueli, Riati) regarding the production data of the RE 2001 aircraft, especially in terms of the division into production series. There are also some inconsistencies concerning the number of aircraft produced in each version.

Production line at the Reggiane plants in Reggio Emilia where RE 2001 wings were assembled.

A series of photos showing the various stages of attaching the wings to the fuselage.

Work on the tail section of the RE 2001 fuselage.

The first series (*Serie I*) was supposed to include 100 aircraft (M.M.6547–6646), which were to be produced at the Caproni Predappio factories. However, the order was changed, and eventually, only 10 aircraft in the version of night fighters, RE 2001 CN (*Caccia Notturna*), were produced in this series.

The second series (*Serie II*) comprised 100 aircraft (M.M.7209-M.M7308), produced by the Reggiane facilities in various versions – 47 of them were finished as day fighters, and 39 as fighter-bombers RE 2001 CB (Caccia Bombardiere). Two aircraft were completed as machines intended for catapult launch trials (M.M.7271 and M.M.7272), which were also prototypes of the naval version RE 2001 OR (*Organizzazione Roma*). Interestingly, the next 12 machines of this series were to be equipped with a hook for carrier landings, although they were intended for use at land bases and for training in landing. During the construction of the *Serie II* aircraft, there was a challenge in maintaining the appropriate production pace. By the end of 1941, 24 *Serie II* aircraft were produced, and the entire order was completed only in August 1942.

The next production series (*Serie III*) included 32 aircraft (M.M.9921–9952), produced at the Reggiane facilities in Reggio Emilia. These were machines in the fighter version – both day and night. Additionally, the first machine from this series was used to build the prototype of the torpedo version – RE 2001G.

The fourth series (*Serie IV*) consisted of 50 aircraft in the night fighter version, ordered from the Reggiane facilities (M.M.90000–M.M.90049). By the time of Italy's capitulation, 34 of these were likely completed, with the remainder at various stages of progress. The unfinished aircraft were probably destroyed during a raid on the Reggiane facilities in January 1944.

The final production series comprised 50 aircraft (M.M.90751–M.M.90800), produced at the Reggiane facilities. The order, placed in April 1942, initially called for an entirely unrealistic number of 550 aircraft in the OR version. By the summer of 1942, this was reduced to 50 aircraft, but

Work on the Alfa Romeo R.A. 1000 R.C. 41-I "Monsone" engine.

in the CN version. Two aircraft from this series were not delivered due to Allied air raids. Interestingly, according to some sources, this was *Serie V*, while others refer to it as *Serie VI*. At least one photograph of a CN version aircraft clearly shows the *Serie VI* designation. This is the aircraft with the military number M.M.90789. It seems that in photos taken after the Allied raid on the Reggiane facilities in January 1944, destroyed RE 2001s can be seen, which also bear the *Serie VI* designation.

The total production amounted to 234 serial RE 2001 aircraft, plus three prototypes (M.M.408, M.M.409, and M.M.538). This was a very small number, starkly illustrating the limited production capabilities of not just the Reggiane facilities, but also the entire Caproni group.

During the production of the RE 2001 aircraft, only minor design changes were introduced. These modifications stemmed from the experiences gathered during their production and operation. Regarding the cockpit interior, some instruments were updated (e.g., the OMI t03 compass) and the clearance

Final assembly hall of RE 2001 aircraft, probably Serie III. *The aircraft in the photo have double Venturi nozzles.*

of the opening near the rudder pedals was widened. The design of the cockpit canopy and windscreen was modified, with the latter receiving an additional armoured glass panel. The gun channels in the wings were extended, and a balancing flap was installed in the right aileron. Additionally, a deployable radio direction-finding antenna was mounted on the vertical and horizontal stabilizers. It appears that individual aircraft, although it's unclear from which version/series, had radio direction-finding antennas placed under the fuselage. It's also worth noting that all aircraft from *Serie I-VI* had slightly modified engine cowls compared to the *Serie 0* machines. The difference lay in the increased number of ventilation holes, which provided better cooling for both the engine and the machine guns.

Versions, Prototypes, and Projects

RE 2001 (*Caccia Diurni*)

This was the basic version, based on the *Serie 0* aircraft. The main difference lay in the previously mentioned minor changes to the engine cowl and the fuselage's weapon compartment. Approximately 87 aircraft were likely produced in this variant.

RE 2001 *Cinematografico and Fotografico*

RE 2001 aircraft were adapted for reconnaissance roles. However, the exact number of aircraft modified in this way is not known. There were two reconnaissance variants. One involved the installation of two Cineavia cameras in streamlined fairings on the leading edges of both wings. The first aircraft converted in this manner was an RE 2001 *Serie 0* with the number M.M.08071, which flew in early 1943. The second variant involved installing a German Robot camera in the right wing. It is important to note that these modifications were not endorsed by the Reggiane company.

RE 2001 CN (*Caccia Notturna*)

The prototype for the night fighter version was a machine belonging to *Serie 0* with the number M.M.08075. In addition to this, around 90 aircraft were produced in this variant. The primary difference compared to the day fighter was the armament – the RE 2001 CN had two German 20 mm Mauser MG 151/20 cannons installed in underwing gondolas (with an ammunition supply of 60 rounds per barrel), instead of the 7.7 mm Breda-SAFAT machine guns. This necessitated minor changes in the wing's skin-

Preparation of RE 2001 aircraft for test flights and acceptance, Reggiane plants, spring of 1943.

ning. However, it is not known how many aircraft were equipped with this armament. It soon became apparent that there were problems with supplying a sufficient number of Mauser cannons. There is information that only about 10 RE 2001 CNs were equipped with cannons. The remaining CN aircraft had the same armament as the day fighters.

Other modifications in the CN version included additional cockpit lighting, two Venturi tubes on the right side of the fuselage (although some CNs had a single tube), and bomb racks mounted under the fuselage.

Finishing work on RE 2001 (M.M.90755). This aircraft was part of Serie V *or* VI.

RE 2001 CB (*Caccia Bombardiere*)

The fighter-bomber version, designated RE 2001 CB, was developed by installing a racks under the fuselage for bombs weighing 160 or 250 kilograms. It was also possible to install an extender that moved the bomb's trajectory beyond the propeller's circle, allowing for dive bombing. There is also mention of bomb racks for bombs up to 100 kg under the wings. However, this seems to have been a theoretical possibility, as No. published photographs show such a configuration. A total of 39 aircraft were produced in the fighter-bomber configuration.

One of the RE 2001 CBs (M.M.90754) was also used as a carrier for a fuel-air bomb. It was tested at the Furbara weapon research centre, but due to a lack of success, the development program was discontinued.

RE 2001 GV

Towards the end of 1940, two Italian pilots, *Ten.* Riccardo Vaccari and *Ten.* Rinaldo "Aldo" Galimberti, independently proposed a concept for attacking enemy ships. Interestingly, their ideas were remarkably similar and developed independently. The Italian pilots envisaged an attack on enemy ships conducted at maximum speed in a dive-bombing approach using a fighter aircraft armed with a heavy bomb. The memorandum presented by both pilots sparked the interest of the Ministry of Aviation and General Mario Bernasconi, the air force inspector, resulting in the authors being given the opportunity to develop their concept practically during tests at the Furbara range. Various aircraft were considered for this purpose, including the Macchi C.202, RE 2001, and even the FIAT CR.42. The RE 2001 was ultimately chosen as the weapon carrier for further research. At the Centro Studi di Guidonia, a special bomb designated 630 PD, capable of penetrating 70 mm of armor, was developed. This bomb was a modification of a 381 mm anti-tank shell used by the "Littorio" class battleships. In early 1942, a modified RE 2001 (M.M.7226) arrived at the Furbara range, equipped to carry this new bomb. The aircraft was designated GV, derived from the initials of the inventors' surnames. There were likely two RE 2001 GV aircraft, although the military number of the second is not known. In spring 1942, *Ten.* Galimberti tragically died during a training flight on a FIAT CR.42, and the subsequent trials were continued by *Ten.* Vacari and *Ten.* Robone. Experienced pilot Giulio Reiner also participated in the tests for a time. The plan was to use these aircraft against British convoys traveling from Gibraltar to Malta. On 8 August 1942, a strong convoy, including the aircraft carrier HMS *Victorious*, was located. On the same day, aircraft piloted by Vaccari and Robone were relocated from Furbara to Elmas airfield in Sardinia. Formally, the aircraft belonged to the Sezione Sperimentale, and the pilots served in the *22° Gruppo Autonomo C.T.* The 630 PD bombs and a mechanic from the Reggiane factories, who was to supervise the correct mounting of the weapons and assist with any technical problems, also arrived at the airfield.

A mechanic in the cockpit of an RE 2001 prepared for a test flight. The aircraft remains unpainted, making the details of the fuselage and wings construction clearly visible.

The attack on the British convoy was carried out by a pair of Reggiane aircraft on 12 August. There is uncertainty about the type of bombs ultimately used. Italian sources suggest either the 630 PD bombs or 500-kilogram fragmentation bombs, while British sources mention 50-kilogram bombs. The latter seems less likely, as attacking an aircraft carrier with such small bombs would be largely ineffective.

The attack by the Italian pilots, which occurred around 13:30 – 13:40, was not the "fatal blow" anticipated. One of the bombs, most likely dropped by Vaccari, hit the deck but failed to explode. It broke apart, and its fragments killed six crew members (including four officers). The second bomb bounced off the carrier's deck and fell into the sea. Shortly after the attack, the Reggiane pair briefly engaged with Fulmars from No. 809 Squadron NAS, but this skirmish had No. significant outcome. Both Reggiane aircraft landed back at Elmas at 14:35. Vaccari's report suggested continuing the production of aircraft and bombs and training more pilots. However, since the mission essentially ended in failure, the Ministerio dell'Aeronautica abandoned further work. It seems that the main cause of the failure was the inadequacy of the bombs (the fuses disintegrated upon contact with armoured plates, preventing explosion).

RE 2001 OR

Regarding the Italian construction plans for the aircraft carriers *Aquillia* and *Sparviero*, there was also a requirement for suitable carrier-based aircraft. The preparation of aerial armament for these carriers was codenamed *Organizzazione Roma*, the same designation given to the naval version of the *Ariete I* – RE 2001 OR. The *160° Gruppo*, which was to be based on the *Aquilla* aircraft carrier, was being prepared under the command of *Magg.* Michele Mandara.

Initially, the plan was to construct several aircraft in the naval version for trials and pilot training. There was also a plan to build 120 aircraft (in two series of 60), which were even assigned military numbers – M.M.92459–92518 and M.M.98718–98777. Later, the idea of constructing 550 RE 2001 OR was proposed. However, due to the failure of the plans to build Italian aircraft carriers, orders for the naval *Ariete I* were cancelled.

Determining the number of produced RE 2001 OR aircraft is quite complicated. Many sources state that two aircraft were made in the Ultralleggeriti variant with reduced weight, intended for catapulting from ship decks, along with 12 carrier-based RE 2001 OR. However, it seems that in reality, there were fewer naval *Ariete I*. According to research conducted by Marco Gueli, the existence of four naval RE 2001s is confirmed, specifically machines with the numbers M.M.7259, 7260, 7271, and 7272. These were essentially prototype aircraft, on which various tests were conducted, including the placement of the landing hook and arresting wire grips, as well as flight testing. Other aircraft, such as M.M.7292, M.M.7307, M.M.90755, described as OR, were most likely not fully configured as naval versions. After the completion of trials conducted at the bases in Perugia and Sarzana, all naval RE 2001s were converted to the fighter version.

An impressive, propaganda photo of finished Reggiane RE 2001 aircraft. Based on them, one might think that the aircraft were mass-produced. However, the production of RE 2001 was very slow and fraught with huge problems. In 3 years, just over 200 aircraft were produced.

RE 2001bis

During the development of the RE 2001, the aerodynamics of the first prototype were improved by placing air intakes for the liquid coolers at the leading edge of the wing. The modified aircraft, designated RE 2001bis (M.M.538), achieved a maximum speed of 600 km/h at an altitude of 6,000 meters. However, this modification was not considered suitable for mass production, and the aircraft was reverted to its initial configuration. It's likely that in the Reggiane factories, the aircraft informally received the name *Falco II*.

RE 2001 *Delta*

Due to the limited availability of DB 601A-1 engines and their licensed version produced by Alfa-Romeo, the aircraft M.M.9920 was equipped with a 12-cylinder, air-cooled Isotta-Fraschini R.C 16/48 "Delta" engine with 840 horsepower. The machine, designated RE 2001 *Delta*, was first flown on 8 September 1942, but its performance was not impressive – the maximum speed at 5,600 meters was 523 km/h, and the time to climb to 6,000 meters was 10.5 minutes. Although there were plans to fulfill an order for 100 aircraft, on 27 January 1943, during a flight on the prototype, the engine caught fire, resulting in the loss of the aircraft. Shortly after this event, the order was cancelled.

Photos of the prototype RE 2001 Delta *(M.M.9920) during tests at the experimental centre in Guidonia. Noteworthy is the unusual placement of the royal house emblem – not in the centre of the white cross, but on its upper part.*

Opposite page: *Engine cowling of the Isotta-Fraschini R.C. 18-48 "Delta".*

Details of the front part of the fuselage with the engine cover open and the cover of the armament compartment in the fuselage removed.

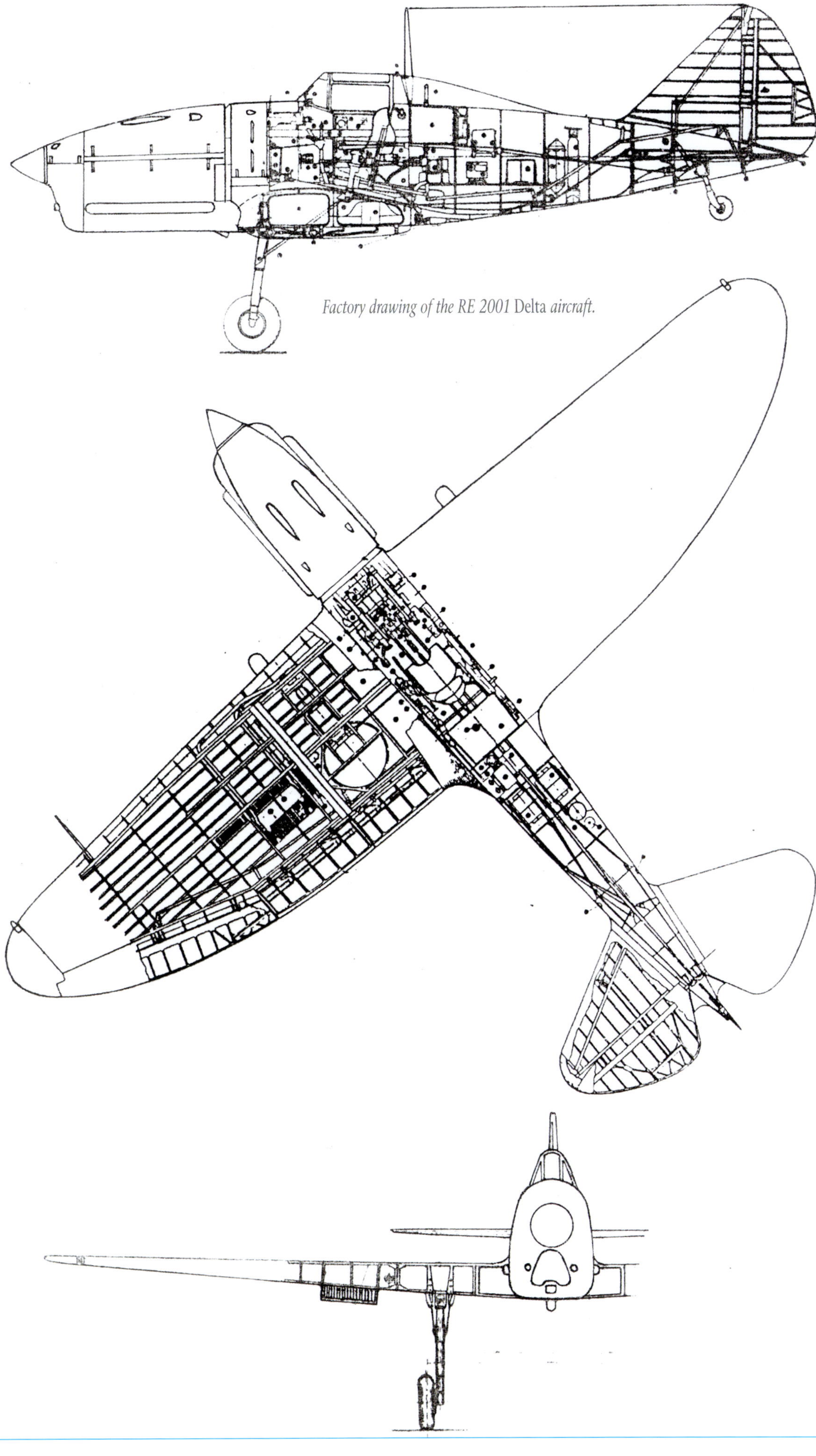

Factory drawing of the RE 2001 Delta *aircraft.*

Painting RE 2001 aircraft "in the open air".

RE 2001 *Ligneo*

This was an unrealized project for a version entirely built of wood, intended as a solution to the scarcity of aeronautical alloys, primarily aluminium.

RE 2001 G

The RE 2001 G (M.M.9921) was an experimental model designed to adapt the RE 2001 for anti-ship warfare. This single prototype was equipped to carry a small aerial torpedo. It underwent testing at the Furbara range but never entered mass production. The subsequent fate of the aircraft remains unclear. After the tests, it was sent to the Scuola Aerosiluranti in Gorizia, and it was likely destroyed in September 1943.

RE 2001 H

This designation referred to a project for an aircraft intended for engaging enemy armoured vehicles. The plan was to arm it with 20 mm cannons and an underbelly bomb. However, this project was never realized.

RE 2001 DB 605

In mid-1941, there was a proposal to equip the RE 2001 with the German Daimler Benz DB 605A engine or its licensed version produced by FIAT. This was seen as a solution to the issues with the supply of Alfa Romeo R.A. 1000 R.C. 41-I "Monsone" engines. Nevertheless, this plan was never implemented.

RE 2001 *Scorta*

In the autumn of 1943, a few RE 2001 aircraft (three or six) that were in the hands of the *Aeronautica Cobelligerante Italiana* were modified to increase their range, a necessity for flights over the Balkans. A "wet" hardpoint was fitted under the fuselage for an additional fuel tank. This attachment could also carry a transport container. This version was unofficially designated as RE 2001 S.

RE 2001 aircraft prepared for acceptance. All machines are painted in the Metropolitan scheme.

*A series of photos from the test flight of RE 2001 CN (M.M.90760) carried out in April 1943 by Alfonso Caracciolo. The aircraft was equipped with 20 mm Mauser MG 151/20 cannons under the wings. The aircraft served in the 358*ª Squadriglia *and 394*ª Squadriglia. *In September 1943, it was destroyed in Venafiorita.*

Reggiane RE 2001 CN Serie VI *(M.M.90789) test-flown on 26 May 1943, by De Prato. Notable is the inscription* Ariete I *on the vertical stabilizer, which appeared practically only on the latest produced aircraft.*

Reggiane RE 2001 CN prepared for acceptance. All aircraft are painted black. All also have flame dampers installed on the exhaust pipes. However, they do not have the underwing 20 mm Mauser MG 151/20 cannon pods.

Front part of the fuselage with Alfa Romeo R.A. 1000 propeller spinner. Also visible is the flame damper on the exhaust pipes.

Reggiane RE 2001 CN entirely painted black. Even the white identification stripe was partially painted over.

Reggiane RE 2001 assigned to the 2° Gruppo Autonomo C.T., Gorizia airfield, early 1942. Notable is the number 4 placed above the Reggiane factory emblem on the vertical stabilizer.

Reggiane RE 2001 CN Serie II *(M.M.7279) after a forced landing at Reggia Emilia airfield, summer of 1942. The aircraft has two Venturi nozzles.*

Reggiane RE 2001 CB aircraft lined up. Under the fuselages, 500-kilogram bombs are visible.

Reggiane plant hall after the Allied raid on 8 January 1944. The photo shows destroyed or damaged RE 2001 aircraft. It seems that the aircraft in the foreground has the inscription Ariete I *on the vertical stabilizer.*

Promotional poster for the RE 2001.

Reggiane RE 2001 in Combat

The Regia Aeronautica

The first unit to receive the RE 2001 fighter planes was the *2° Gruppo Autonomo C.T.*, which previously operated FIAT G.50bis aircraft. This unit had been engaged in North Africa from December 1940 to July 1941 before returning to Italy. In January 1942, the group began reequipping with the RE 2001, starting with the *152ª Squadriglia* at Gorizia airfield. By April, the pilots from this squadron had trained their colleagues from the *150ª* and *358ª Squadriglia* at CiampiNo. airfield, completing the rearming of the *2° Gruppo*.

In early May 1942, 18 RE 2001s from the *2° Gruppo* were transferred to the Sicilian airfield of Santo Pietro di Caltagirone (commonly shortened to Caltagirone), from where they were to participate in an offensive against Malta. However, the timing was not ideal for their debut. The *Luftwaffe's* offensive against the island was drawing to a close, with most of its units redeployed elsewhere. This left the main burden of the operations on the *Regia Aeronautica*, supported only by *Luftwaffe* units including Messerschmitt Bf 109s (II. and III./JG 53) and Junkers Ju 88s (I./KG 54, KGr 806). Significantly, the RAF's defensive squadrons on Malta (126th, 185th, 249th, 601st, and 603rd Squadrons) had been equipped with the more advanced Spitfire V by this time.

The RE 2001's combat debut occurred on 10 May 1942, when pilots from the *2° Gruppo*, along with Macchi C.202s from the *4° Stormo*, were tasked with escorting five Cant Z.1007bis bombers. The Italian fighters reported shooting down six Spitfires while losing one C.202 and one Z.1007bis, with another bomber heavily damaged. Three Spitfires were claimed by the *2° Gruppo* pilots, at the cost of damage to two RE 2001s. However, the RAF squadrons involved in the encounter, No. 601 Squadron and No. 126 Squadron, reported No. losses.

The next day, 11 May 1942, eight RE 2001s patrolled over Malta without encountering enemy aircraft and returned to Sicily. During their return, they were surprised by three aircraft from No. 249 Squadron. One Italian pilot, attempting to evade, crashed into the sea and was credited as a kill to Rhodesian ace of Greek descent P/O John Agorastos Plagis, who achieved 15 individual and 2 shared kills during the war. Interestingly, Plagis was officially credited with destroying a C.202.

In the late afternoon of 12 May 1942, while escorting three S.84 torpedo bombers from the *4° Gruppo* Autonomo A.S., pilots from the 15 C.202 of the *4° Stormo* and 15 RE 2001 from the *2° Gruppo* reported shooting down three Spitfires, three probably, and damaging two others. In reality, the RAF lost three Spitfires, but it's important to note that the destruction of three British fighters in this encounter was also claimed by German pilots from III./JG 53.

RE 2001 Serie 0 *marked for the* 150ª Squadriglia, *but without an individual number.*

RE 2001 Serie II *(M.M.7216) from the* 150ª Squadriglia *(marking 150-7) after a forced landing on 2 June 1942, at Comiso.* Sergente Maggiore *Giovanni Dringoli, the aircraft's pilot, is standing on the wing.*

RE 2001 CN from the 150ª Squadriglia *(*2° Gruppo Intercettori*), spring 1943. Note is the small size of the tactical marking, likely due to the unit's shift to defense duties in Italy and night operations.*

Italian pilots from the 2° Gruppo Autonomo C.T. *relaxing in front of an RE 2001 with the marking 152-2.*

Reggiane RE 2001 Serie II *(M.M.7209) from the* 152ª Squadriglia *(marking 152-1), Santo Pietro di Caltagirone airfield, May 1942. This aircraft was flown by* Ten. *Remo Cazzolli, who was shot down over Malta on 18 May 1942 and captured. The engine cover featured the coat of arms of Trento,* Ten. *Cazzolli's hometown.*

Two Reggiane aircraft were seriously damaged in the encounter and made emergency landings in Sicily. *Serg.* Mario Marchio managed to land his burning fighter on the shore of the island but succumbed to severe injuries a month later. Notably, he was credited with two aerial victories in this battle. The group commander, *Ten.Col.* Aldo Quarantotti, who made a forced landing in Catania with his damaged RE 2001, was uninjured. Additionally, one of the escorted bombers was lost, and another was seriously damaged.

Two days later, during an escort mission for three German Ju 88A bombers from KGr 806, two victories were reported (by *Ten.* Carlo Seganti and *Ten.* Leo Venturini). However, these claims do not find confirmation in British losses.

On the morning of 16 May, the Italians, with fifteen RE 2001s and 26 Bf 109Fs from the *Luftwaffe*, undertook a mission in the Kalafrana area. During an encounter with Spitfires from No. 126 Squadron RAF, the aircraft piloted by *S.Ten.* Carlo Grillo was seriously damaged, leading him to make a forced landing in Sicily. The Germans lost one of their five fighter-bomber Bf 109Fs, whose pilot was rescued after spending eight days at sea. The defenders of Malta did not report any losses again.

The next day, 19 RE 2001s were tasked with covering a Cant Z.506B seaplane on a rescue mission. The Italians were intercepted by seven Spitfires, which damaged the seaplane and one of the fighters. The Italians claimed two Spitfires definitely downed, one probably, and three enemy aircraft damaged. In fact, Sgt. Frank S. Howard's aircraft (from No. 249 Squadron) was hit by the escort during an attack on the seaplane. The Rhodesian crashed his Spitfire BR344 on landing at Luqa airfield and died four days later due to his injuries.

On 18 May, eight RE 2001s, along with sixteen C.202 Folgores, were escorting MAS torpedo boats operating near Malta. The Italians were surprised by four pilots from No. 249 Squadron, who claimed three kills, though in reality, they only shot down the aircraft of *Ten.* Remo Cazzolli from the *152ª Squadriglia*, who survived the crash into the water and was captured. The next day, Reggianes, along with C.202s, escorted three Cant Z.1007bis bombers. All three bombers were damaged, with one making a water landing on the return trip. Twenty Spitfires from No. 126 and No. 601 Squadron participated in the action against the Italian expedition. The aircraft of F/O C.M. Hone from No. 601 Squadron was damaged by an RE 2001, but the pilot landed at Takali airfield. He was likely hit by *S.Ten.* Carlo Seganti, who claimed a confirmed kill. In addition, the pilots of the *2° Gruppo* reported five probable kills and claimed to have shot down a Beaufighter, which, however, is not confirmed in RAF losses.

On the morning of 20 May, the task of the RE 2001s was to escort a Cant Z.506B seaplane (from the *612ª Squadriglia Soccorso*) tasked with finding Italian pilots shot down at night. Due to engine problems, *Ten.* Giorgio Pocek detached from the formation but reported shooting down a Spitfire on his return journey, a victory that is difficult to verify.

On the morning of 23 May 1942, sixteen RE 2001s, supported by four Bf 109Fs from 4./JG 53, provided escort to five Cant Z.1007bis bombers from the *50° Gruppo*. Despite two *Ariete I* being damaged and one Z.1007bis lost, the Italian fighters claimed three Spitfires shot down. However, there is No. confirmation of these losses from the RAF. It should also be noted that the British claims of several victories in this encounter do not find confirmation in actual German and Italian losses.

Reggiane RE 2001 Serie II *(M.M.7214) from the* 152ª Squadriglia, *which made a forced landing in Comiso with* Capitano *Salvatore Teja. The aircraft, marked 152-4, was damaged during a combat flight over Malta.*

A pair of RE 2001s from the 2° Gruppo Autonomo *C.T. in flight, summer 1942. The lead aircraft is marked for the* 358ª Squadriglia *(358-4), and the second bears the markings of the* 150ª Squadriglia.

On 25 May, a similar operation was carried out, but this time with three S.84s from the *4° Gruppo*, escorted by sixteen RE 2001s. All bombers sustained damage, but the pilots of the *2° Gruppo* claimed four kills. Indeed, their victim was 19-year-old P/O Walter "Wally" Caldwell from No. 601 Squadron, who died in his aircraft.

The next day, pilots from No. 603 Squadron took their revenge on the Italians, shooting down the commander of the *358ª Squadriglia*, *Cap*. Annibale Sterzi (with 6 victories, including one in Spain). Although Sterzi managed to bail out, his parachute failed, and his body fell near Luqa airfield. In this skirmish, the RAF pilots claimed two kills, while the Italians claimed one. Their victim was Australian Sgt. Jack "Slim" Yarra (with 12 victories).

On 30 May, three S.84s were sent to bomb targets in Malta, escorted by 22 Reggiane and 12 Bf 109s. One bomber was damaged in a Spitfire attack. Meanwhile, pilots from the *2° Gruppo* claimed three kills and the damaging of as many as 15 enemy fighters, all without suffering any losses themselves. However, the British squadrons (No. 126 and 185) reported No. losses in this engagement.

On 2 June, a similar operation took place with three S.84 bombers escorted by 24 RE 2001s and 32 C.202s from the newly arrived *155° Gruppo* in the combat zone. Despite sustaining damage to three RE 2001s, the Italians reported three victories – two were credited to pilots from the *2° Gruppo* (L. Jellici and G. Dringoli), and one to fighters from the *155° Gruppo*. In reality, the only victim of the Italians was a Spitfire BR285, piloted by P/O John R. Halford from No. 185 Squadron, who made a water landing in Kalafrana Bay but was rescued.

On the Italian side, there were two RE 2001 losses. One of them was flown by *Serg*. Giovanni Dringoli, who made a belly landing in Comiso. The other aircraft (M.M.7752) was forced to land in Sicily, likely due to an oxygen system failure and the pilot's hypoxia.

On the morning of 6 June 1942, twelve RE 2001s along with 24 C.202s from the *155° Gruppo* escorted five Z.1007bis bombers from the *50° Gruppo*. The Italian formation was intercepted by Spitfires from No. 249 Squadron and No. 603 Squadron. RAF pilots reported two definite and two probable victories of RE 2001s, but in reality, only *S.Ten*. Leonardo Venturini was shot down. Pilots from the *2° Gruppo* reported one certain and one probable kill, and an additional victory was claimed by a C.202 pilot. However, the only RAF loss was a Spitfire damaged by bomber gunners' fire. As Venturini had radioed about ditching, after the mission, 11 pilots led by the commander of the *2° Gruppo*, *Ten.Col*. Quarantotti, began searching for their comrade. During the mission, the Italians were surprised by Spitfires from No. 249 Squadron, who claimed two victories. Their victims were *Ten*. Arnaldo de Merich, while *Cap*. Salvatore Teja made a belly landing near Caltagirone airfield with a damaged right horizontal stabilizer. The searched pilot was also not found.

The Italians returned over Malta in the afternoon, with 13 RE 2001s and 6 C.202s escorting a Z.506B seaplane on a rescue mission. They were again intercepted by Spitfires, this time from No. 185 Squadron. F/O Plagis claimed two victories, and F/Sgt Reid one. In fact, two pilots were shot down – *Serg*. Giuseppe Baraldi and *Serg.M*. Aldo Geminiani, both of whom died. Three Canadian pilots also shot down the Red

Reggiane RE 2001 from the 2° Gruppo *on an airfield, with a S.79 bomber approaching for landing in the background.*

Reggiane RE 2001 from the 152ª Squadriglia *(marking 152-2) prepared for a combat mission over Malta.*

Cross-marked white Cant Z.506B, whose crew died when the plane exploded. The *2° Gruppo* claimed one victory, and another was by a C.202 pilot. The British loss was P/O Sherlock, who made a forced landing, but his aircraft was repairable.

The next engagement involving pilots from the *2° Gruppo* occurred on 10 June 1942, when, in the evening, five Z.1007bis bombers escorted by 19 RE 2001s, 27 C.202s, and Bf 109Fs flew over Malta. S/L Stanley Grant from No. 249 Squadron shot down the Reggiane flown by *Serg*. Giovanni Dringoli, who was killed. Meanwhile, F/Sgt John Williams damaged the aircraft of *S.Ten.* Agostino Celentano, who, however, managed to return to Sicily. RAF pilots also brought down one Bf 109F and one C.202. Only the pilots of the *155° Gruppo* claimed four victories in retaliation, though in reality, only the destruction of P/O Innes' Spitfire from No. 601 Squadron, who bailed out safely, is confirmed.

From 4 May to 10 June 1942, to cover the increasing losses, the unit received 8 RE 2001s, allowing it to continue flights against Malta. On the late afternoon of 14 June, starting from Sardinia, the *2° Gruppo* with 15 aircraft, supported by seven C.200s from the *54° Stormo*, escorted 14 S.79 torpedo bombers attacking the "Harpoon" convoy en route to Malta. The Italians were intercepted by six Sea Hurricanes from No. 813 Squadron NAS. Two of these attacked the S.79s, shooting down two Italian aircraft. The remaining four British planes engaged in combat with the Italian fighters. As a result, a Sea Hurricane piloted by Sub.Lt B.E. Bullivant was shot down, but he was rescued by parachute. Two more British fighters were damaged. One of them, piloted by Sub.Lt H.R. Spedding, crashed during landing on the aircraft carrier, but not before shooting down an RE 2001 flown by *M.llo.* Giovanni Treggia (who was rescued by fishermen). The Italian pilot had scored one victory in this battle before being shot down. Two victories in this battle were claimed by *Ten.Col.* Quarantotti and *S.Ten.* Celentano. In total, pilots from the *2° Gruppo* claimed to have shot down as many as 11 Hurricanes! One of the damaged RE 2001s, piloted by *M.llo* Olindo Simionato, landed in Tunisia and, after repairs, returned to Sicily.

The next day, nine RE 2001s provided cover for Regia Marina ships. Near Pantelleria, the Italian aircraft encountered a British formation consisting of a single Beaufighter VI from No. 235 Squadron and three Fairey Albacore torpedo bombers, escorted by Spitfires. The Italian leader, *Ten.* Giorgio Gasperoni, shot down the Beaufighter X8078 piloted by Sgt. C. Armitage, killing the observer Sgt C.W. Hector. Additionally, the Italians reported shooting down four Swordfish torpedo bombers (more than were actually in the air), mistakenly identifying the Albacores as such. In reality, they only managed to shoot down one Albacore, whose crew, Sub.Lt C. Casey and Lt. W. Paton, died.

On the afternoon of 23 June, 18 aircraft from the *2° Gruppo* conducted a sweep in the area of Takali. This was a prelude to an attack by three S.84s escorted by 27 Macchi C.202s. Such proportions were typical for operations over Malta in May and June. The concept of "clearing" the skies before a bomber raid and providing strong escort for them is understandable. However, the presence of a few bombers could hardly make a significant impression on the defenders of Malta, and in reality, it didn't.

The next day, an S.81 piloted by Duce landed at Caltagirone airfield. Mussolini himself arrived to personally award distinguished pilots. Among the pilots of the 2° *Gruppo* who were awarded the Silver Medal (*Medaglia d'Argento*) were *Cap*. Salvatore Teja, *Ten*. Giorgio Pocek, and *S.Ten*. Agostino Celentano. The Bronze Medal (*Medaglia di Bronzo*) recipients included Larese, Vichi, Seganti, Jellici, Fabri, Patriarca, and Cesaro. The following day, 6 RE 2001s provided an escort for Mussolini's aircraft on his flight from Sicily to Grottagile.

On 26 June 1942, during another bomber escort mission over Malta, pilots of the RE 2001 reported one victory and did not suffer any losses. Two additional victories were credited to the C.202s, which also participated in this mission. The only British loss was a wounded Canadian, Sgt C.P.J. Taylor from No. 601 Squadron, who landed his engine-less, shot-up machine. On the other hand, RAF pilots also displayed excessive optimism by claiming several victories, while the only Italian loss was a damaged C.202. The phenomenon of overestimating one's own successes (known as 'overclaiming') was common in the battles over Malta and affected pilots from both fighting sides.

Maintenance work on a Reggiane RE 2001 from the 2° Gruppo *(marking 150-5).*

Aircraft from the 2° Gruppo ready for departure to Malta, probably Gerbini airfield, summer 1942. The centre aircraft is from the 358ª Squadriglia, marked 358-5.

At the end of June, Axis forces in Sicily were reinforced, leading to more intense operations against Malta. On 1 July 1942, fifteen RE 2001s, along with 70 C.202s, participated in an evening action, escorting five S.84bis bombers. This time, they achieved success, reporting eight victories, including two by pilots from the *2° Gruppo* (*S.Ten.* Vichi and *M.llo* Jellici). In this encounter, No. 603 Squadron lost one Spitfire shot down and another damaged. The Italian losses were two damaged C.202s.

The next day, 15 RE 2001s, along with 24 C.202s, escorted five Z.1007bis bombers. One C.202 was shot down and another seriously damaged, and their pilots claimed three victories. Although several RE 2001s sustained damage, all returned, with their pilots reporting seven victories, including two each by *Serg.M.* Rino Ricci and *Serg.* Cesare Di Bert. In reality, only two Spitfires from No. 603 Squadron were forced to land.

The following day, RAF pilots heavily damaged two Z.1007bis bombers, while C.202 pilots claimed two, and RE 2001 pilots three victories, although only F/O King's fighter from No. 603 Squadron was damaged.

On 6 July 1942, 14 fighters from the *2° Gruppo* directly escorted three Z.1007bis from the *9° Stormo*, while the C.202s conducted a sweep. This day, pilots of the Reggiane encountered Canadian Sgt. George "Buzz" Beurling, who had recently arrived on the island and soon became a leading ace in the battle over Malta. In this sortie, Beurling claimed two C.202s, but actually, his victims were Macchi Ilo. Francesco Pecchiari from the *352ª Squadriglia* and an RE 2001 flown by *S.Ten.* Romano Pagliani.

The next day, five Z.1007bis bombers from the *9° Stormo* appeared over the island, escorted by 35 C.202s and 12 Reggiane, supported by German Bf 109s.

One of the bombers was shot down by anti-aircraft artillery, while pilots of 22 Spitfires engaged in combat with the fighters. As a result, the Italians lost a C.202 piloted by *Ten.* Cherubini, and his colleagues reported five damaged enemy fighters. Pilot *M.llo* Olindo Simionato from the *2° Gruppo* claimed one victory, and Fw. Feyerlein from 6./JG 53 claimed two. The RAF indeed lost two Spitfires along with their pilots, and another aircraft was shot and forced to land.

On 11 July, eight RE 2001s along with Bf 109s from I./JG 77 escorted German Ju 88 bombers. The Italians reported two victories, one of which was by *Ten.Col.* Quarantotti, and five damages, while the Germans claimed one victory. In fact, two Spitfires were damaged.

The next day, 12 July, was another dark day for the *2° Gruppo*, largely due to Canadian pilot George "Buzz" Beurling. First, Beurling hit the RE 2001 of *Ten.* Francesco Vichi, who bailed out successfully. P/O Berkeley-Hill may have had a part in this success, but he was shortly shot down by a Bf 109 from I./JG 77. The commander of the *2° Gruppo* led three other pilots in search of Vichi, but two RE 2001s turned back due to malfunctions. Beurling, along with his wingman, was on a similar mission looking for Berkeley-Hill. However, it was the RAF pilots who first spotted the enemy, realizing the Italians were searching for their pilot. Beurling ordered his wingman to climb for cover and closed in on the two Italians. He first fired at *Ten.* Carlo Seganti's aircraft, which caught fire after a short burst. Then he quickly positioned himself on the tail of *Ten.Col.* Quarantotti's plane, firing a burst from about 30 meters away. Shortly after, the Reggiane, likely with a dead pilot, plunged into the water. The entire action took the Canadian ace about seven seconds. Beurling mistakenly identified his victims as C.202s, a common error among Allied pilots.

By 13 July 1942, out of the 22 aircraft initially equipped to the *2° Gruppo*, only six remained operational. The next day, all serviceable machines participated in another mission over Malta, which was

Technical inspection of RE 2001 aircraft from the 2° Gruppo Autonomo C.T.

An American soldier posing with an abandoned RE 2001 Serie II *(M.M.7227).*

to provide cover for 18 Junkers Ju 88As. In the encounter with RAF aircraft, *Ten.* Pocek recorded one victory, C.202 pilots claimed three (at the cost of two of their own aircraft), and a German Bf 109 pilot reported one victory. In reality, one Spitfire was shot down, and three others were damaged. However, determining who was responsible for this sole confirmed victory is not possible.

In the following days, the activity of the *2° Gruppo* pilots drastically decreased. The unit, exhausted by combat, was effectively withdrawn from active operations. Additionally, after the death of *Ten. Col* Aldo Quarantotti, the group lacked a new commander. On 24 July, *Magg.* Pier Giuseppe Scarpetta (with 6 victories, including one in Spain) was appointed to this position.

The *2° Gruppo*'s first operation after a forced break was on 5 August 1942, providing escort for Italian bombers attacking targets in Malta with a few RE 2001s. On 11 August 1942, the unit was transferred to Sardinia (20 aircraft to Monserrato airfield) in anticipation of another skirmish with Allied convoys (Operation "Pedestal"). However, during the first mission conducted by 16 RE 2001s, they failed to locate the bombers they were supposed to escort. In a second escort mission involving nine aircraft, although three Sea Hurricanes were claimed shot down, none of these claims are confirmed in

"Pulcino con mitra" – the emblem of the 2° Gruppo, *designed by* Sergente Maggiore *Giovanni Dringoli.*

British losses. However, *Ten.* Bizio was shot down by Sub.Lt. Hutton and captured by the destroyer HMS *Pathfinder*, and another RE 2001 sustained heavy damage.

On 14 August, He 111 torpedo bombers were sent against a British convoy, escorted by Italian RE 2001s. Due to bad weather, only three *Ariete I* accompanied the German aircraft. This German-Italian formation was intercepted by four Spitfires from No. 126 Squadron. The RAF pilots only spotted the Italian fighters and caught them by surprise, with F/L Johnson and Sgt. Marshall shooting down the entire Italian section. Johnson claimed two victories, including *Ten.* Giorgio Pocek (who was rescued by a *Luftwaffe* Do 24T seaplane). The other two Italians, *Magg.* Pier Giuseppe Scarpetta, the then commander of the *2° Gruppo Autonomo C.T.*, and *Ten.* Isidoro Disinta, were killed. *Cap.* Angelo Merato was temporarily appointed as the commander of the *2° Gruppo*, and in September 1942, he was replaced by *Magg.* Edoardo Molinari.

One of the last clashes over Malta occurred on 17 September when Italian *Ariete I* engaged with Spitfires from No. 126 and No. 229 Squadron RAF. The encounter was inconclusive – the British reported two probable victories, but these were likely only damaged aircraft.

During the battles over Malta, the *2° Gruppo* operated 64 RE 2001 fighters from both *Serie 0* and *Serie II*. The aircraft were particularly intensively used by the *150ª Squadriglia*, whose pilots conducted 107 combat sorties in May alone. In the following months, pilots from this squadron continued to fly more frequently than those from the other two squadrons. For instance, in July 1942, pilots of the *150ª Squadriglia* carried out 91 sorties, while the *152ª Squadriglia* only executed 8, and the *358ª Squadriglia* 18.

Several Italian pilots demonstrated great skills and bravery, achieving multiple downings. Among the most successful were *Sottotenente* Agostino Celentano, who achieved six of his seven victories over Malta, *Sergente Maggiore* Cesare Di Bert (6 downings), *Tenente* Giorgio Pocek, *Tenente* Carlo Seganti, and Maresciallo Olindo Simionato (each with 5 downings). Notably, three pilots from the *2° Gruppo* were posthumously awarded Italy's highest military decoration – the *Medaglia d'Oro*: Aldo Quarantotti, Pier Giuseppe Scarpetta, and Carlo Seganti. This highlights the challenging and often perilous nature of the aerial combat faced by Italian aviators over Malta.

A pilot from the 150ª Squadriglia *posing next to the tail of an RE 2001 with the emblem of the* 2° Gruppo Autonomo C.T. *and the squadron pennant.*

At the beginning of November 1942, the squadrons of the group arrived at the Campino airfield near Rome. By the end of the month, the unit was renamed as *2° Gruppo* Autonomo Intercettori, which was under the Commando Intercettori "Leone", responsible for the air defence of Italy. The equipment, besides the RE 2001 CN, also included the outdated FIAT CR. 42 and the slightly better Dewoitine D.520. The mission of the pilots from *152ª* and *358ª Squadriglia* was to defend Liguria (mainly the area of Genoa and La Spezia), while *150ª Squadriglia* was tasked with protecting the Campania region. Interestingly, formally this squadron was incorporated into the structure of the *22° Gruppo*. In June 1943, the individual squadrons were relocated to the following airfields: Sarzana (*150ª Squadriglia*), Capua (*152ª Squadriglia*), and Albegna (*358ª Squadriglia*). However, their pilots did not achieve significant successes, although it was probably one of them who reported the last shooting down by a pilot flying an RE 2001 in the colours of the *Regia Aeronautica*. On 31 August 1943, around 12:20, *M.llo* Ricardo Castelletti reported shooting down a B-17 in the area of Leghorn – Caprala. Indeed, the B-17F "Able Mable" (42-5477) from the 99th Bomber Group was damaged in that area, but the Italian anti-aircraft defence also claims this success.

Other units equipped with the Reggiane RE 2001 fighters did not participate as actively in combat as the *2° Gruppo*. At the end of June 1942, the *22° Gruppo Autonomo C.T.* (consisting of *359ª*, *362ª*, and *369ª Squadriglia*), commanded by *Cap.* Vittorio Minguzzi, was equipped with the fighter-bomber RE 2001. This unit had already completed a combat tour on the Eastern Front flying Macchi C.200 Saetta aircraft. The rearmament to Reggiane fighters was preceded by a short training conducted at the Ciampino airport in Rome. In August 1942, the unit was transferred to the Monserrato airfield in Sardinia. The combat debut of the RE 2001 occurred on 12 August 1942, when the unit participated in attacks on a heavily protected British convoy heading to Malta (Operation "Pedestal"). The unit included the previously mentioned pilots *Ten.* Vaccari and *Ten.* Robone, who had participated in the tests of the RE 2001 GV, and on that day carried out an unsuccessful attack on the aircraft carrier HMS *Victorious*.

Pilot Sergente Maggiore *Gino Pizzati from the* 150ª Squadriglia *after returning from a combat mission over Malta, summer 1942.*

At the beginning of September, the unit was transferred to the Sicilian airfield Santo Pietro di Caltagirone, from where it was to participate in planned attacks on Malta. For a time, two squadrons, *362ª* and *369ª Squadriglia*, also operated from the airfield on Pantelleria.

The last offensive against Malta, which began on 11 October 1942, indeed meant greater involvement of the Reggiane pilots from the *22° Gruppo*, but their primary task was to carry out fighter-bomber missions. On the first day of the offensive, 17 bomb-armed RE 2001s participated in operations over Malta, escorted by 25 C.202s. In this mission, *M.llo* Romano Pesavento was killed, most likely shot down by F/O William Rolls from No. 126 Squadron, who reported shooting down two RE 2001s in this skirmish. The next day, 13 RE 2001s participated in an attack on Malta, and on the 18th, 21st, 22nd, and 25th of October, three aircraft each were engaged in strong fighter cover, allowing them to avoid losses.

Following the Allied landing in North Africa, the *22° Gruppo* was utilized for operations against targets in Algeria. For this reason, at the beginning of November, the unit was relocated to the Elmas airfield. For several days, the unit also operated from Pantelleria, and fairly quickly returned to its Sardinian bases (Monserrato, Elmas). On 23 and 28 November, the Reggiane carried out fighter-bomber attacks on the Algerian port of Bone. The pilots of the *22° Gruppo* found themselves over this target again on 1 December 1942. However, this time their task was to escort 10 torpedo aircraft S.84 from *89° Gruppo* A.S. The five machines led by *Capitano* Germano La Ferla (who ended the war with 5 victories) were not able to effectively protect the torpedo planes. A pair of Spitfires from No. 242 Squadron RAF shot down three S.84s.

Over Algeria, the RE 2001s also appeared in the subsequent days. Fighter-bomber missions in the Bone area were carried out on 3 and 6 December. During the latter mission, two Spitfires shot down the aircraft of *S.Ten.* Arrigo Pederzoli. The last patrol from Sardinia by pilots of the *22° Gruppo* was conducted on 25 December 1942. The next day, the unit's personnel were airlifted to the Naples-Capodichino airfield, while the aircraft were transferred to the *24° Gruppo*. At the beginning of 1943, the *22° Gruppo* was equipped with various types of aircraft, mainly C.202 and the French Dewoitine D.520. The most valuable in combat were the RE 2005s, which were assigned to the *362ª Squadriglia*. However, the delivery of these aircraft to the *22° Gruppo* was insufficient, so the RE 2001 continued to participate in operational activities. This is evidenced by the combat reports of the unit, which in the spring and summer of 1943 mention this type of aircraft. They were flown by pilots from different squadrons, but perhaps the most intensive use of these aircraft was by pilots of the *150ª Squadriglia*, which had been added to the group. In July and August 1943, pilots of the RE 2001 from the "twenty-second" reported successes achieved both by day and night. On the night of 16/17 July, *Serg.* Pietro Sguotti (*150ª Squadriglia*) shot

A pair of Reggiane RE 2001 aircraft from the 359ª Squadriglia, taxiing at Santo Pietro di Caltagirone airfield, summer/autumn 1942. The aircraft on the left is marked 359-4. Both machines only have white triangles painted on the fuselage, without the unit emblem.

Reggiane RE 2001 aircraft from the 359ª Squadriglia, summer 1942, with a visible part of the under-fuselage bomb rack.

down a British Wellington X from No. 147 Squadron over Naples. During the action on 17 July also over Naples, pilots of the *150ª Squadriglia* reported shooting down a B-24 (*Ten.* Bartolozzi and *Serg.* Pizzati) and a B-17 (*Cap.* Bonet and *Serg.* Prati) for sure, and possibly another "Fortress" (*Ten.* Prete). Meanwhile, *Cap.* Giovanni Bonet added a Mosquito to his tally. However, the loss list includes only one B-24 (an aircraft from the 44th Bomber Group). The next night, three RE 2001 pilots reported shooting down an allied twin-engine aircraft in the Torre del Greco area. On 4 August, in the Ventotene – Ischia – Capri area, RE 2001 pilots shot down two B-17Fs. One was credited to *Serg.M.* Di Berti, and the other to the pair of pilots: *Cap.* Bartolozzi and *Serg.* Pizzati. During the action over Italy, the Americans indeed lost two "Flying Fortresses" from the 2nd Bomber Group. It is difficult, however, to determine the extent of the fighters' involvement versus that of the anti-aircraft defence. The last time RE 2001s appear in the reports of the *22° Gruppo* was on 21 August 1943. Pilots of these aircraft recorded their involvement in two reported probable victories.

As mentioned earlier, the first RE 2001s were transferred to the *24° Gruppo* at the end of 1942, and these were machines handed over by the *22° Gruppo*. At the beginning of 1943, the *24° Gruppo*, which

A pair of RE 2001s from the 362ª Squadriglia *during technical inspection.*

included the *354ª* and *370ª Squadriglia*, had 20 *Ariete I* aircraft, of which 13 were operational. Additionally, the unit also had other types of aircraft – 19 FIAT CR. 42s (13 operational) and 14 FIAT G.50s (9 operational). Soon, the *355ª Squadriglia*, equipped with Macchi C.202s, was incorporated into the *24° Gruppo*. The combat debut of the RE 2001 occurred on 13th January with an attack on a submarine in the Monte Arista region (Sardinia). In the later period, the main task of the unit's pilots was to defend Sardinian airfields against attacks by Allied aircraft. However, these encounters did not yield spectacular successes, and the reported victories were not always confirmed in the actual losses of the opponents. On 7th February at 15:05, *Serg*. Enrico Canepa from the *370ª Squadriglia* reported shooting down a P-38 in the Capo Spartivento area (southern part of Sardinia). In the same skirmish, pilots of the *24° Gruppo* collectively reported probably shooting down 4 enemy aircraft of an unspecified type. However, none of these reported successes are confirmed by American losses. On 17 February 1943, ten RE 2001s and four C.202s from the *24° Gruppo* clashed with B-26B Marauder bombers from the 17th Bomber Group, escorted by P-38F Lightnings from the 82nd Fighter Group. The RE 2001 pilots reported a probable victory of a Lightning and damage to two Marauders, while the Folgore pilots added a damaged Marauder and Lightning. However, in the encounter with P-38s from the 1st Fighter Group and 82nd Fighter Group on 28 February, five RE 2001s were damaged, and one crashed on landing. The Reggiane pilots reported damaging 4 American aircraft, but this is not confirmed. On 31 March a formation of C.202s and RE 2001s from the *24° Gruppo*, acting together with fighters from the *160° Gruppo*, was scrambled to repel an American heavy bomber raid escorted by P-40 fighters. In total, 15 RE 2001s and 12 C.202s participated in the action. The Italians reported shooting down 4 bombers probably. However, in this mission, the Americans did not lose any "Fortresses". On the Italian side, there was one damaged RE 2001, whose pilot was injured. Additionally, 3 RE 2001s were damaged during an Allied attack on the Monserrato airfield. The last action of the *24° Gruppo* involving Reggiane took place on 14 April 1943. An attack on a formation of 40 heavy bombers escorted by 20 P-38 Lightnings was conducted

Reggiane RE 2001 from the 362ª Squadriglia *(marking 362-7). Under the cockpit, a white triangle is painted, but without the emblem (scarecrow Lo Spuracchio).*

Reggiane RE 2001 Serie II *(M.M.7303) with the unit marking (*362ª Squadriglia*) on the white identification stripe. The aircraft's paint scheme is quite mysterious – two colors are visible. The front part is darker, while the middle is significantly lighter. It seems that the front and rear of the aircraft were refreshed, but these are only speculations. Visible are two Venturi tubes and a mount for a photo-gun on the wing.*

by 22 Italian fighters. Among them, however, was only one RE 2001. In this skirmish, the pilots of the *Regia Aeronautica* reported 4 victories. Subsequently, all RE 2001s were transferred to the *160° Gruppo*.

This transfer marked a shift in the utilization of the RE 2001 aircraft within the Italian air force. The involvement of the RE 2001 in various operations, from defensive missions to escort and fighter-bomber roles, demonstrates the versatility of the aircraft despite the mixed results in terms of confirmed enemy losses. The transition of these aircraft to the *160° Gruppo* likely indicated a reorganization or a strategic shift in their deployment during the ongoing war efforts.

At the beginning of 1943, the *160° Gruppo Autonomo C.T.* began to be equipped with RE 2001 aircraft. By April, Reggiane fighters had been allocated to all three of its squadrons: *375ª*, *393ª*, and *394ª Squadriglia*. In total, there were only 16 aircraft, meaning that the group also operated other types of fighters: two FIAT G.50s and two FIAT CR.42s. The situation was not significantly improved by the transfer of several RE 2001s from the *24° Gruppo* in April 1943, mainly because these aircraft were heavily used. A substantial reinforcement occurred in May 1943 when the *358ª Squadriglia*, equipped with six Reggiane, joined the *160° Gruppo*. This unit was stationed at airfields in Perugia, Decimomannu

Reggiane RE 2001 from the 362ª Squadriglia *(marking 362-4) during fueling. The aircraft is painted in the "Metropolitano" scheme –* Verde Oliva Scuro 2/Grigio Azzuro Chiaro 1. *Although some publications show the aircraft in a two-tone paint scheme, there is no photographic evidence to support this.*

RE 2001 aircraft from 362ª Squadriglia (22° Gruppo Autonomo C.T.), likely at Santo Pietro di Caltagirone airfield, September 1942. In the foreground, aircraft with markings 362-11 and 362-6, but only the first one has the unit's emblem painted.

(Sardinia), and Sarzana near Pisa. Due to plans for the unit to be based on the aircraft carrier *Aquila*, the *160° Gruppo* was formally under the command of the Regia Marina. Between March and September 1943, the unit completed 1206 combat flights, engaging in numerous air battles.

On 31 March, the Reggiane RE 2001, along with aircraft from the *24° Gruppo*, clashed over southern Sardinia with an American bombing expedition. No losses were incurred in the air, but during takeoff from Decimomannu airfield, three RE 2001s were destroyed in an attack by American aircraft, and the pilots were killed. Another aircraft of this type was seriously damaged. On 14 May, 1943, while repelling an American air attack on targets in the Olbia region, *Serg*. Dante Baiutti reported damaging a P-38. It is possible that his victim was one of the three Lightnings lost by the 82nd Fighter Group that day. On 24 May, six RE 2001s along with five C.202s from the *24° Gruppo*, participated in a battle with Lightnings from the 82nd Fighter Group, which were escorting bombers attacking targets in the Olbia and Venafiority areas. In the clash, both Italian units reported 7 confirmed and 2 probable victories (all against P-38s). Among the Reggiane pilots, confirmed victories were credited to *Serg*. Baiutti, *Serg.M.* Crabbia, and *Serg*. Valentini. Additionally, *Serg*. Baiutti reported a probable kill of a Lightning. The only American loss was a P-38 piloted by 1/Lt. "Ricky" Zubarika (an ace with 8 victories), who was captured. However, several other P-38s were damaged. In the engagement over Sardinia, the USAAF pilots also demonstrated creativity – they reported 5 confirmed victories, 1 probable, and 7 damages, with one Italian loss being a C.202.

On 1 June, in the Olbia region, S.Ten Pezzi and *Serg*. Baiutti reported shooting down two twin-engine bombers (identified as Bostons). These were likely B-25 Mitchells from the 310th Bomber Group. The American unit lost two aircraft – one ditched off the North African coast due to damage, and the

Reggiane RE 2001 with marking 1-1 from 1ª Squadriglia (1° Nucleo Addestramento Intercettori), Treviso airfield, June 1943.

A pilot of RE 2001 from 303ª Squadriglia *before a combat flight.*

Reggiane RE 2001 CN from 234ª Squadriglia *(marking 234-2) in uniform black paint, at Ciampino (or Rimini) airfield, summer 1943.*

Reggiane RE 2001 from an undetermined Italian unit, likely spring 1943. Notable is the very wide, white identification stripe on the fuselage.

Maintenance work on a Reggiane RE 2001. The photo clearly shows the shape of the fuselage behind the pilot's cockpit. The indentations in the "hump" were meant to provide the pilot with better rear visibility. Considering that the pilot only had a single rearview mirror placed centrally, it seems that it improved visibility only to a small extent.

other was likely damaged by anti-aircraft fire. Pilots of the C.202 from the *24° Gruppo* also claimed victories over the Bostons in this engagement.

On 18 June, in a fight with Lightnings, *Serg*. Dante Baiutti was killed, and the aircraft of *Serg*. Angelo Birago was damaged. In this encounter, the Italian fighters claimed a P-38 and a Boston (this time a B-26 Marauder from the 19th Bomber Group). Another P-38 was shot down jointly by *M.llo* Dulio Bernardi and a pilot from the *Luftwaffe* (either from JG 51 or JG 77). On 24 June, during a fierce battle over Olbia, Reggiane pilots claimed definite kills of two P-38s and two Bostons (likely B-26s), as well as two B-24s probably. Pilots of the C.202 from the *24° Gruppo* added 2 shot down Lightnings. Meanwhile, *Luftwaffe* fighters (JG 77) claimed as many as 14 P-38 downed. The actual American losses were 5 Lightnings shot down and 9 damaged. There was also one B-24D lost and one damaged Marauder that landed forcibly at its base. During the aerial duel, two Reggiane from the *375a Squadriglia* were damaged, but the pilots emerged unscathed.

There were also occasional flights against British aircraft attacking at night. On 14 July, three RE 2001s from the *160° Gruppo* intercepted a pair of Beaufighters from No. 47 Squadron RAF attacking a convoy near Corsica. The Italians claimed to have shot down both opponents, but this is not confirmed in British losses. However, on 26 July *Cap*. Tito Valtancoli of the *375a Squadriglia* shot down a Beaufighter X (LX784, crew: F/O King, F/Sgt Tinham – listed as missing) south of Caprera Island. This was one of the last combat actions of this group.

In August 1942, the first RE 2001 CB aircraft arrived at the *102° Gruppo Tuffatori*, a dive bomber unit equipped with Junkers Ju 87R. The first familiarisation flight in an *Ariete I* was carried out on 26 August by Captain Giuseppe Cenni – a legend of Italian aviation. After getting to know the aircraft and its capabilities, Cenni prepared a report on the use of the RE 2001 by the dive bomber unit. It was planned that they would be used for night attacks on targets in Malta together with the "Stukas". After carrying out a bombing attack, the aircraft could provide cover for the dive bombers. One such flight took place on 22 September, when seven Italian "Stukas" and one RE 2001 piloted by Captain Giuseppe Cenni attacked targets on the island of Gozo. It is said that Cenni attracted the attention of enemy fighters, allowing the Italian Ju 87R to complete their mission. In the spring of 1943, however, the group was re-equipped with RE 2002 aircraft, which were much better suited for bombing attacks.

In February 1943, familiarisation flights in the RE 2001 were carried out by Lt. Col. Guido Nobili, commander of the *101° Gruppo Tuffatori*, and one of the most experienced pilots of this unit – Lt. Gino Priolo. Earlier, fighting in North Africa, pilots of the *101st Gruppo* flew FIAT CR. 42 and Junkers Ju 87R. Initially, it was planned that their new aircraft would be Junkers Ju 87D, but this changed. At Lonate Pozzolo airfield, the Italian pilots had the opportunity to familiarise themselves with the Reggiane RE 2001. The unit also had D.520 and two-seater FIAT G.50B aircraft. However, in April 1943, Reggiane RE 2002 arrived, which were assessed as the optimal solution.

Above: Loading ammunition into the fuselage-mounted 12.7 mm Breda-SAFAT machine guns.

Above, right: A photo of an RE 2001 just before takeoff. The photo shows in detail the front part of the fuselage. Notable are the intense paint wear on the wings. The durability of the paint coating on Reggiane aircraft was not the highest.

At the end of 1942, about 10 RE 2001 CN aircraft were delivered to two groups forming the *41° Stormo Intercettori* – the *59° Gruppo Intercettori* (*232ª* and *233ª Squadriglia*) and the *60° Gruppo Intercettori* (*234ª* and *235ª Squadriglia*). Among the RE 2001s used by the *59° Gruppo* were at least three aircraft equipped with 20 mm cannons. The *41° Stormo*, previously a bomber unit, was reorganized primarily for night operations. Besides the *Ariete I*, the unit also used other types of aircraft, including 3 Bf 110C, 15 Do 217J, CR. 42, and D.520. The main task was the air defense of industrial centers in northern Italy. In the spring and summer of 1943, there were interceptions of American and British bombing raids, but no spectacular successes were recorded. Italian pilots reported shooting down and damaging enemy bombers, but these were not always reflected in the actual losses. On 28 May, 6 RE 2001 CN aircraft and three D.520s took off after 11:00 from the Metato airfield near Pisa and intercepted a formation of 17 American heavy bombers in the Livorno area. After the battle, the Italian pilots reported 2 certain and one probable "quadrimotori" shootdowns. Additionally, Capt. Ottorino Triboldi reported shooting down a twin-engine aircraft. However, this was not confirmed in the list of American losses.

Towards the end of 1942, about 10 RE 2001 CN aircraft were received by two groups forming the *41° Stormo Intercettori* – the *59° Gruppo Intercettori* (*232ª* and *233ª Squadriglia*) and the *60° Gruppo Intercettori* (*234ª* and *235ª Squadriglia*). Among the RE 2001s used by the *59° Gruppo* were at least three aircraft armed with 20 mm cannons. The *41° Stormo*, previously a bomber unit, was reorganized mainly for night operations. In addition to *Ariete I*, the unit also used other types of aircraft, including 3 Bf 110C, 15 Do 217J, CR. 42, and D.520. The main task was air defense of industrial centres in northern Italy. In spring and summer of 1943, there were interceptions of American and British bombing raids, but no spectacular successes were recorded. Italian pilots did report shooting down and damaging enemy bombers, but these were not always confirmed in actual losses. On 28 May 1943, 6 RE 2001 CNs and three D.520s took off after 11:00 from Metato airfield near Pisa and intercepted a formation of 17 American heavy bombers in the Livorno area. After the battle, Italian pilots reported 2 definite and one probable "quadrimotori" shootdowns. Additionally, Captain Ottorino Triboldi reported shooting down a twin-engine aircraft. However, this was not confirmed in the American loss records. On the morning of 28 June 1943, in the Livorno – Pisa area, pilots of the *59° Gruppo* reported shooting down 2 four-engine aircraft. Again, there were no B-17s or B-24s listed in the USAAF losses. On the night of 18/19 July 1943, Lieutenant Carlo Medun reported a probable aerial victory over a four-engine aircraft, but the location of the engagement was not specified. It should be noted that neither the British nor the Americans lost any heavy bombers that night. The effectiveness of Italian fighters was demonstrated on the night of 16/17 August 1943 when three RE 2001s from the *59° Gruppo* were scrambled to repel an attack by British bombers on Turin. Sergeants M. Gaetano Tonini and Lieutenant Cesare Balli reported shooting down two bombers – one near Altessano and the other near Rivara. Indeed, during the raid on Turin, two Halifax II bombers were lost (one from No. 35 Squadron RAF and one from No. 405 Squadron RCAF). On the day of the armistice, the unit had, among others, 19 operational RE 2001 CNs (11 of them serviceable).

From January to September 1943, the RE 2001 fighters were equipped to the *167° Gruppo* (*300ª* and *303ª Squadriglia*). The unit was stationed at Ciampino, Grottagile, and Littoria airfields. The aircraft were primarily used to repel American raids on Italian cities and industrial centres. During one such mission, on 17 July 1943, near the island of Ischia, *M.llo* Erminio Crescenzi and *Cap*. Paolo Spadiccini claimed a joint victory over a P-38, which, however, is not confirmed in the USAAF loss records. Two days later, over the Italian capital, a confrontation occurred with USAAF bombers in which *Cap*. Spadaccini reported shooting down a B-17, and *Ten*. Bruno Serotini a B-25. It is possible that Spadiccini's victim was a B-24D (s/n 42-40665, "Ten High") from the 389th Bomber Group, which, damaged, landed in Malta. Serotini's victim could have been a Mitchell from the 321st Bomber Group. Shortly after, his Reggiane was hit by fire from an American gunner. Although the Italian managed to eject from the burning aircraft, his parachute did not open. Ten. Serotini was posthumously awarded the Medaglia d'Oro. Another pilot from the *303ª Squadriglia* (*Cap*. Edmondo Massi) died when his RE 2001 collided with a German aircraft during takeoff. It should be added that pilots from the *59° Gruppo*, who also participated in the skirmish over Rome, reported a probable B-17 shootdown. On 11 August *M.llo* Erminio Crescenzi from the *167° Gruppo* reported shooting down a B-17 near Ostia, but there is no unequivocal confirmation of this success.

Italian personnel inspecting a Reggiane RE 2001 that "nosedived". The photo clearly shows two Venturi tubes, the method of opening the pilot's canopy cover, and a mount for a photo-gun on the right wing.

The *1° Nucleo Addestramento Intercettori* was a training unit for night fighter and interceptor squadrons. In its three squadrons, there were nearly 40 RE 2001s in total, with the most in the *1ª Squadriglia*, which was responsible for pilot training. The *Ariete I* fighters were also in the aviation schools at Osoppo and Venaria Reale.

On the day of the armistice, over 70 RE 2001s were in the Regia Aeronautica units, but only 33 aircraft were operational. Some of the aircraft were destroyed to prevent them from falling into German hands, and those that survived were split between the south (*Aeronautica Cobelligerante Italiana*) and the north (*Aviazione Nationale Repubblicana* and *Luftwaffe*).

RE 2001 aircraft from 2° Gruppo Autonomo C.T. *at an airfield on Pantalleria, summer 1942.*

Reggiane RE 2001 from 2° Gruppo Autonomo C.T. *with the unusually placed personal name "Pierino" above the phalanx symbol.*

Reggiane RE 2001 GV (M.M.7226) from Sezione Speciale with a 630 PD bomb under the fuselage, Elmas airfield, August 1942.

Work on attaching a 630 PD bomb under the fuselage of RE 2001 G.V.

Details of the of a 630 PD bomb under the fuselage of RE 2001 G.V.

Prototype RE 2001 GV (M.M.7226) in the Reggiane factory hangar, February 1942.

Reggiane RE 2001 (M.M.08071) in the Fotografico *version with two Cineavia cameras mounted on the leading edges of the wings, Guidonia, spring 1943.*

A German Robot camera experimentally mounted on the wing of an RE 2001. The tests did not result in the implementation of this version into production and operational use.

Reggiane RE 2001 OR with markings of 394ª Squadriglia *during trials in Perugia in 1943.*

On 24 June 1942, Benito Mussolini visited 2° Gruppo Autonomo C.T. and awarded distinguished pilots. One of them was Ten. Giorgio Pocek, shown in the photo, who received the Medaglia d'Argento.

Visit by King Victor Emmanuel III and high Italian commanders to the Furbara air base in March 1943, on the occasion of the 20th anniversary of the founding of Regia Aeronautica. Two RE 2001 aircraft are in the background.

Reggiane RE 2001 from 369ª Squadriglia (marking 369-1) during refueling. Notable is the dust filter on the air intake. From photo analysis, it seems that such a solution was used relatively infrequently.

Aeronautica Cobelligerante Italiana and *Aeronautica Militare*

Soon after the Italian capitulation, at least a dozen RE 2001 aircraft flew over to the Allied side. These were machines previously serving in the 160° and *167° Gruppo*. It cannot be ruled out that later the inventory of Reggiane RE 2001 aircraft under the *Aeronautica Cobelligerante Italiana* (until 1946 also referred to as Regia Aeronautica) increased with machines located in various repair bases. However, this likely involved only a few aircraft.

Six aircraft were allocated to the *82ª Squadriglia*, part of the *155° Gruppo Autonomo*, based at the Elmas airfield in Sardinia. Meanwhile, seven aircraft (of which 3 were technically operational) were assigned to the *356ª Squadriglia* (*21° Gruppo*), stationed at the Brindisi-Casale airfield in southern Italy.

The first combat mission of the RE 2001 was a reconnaissance flight carried out by two *Ariete I* on 5 October 1943. It was a visual reconnaissance of airfields located in Albania (Valona, Carpi) and Greece (Paramythia and Ioannina). On 12 November 1943, five RE 2001s participated in an attack on the German-occupied Berat airfield in Albania. On 28 November, the commander of the *356ª Squadriglia*, *Capitano* Paolo Spadicchini, undertook an unusual mission in a modified RE 2001 *Scorta*. A container suspended under the aircraft's fuselage carried money (about 12 million lire) as aid for the soldiers of the *19ª Divisione Fanteria "Venezia"* (19th Infantry Division "Venezia"), who were in the Pljevlja area in Montenegro. After 8 September 1943, the unit's commander, General Giovanni Batista Oxilla, refused to surrender to the Germans. This decision led to the commencement of fighting against their recent allies alongside Josif "Broz" Tito's Yugoslav partisans. The money was intended to supply the unit, which in early December 1943 was transformed into the *Divisione Italiana Partigiana "Garibaldi"* (Italian Partisan Division "Garibaldi"). The lone RE 2001 *Scorta* was escorted by six C.205V *Veltro* for the 2 hours and 35 minutes flight, and the mission was a success.

In early 1944, all operational RE 2001s were transferred to the *20° Gruppo* and then to the *101° Gruppo Tuffatori*. Both units were based at the Lecce-Galatina airfield. RE 2001s were used for combat missions in a limited capacity until May 1944. The missions mainly involved supporting Yugoslav partisan units. Subsequently, the aircraft were transferred to the Scuola Addestramento Caccia in Leverano.

After the war, it was discovered that in addition to the aircraft used in the school in Leverano, many other RE 2001s were still present in Italy. At the airfield in Ferrara, about 20 machines were identified as suitable for repair. Other airfields, repair bases, and aircraft factories contained components and parts of the *Ariete I*. In the Caproni factories in Predappio alone, about 30 fuselages were found. There was an idea to restore several dozen RE 2001s to service, but this was abandoned due to the significant costs involved. Another factor was the aircraft's poor performance and the rearming of Italian air units with American and British aircraft. Eventually, the newly formed Italian Air Force (*Aeronautica Militare*) only used five RE 2001 aircraft. Three of them were assigned to the unit commanded by Lt. Enrico Dallari – Sezione Meteorologica – stationed at the Venice-Lido (S.Nicolo) airfield. These aircraft had the markings U-31, U-32, and U-34. In May 1947, two of the aircraft were damaged in an act of sabotage, suspected to have been carried out by the Israeli organization Haganah. Apparently, this was due to a mistake – the RE 2001s were mistaken for Macchi C.205Vs, which were supposed to be sent to Egypt.

A pair of RE 2001 aircraft of the Cobelligerante Air Force, likely in the autumn of 1943. The planes have transport containers under the fuselage. The aircraft in the background likely has a circular antenna for a directional radio finder mounted underneath.

An RE 2001 taxiing at Galatina airfield, probably from the 356ª Squadriglia *(*20° Gruppo, 51° Stormo*), early 1944. The emblem of the* 51° Stormo *is visible on the vertical stabilizer. The positioning of the Italian national markings on the lower wing surfaces is clearly visible.*

RE 2001 S with tactical number 5 in flight – one of the few photos of Ariete I *in flight. The photo shows the placement of national markings on the upper and side surfaces of the aircraft.*

Two other *Ariete Is* were assigned as liaison aircraft to units stationed at the Rome-Centocelle and Giota del Colle airfields. In the Italian Air Force, the RE 2001s served until the end of the 1940s and were then scrapped.

Aviazione Nationale Repubblicana

On the northern side (Repubblica Sociale Italiana), a total of several dozen RE 2001 aircraft were found, but most likely only 5–6 of them were incorporated into the service of the *Aviazione Nationale Repubblicana*. The aircraft were used for training at the Scuola Addestramento CN in Albenga, which trained night fighter pilots. The *Ariete I* was also used as a liaison aircraft in the Reparto Aereo Collegamenti at the Bresso (MI) airfield. Reports of the *Ariete I's* combat use by the *170ª Squadriglia Autonoma* Caccia Noturna have not been unequivocally confirmed.

It is also worth mentioning an interesting aspect related to the RE 2001s found in northern Italy. Photographs of the Reggiane plants taken after the Allied raid on 8 January 1944, show at least a dozen destroyed *Ariete Is* that were in the factory hall. About 20 more RE 2001s were located at various airfields in northern Italy – Bologna, Pavullo, Formignie. These aircraft were not used operationally and were destroyed by the Germans in the spring of 1944.

*RE 2001 CN (likely M.M.90075) with tactical number 1 in non-standard paint, Lecce-Galatina, February 1944. This paint scheme, known as "Estiva" (summer), was created during the aircraft's overhaul at SRAM Monrerrato. Initially, the aircraft served in the 82*ª Squadriglia *(*155° Gruppo*), and was later transferred to the* 101° Gruppo *(*5° Stormo*).*

RE 2001 with marking 5-82 from the 82ª Squadriglia *(*155° Gruppo*), Elmas airfield, November 1943. The aircraft is in an unusual paint scheme, likely applied during an overhaul. It is difficult to determine whether the camouflage blotches on the upper surfaces were bi – or tri-colour.*

RE 2001 in natural aluminium (or silver) colour, but without any tactical markings. Italian national markings were located on the fuselage and wings, and the rear part of the fuselage had the type description and the military number M.M. These photos were likely taken after the end of the war.

Luftwaffe

As for the *Luftwaffe*, the exact number of RE 2001s used by the Germans is not known, but it was likely small. The use of the aircraft with the serial number M.M.90790 in the *Luftwaffe* training unit – JG 107, stationed in Bad Vöslau, is confirmed. On 1 April 1944, the aircraft was damaged (left wing) following a collision with a Messerschmitt Bf 109.

One of the few photos of the RE 2001 in Luftwaffe *service. Most likely, this is an aircraft that served in the training unit JG 107 stationed in Bad Vöslau. According to some sources, the aircraft had an Italian military number M.M. 90790 and a German number, probably 8553. The photo shows a damaged wingtip, which was the result of a collision with a Messerschmitt Bf 109 on 1 April 1944. There is also a trace of the white cross on the tail fin being painted over.*

Camouflage and markings

Regia Aeronautica

The first prototype of the RE 2001, M.M.409, initially featured a natural aluminium colour. The only parts painted in the Italian national colours were the rudder and elevators, which had green-white-red stripes. Later on, the aircraft received a typical Reggiane camouflage pattern for that period. The upper surfaces were painted in a light brown colour (*Giallo Mimetico 3* or *4*), with small masking spots in dark green (*Verde Mimetico 2*) and brown (*Marrone Mimetico 2*). The lower surfaces were painted in a light grey colour (Grigio Mimetico). The second prototype, M.M.408, was painted in the same manner.

For the serial production aircraft, the basic painting scheme was named "Metropolitano." This involved painting the upper surfaces in an olive green colour (*Verde Oliva Scuro 2*), while the lower surfaces were painted in a light grey-blue colour (*Grigio Azzuro Chiaro 1*). A distinctive feature of this scheme was that the olive green colour also covered part of the lower surfaces of the wings. A white identification stripe was present on the fuselage. The rudder featured a white cross with the coat of arms of the royal house, usually positioned in the centre. Standardly, the aircraft also had a phalanx emblem on the fuselage (below the cockpit). The national markings were in a reduced visibility version – black fasces in a black circle. The fuselage also carried the type and production series designation (although not always) and the military serial number M.M. (Matricolo Militare), usually in black with white shading. Additionally, the vertical stabilizer bore descriptions of weight (in black or white). Most aircraft had the Reggiane factory logo on their tail units. Meanwhile, a few aircraft from the last production series had the name *Ariete I* painted on, usually in white. As for the propeller spinner, it was either olive green (*Verde Oliva Scuro 2*) or white. Sometimes the spinners had squadron markings – typically, the tip of the spinner was painted in the squadron colour, less frequently stripes were painted on the spinners.

In July 1943, following the overthrow of Benito Mussolini, the fasces symbols and the national markings on the wings of the aircraft were painted over (although sometimes the black outline of the mark was left intact).

Some aircraft that were produced in the night fighter version, RE 2001 CN, were uniformly painted in black (*Nero 12*). These aircraft did not have national markings on the wings, and the fasces symbol was not placed on the fuselages. Identifying elements included a white stripe on the fuselage (though on many aircraft this was painted over, either completely or partially) and a white cross on the rudder. If the aircraft in the night paint scheme had the type and production series designation and the military serial number M.M., these were in blue.

The tactical markings of the RE 2001 in *Regia Aeronautica* units consisted of the squadron number (*Squadriglia*) and an individual aircraft number. Both their colour and placement on the fuselage varied and were related to the specificities of the units.

On the aircraft of the *2° Gruppo*, the *Squadriglia* number was usually placed before the white identification stripe. In the *150ª* and *152ª Squadriglia*, the numbers were light blue (or light grey-blue). However, in the *358ª Squadriglia*, the number was most likely white. In the *152ª* and *358ª Squadriglia*, the individual numbers were red and typically placed on the white identification stripe. In the *150ª Squadriglia*, the individual number was also red, but it was placed behind the white identification stripe. There were also deviations from these standard practices. There are known photographs of at least two aircraft from the *150ª Squadriglia*, which had tactical markings – the unit number (white) and the aircraft number (red) – placed on the fuselage between the identification stripe and the cockpit. Additionally, these were significantly smaller than the standard markings. This variant of markings likely appeared at the beginning of 1943 when the unit was active in defending Italian territory from Allied raids.

On at least several photographs, individual tactical numbers of aircraft are visible, painted on the main landing gear covers or on the vertical stabilizer. It is difficult to definitively determine which *Squadriglia* these aircraft served in, and information about their affiliation with the *2° Gruppo* is not unequivocally confirmed.

In the spring of 1941, Italian fighters introduced an identification marking in the form of noses painted yellow (the band was about 60 cm wide). Officially, this way of marking aircraft was discontinued in October 1941. However, it seems that some RE 2001s of the *2° Gruppo* might still have had such identification markings in early 1942.

Many aircraft serving in the *2° Gruppo* had the unit's emblem on the vertical stabilizer – a "pulcino con mitra" (chick with a machine gun), designed by pilot *Sergente* Giovanni Dringoli of the *150ª Squadriglia*. A few aircraft from the *152ª Squadriglia* had individual emblems painted on the engine cowls. The aircraft marked 152-1 featured the coat of arms of the city of Trento, 152-4 the coat of arms of the city of Zara (now Zadar), and 152-10 had a Joker emblem. Two other aircraft had emblems in the form of a girl in clogs and a duckling.

For the aircraft of the *22° Gruppo* (*359ª*, *362ª*, and *369ª Squadriglia*), the rules were slightly more uniform. The unit number was placed on the identification stripe in red or black, followed by the individual aircraft number (in red or white). This approach meant that from the left side, the individual number was behind the stripe, but from the right side, it was in front of the identification stripe. The propeller spinners of aircraft from this group were usually white.

Many publications mention the RE 2001s of the *362ª Squadriglia*, which were supposed to have paint schemes consistent with one of the North African (A.S. – *Africa Settentrionale*) variants, i.e., a sandy base colour with olive-green "smoke rings" camouflage. However, a photo of the aircraft marked 362-4 clearly shows that it had the standard "Metropolitano" paint scheme. There is also no known photograph of any other aircraft from this unit in the A.S. paint scheme.

Some aircraft had the emblem of the *22° Gruppo – Lo Spauracchio* (scarecrow) – painted on their fuselages, usually just behind the cockpit. Interestingly, in some photos, it is visible that some aircraft had only a white triangle painted, without the silhouette of the scarecrow.

Aircraft from the *234ª Squadriglia* in the night scheme (uniformly painted black) had tactical markings in blue on the fuselage. An example is the RE 2001 with the marking 234-2, which also had the white identification stripe partially painted over.

In the *303ª Squadriglia*, the light blue unit designation was placed before the identification stripe, and the individual aircraft number in red was placed on the stripe. An example is the aircraft with the marking 303-5.

In the *394ª Squadriglia*, the squadron number was black, starting before the identification stripe and ending on it, while the red, individual aircraft number was placed behind the stripe. An example is the RE 2001 OR with the marking 394-1.

On the *Ariete* aircraft that were part of the fighter pilot training unit *1° Nucleo Addestramento Intercettori*, tactical markings were painted on the white identification stripe. The first digit, indicating the unit, was in black, and the second digit, assigned to the specific aircraft, was in red. An example from this unit is the RE 2001 with the marking 1-1.

There is also a very unusual RE 2001 to mention. This is an aircraft from *Serie 0* with the serial number M.M. 08071, which was fitted with two Cineavia cameras, making it the first *Ariete* in a reconnaissance configuration. The aircraft was used in the promotional film "Primo Volo" produced by the Instituto Nazionale Luce. According to Marco Gueli, for better contrast in aerial photography, the aircraft was painted entirely yellow, except for the olive green rudder and a white identification cross (without the royal house's coat of arms). The fuselage also had a white identification stripe. However, it had neither the fasces symbol nor the Italian national markings. In this unusual paint scheme, the aircraft was used by the Reparto "T" at the Rome-Centocelle airfield in early 1943.

However, the information that one of the RE 2001 OR prototypes was uniformly painted in light blue has not been confirmed by photographs.

Aeronautica Cobelligerante Italiana

The RE 2001 aircraft that joined the Allied side under the *Aeronautica Cobelligerante Italiana* had varied paint schemes. Some machines retained their original paint, such as the "Metropolitano" scheme or the uniform black colour. Old markings were painted over, and new ones were applied. The identifying marks were red-white-green roundels. Some aircraft had tactical markings in the style of Regia Aeronautica – with the unit designation and individual aircraft number on the fuselage. An example is the RE 2001 from *82ª Squadriglia* with the marking 5-82. However, it seems that most aircraft only had an individual tactical number. According to some sources, the individual tactical number was also placed on the landing gear covers, but due to the small number of photos and their poor quality, this is hard to confirm. The situation with the colour of the propeller spinners is similar. Were they painted red, which was an identifying feature of Allied aircraft in the Mediterranean region, or were they blue or olive green?

The aircraft that underwent repairs at SRAM in Monserrato, Sardinia, received new paint schemes – the upper surfaces were sand-coloured, with green masking spots resembling "snakes." This likely happened in the autumn of 1943. This scheme somewhat resembled the famous Italian "smoke rings," but was different. The lower surfaces were light grey. This painting scheme is sometimes referred to as "Estiva" (summer). It is unclear exactly what paints were used for this camouflage – whether they were still Italian stocks or already Allied colours. The most well-known example of an aircraft in this scheme is an RE 2001 CN with 20 mm cannons and a white tactical number 1. Identifying the paint scheme of the previously mentioned aircraft with the marking 5-82 is more challenging. It seems that the camouflage spots on the upper surfaces of this RE 2001, applied over a sand-coloured base, were in two colours: green (dark green) and brown.

Aeronautica Militare

The aircraft that were part of the Sezione Meteorologica at the Venice-Lido (S.Nicolo) airfield were in natural aluminium (or silver) colour. The markings in the form of codes (U-31, U-32, and U-34) were applied in black on the lower surfaces of the wings in such a way that on the right wing, it was aligned with the direction of flight, and on the left, it was reversed. The number (e.g., 32) in black was also located on the vertical stabilizer.

Aviazione Nationale Repubblicana

To date, no photograph of an RE 2001 serving in the ANR has been published. Therefore, it is only possible to speculate that, like other aircraft previously belonging to the *Regia Aeronautica*, changes were limited to new national markings. However, there is no information preserved about the tactical markings of these aircraft.

Luftwaffe

The aircraft that came into German hands likely retained their original Italian paint schemes, namely the "Metropolitano" scheme. Only *Luftwaffe* national markings and German registration numbers were added. The aircraft (M.M. 90790, German number likely 8553) serving in JG 107 had a wide identification stripe on the fuselage, probably yellow in colour. It is uncertain whether the wingtips were painted and, if so, what colour they were (white, yellow?). The propeller spinner was most likely white.

*The prototype Reggiane RE 2001 Delta prepared for a test flight. The aircraft was in standard livery (the "Metropolitano" scheme) – the upper surfaces in dark olive green (*Verde Oliva Scuro 2*), and the lower surfaces in light grey-blue (*Grigio Azzurro Chiaro 1*). There was a white stripe on the fuselage. Note, a white cross on the vertical stabilizer larger than the standard marking of this type.*

The first prototype RE 2001 M.M.409, Reggio Emilia, June 1940. The upper surfaces of the aircraft were light brown (Giallo Mimetico 3 or 4), onto which small camouflage spots of dark green (Verde Mimetico 2) and brown (Marrone Mimetico 2) were applied. The lower surfaces were light grey (Grigio Mimetico). The aircraft had early type national markings on the wings. On the rudder, a white cross with the emblem of the royal coat of arms, and under the cockpit, a phalanx emblem.

Reggiane RE 2001 CN Serie VI (M.M. 90789), Reggio Emilia, Spring 1943. The aircraft was black (Nero 12) overall. The exception was the rudder, which was probably dark green (Verde Oliva Scuro 2). The machine did not have national marking on the wings, and the phalanx emblem was not placed on the fuselage. An identification white stripe on the fuselage was partially painted over. The type designation and military number were in white. On the vertical stabilizer, there was the inscription Ariete I – which was a rarity.

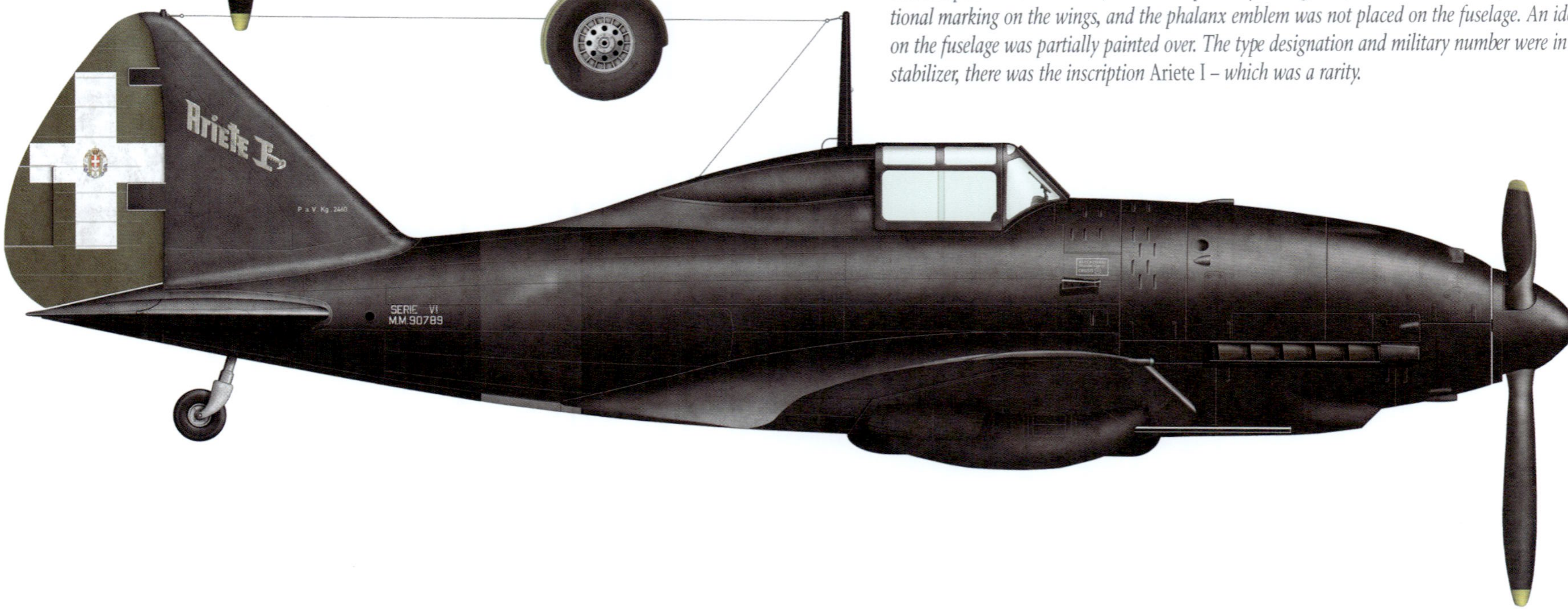

Reggiane RE 2001 Serie 0 *(M.M.08071), Reparto "T", Rome-Centocelle, early 1943. The aircraft was converted into a reconnaissance variant – with two Cineavia cameras fitted in the wing fairings. The aircraft was used in the promotional film "Primo Volo" produced by the* Instituto Nazionale *Luce. To ensure better contrast during aerial photography, the aircraft was entirely painted yellow, except for the rudder which was olive-green with a white identification cross (but without the emblem of the royal house). A white identification stripe was present on the fuselage. However, there were neither phalanx emblems nor Italian national markings.*

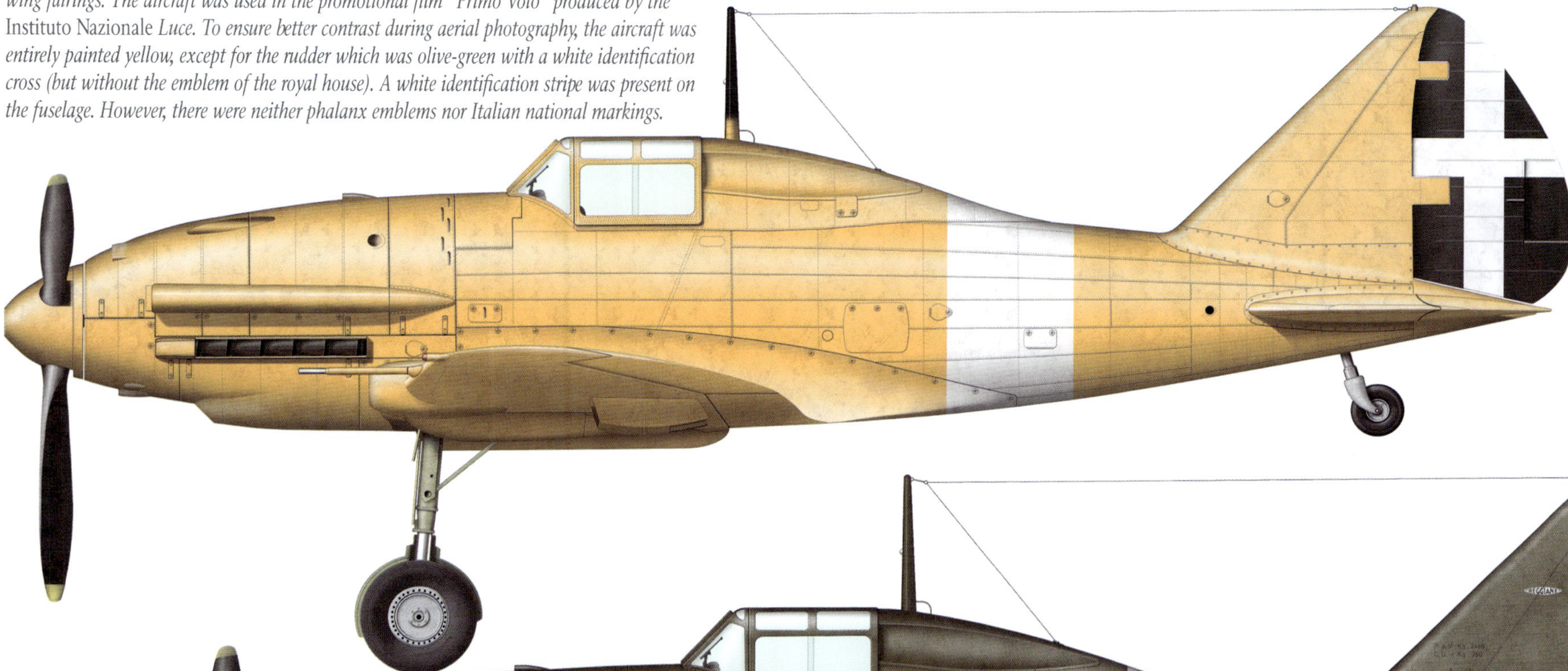

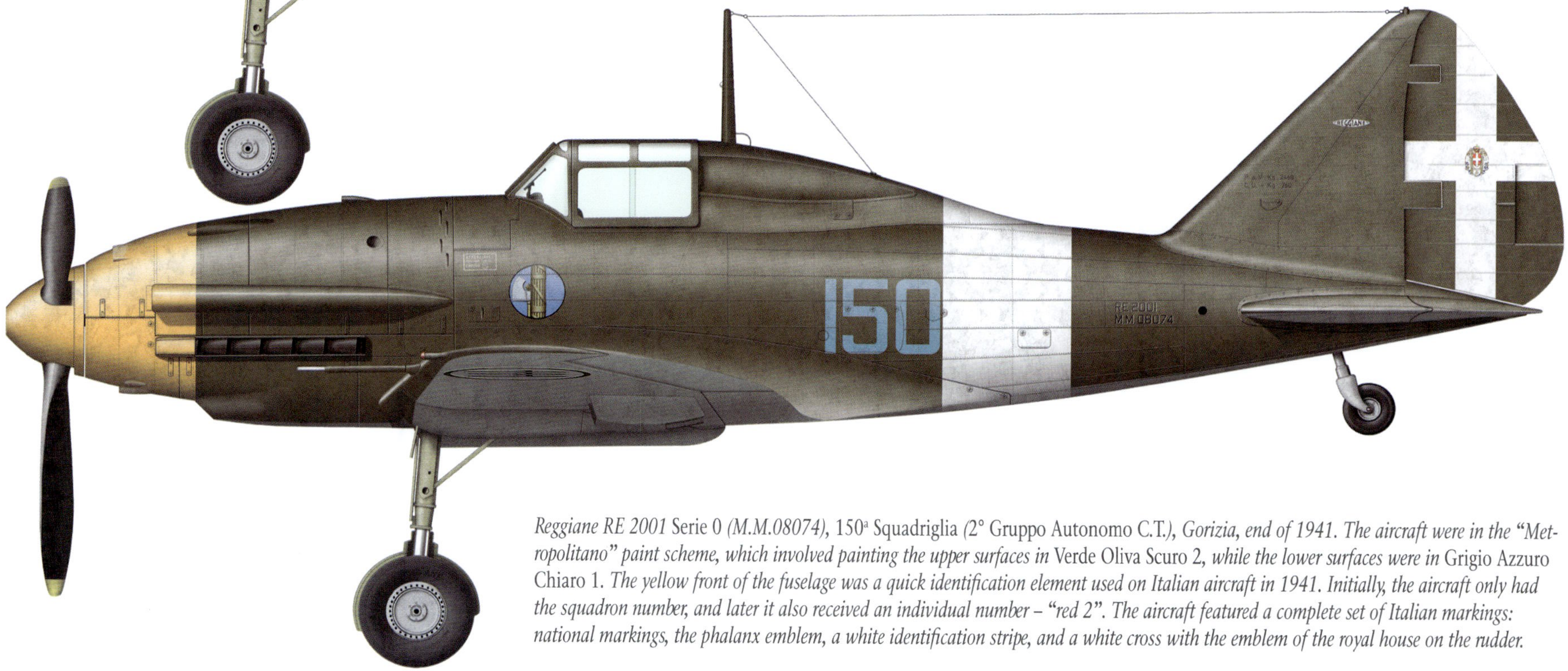

Reggiane RE 2001 Serie 0 *(M.M.08074)*, 150ª Squadriglia *(*2° Gruppo Autonomo *C.T.), Gorizia, end of 1941. The aircraft were in the "Metropolitano" paint scheme, which involved painting the upper surfaces in* Verde Oliva Scuro 2, *while the lower surfaces were in* Grigio Azzuro Chiaro 1. *The yellow front of the fuselage was a quick identification element used on Italian aircraft in 1941. Initially, the aircraft only had the squadron number, and later it also received an individual number – "red 2". The aircraft featured a complete set of Italian markings: national markings, the phalanx emblem, a white identification stripe, and a white cross with the emblem of the royal house on the rudder.*

Reggiane RE 2001 with the designation 1-1 from 1ª Squadriglia *(*1° Nucleo Addestramento Intercettori*), Treviso airfield, June 1943. The aircraft were in the "Metropolitano" paint scheme – upper surfaces in* Verde Oliva Scuro 2, *lower surfaces in* Grigio Azzuro Chiaro 1. *The aircraft featured a complete set of Italian markings.*

Reggiane RE 2001 S (likely M.M.9926, Serie III*),* Aeronautica Cobelligerante Italiana, *"white 5", from* 356ª Squadriglia *(*21° Gruppo*), Brindisi-Casale, November 1943. The aircraft was black (*Nero 12*) overall, which may indicate that it was a RE 2001 CN converted to the* Scorta *version.*

*RE 2001 with the tactical designation 5-82 belonging to 82*ª Squadriglia *(*155° Gruppo*),* Aeronautica Cobelligerante Italiana, *Cagliari-Elmas airfield, November 1943. The aircraft featured an unusual paint scheme applied during its overhaul at the SRAM facilities in Monserrato. The upper surfaces had a sandy base color onto which dark green and brown camouflage spots were applied (it cannot be excluded that the spots were only dark green). The lower surfaces were light grey. It is difficult to definitively determine which paints were used for this scheme. The propeller spinner was white.*

Reggiane RE 2001 from 150ª Squadriglia *(*2° Gruppo Intercettori*) with the marking 150-2, Rome-Ciampino, Spring 1943. The aircraft were in the "Metropolitano" paint scheme – upper surfaces in* Verde Oliva Scuro 2*, and lower surfaces in* Grigio Azzuro Chiaro 1*. The aircraft featured a complete set of Italian markings.*

Reggiane RE 2001 Serie II *(M.M.7216)*, 150ª Squadriglia *(*2° Gruppo Autonomo C.T.*)*, *Santo Pietro di Caltagirone, June 1942. The aircraft, marked as 150-7, was piloted by* Sergente *Giovanni Dringoli – the creator of the group's emblem, which was placed on the vertical stabilizer. The aircraft were in the "Metropolitano" paint scheme – upper surfaces in* Verde Oliva Scuro 2, *and lower surfaces in* Grigio Azzuro Chiaro 1. *The aircraft featured a complete set of Italian markings. The propeller spinner was white.*

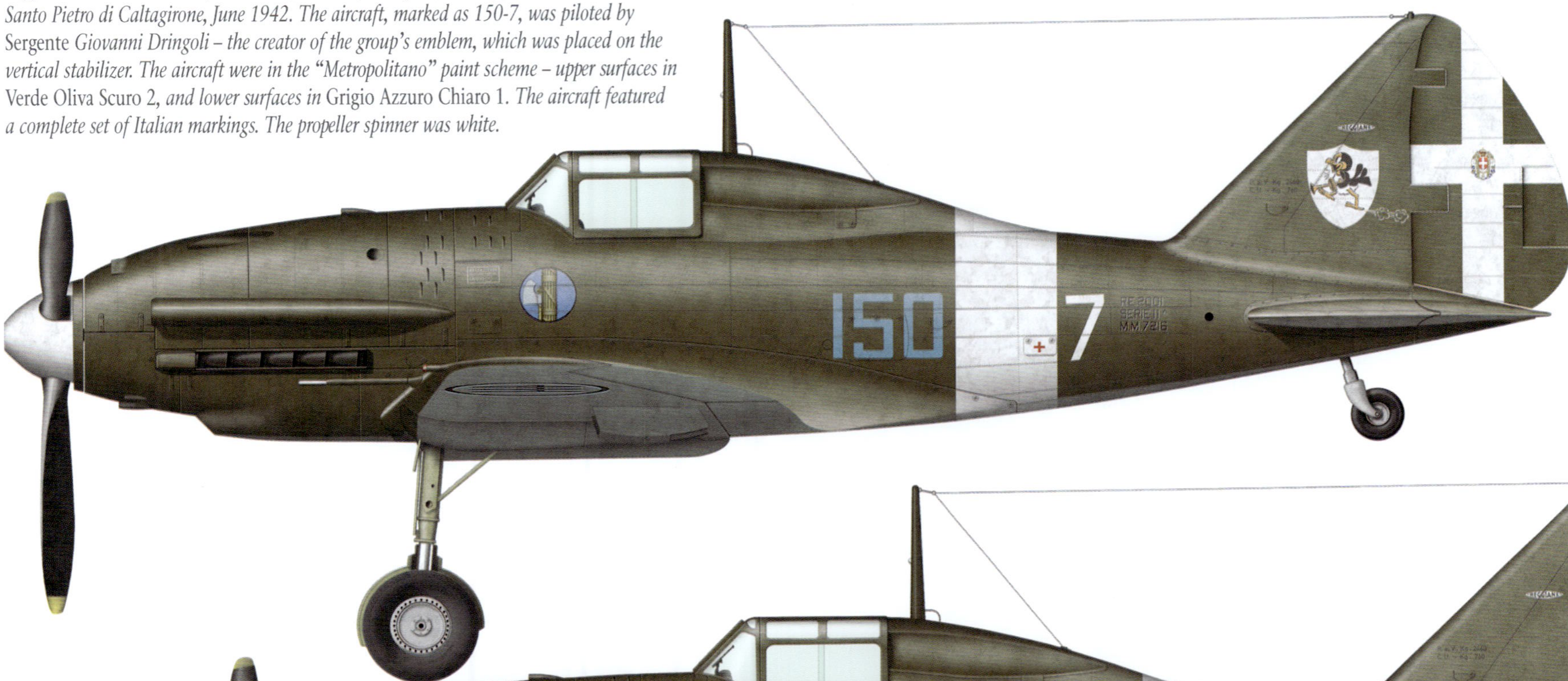

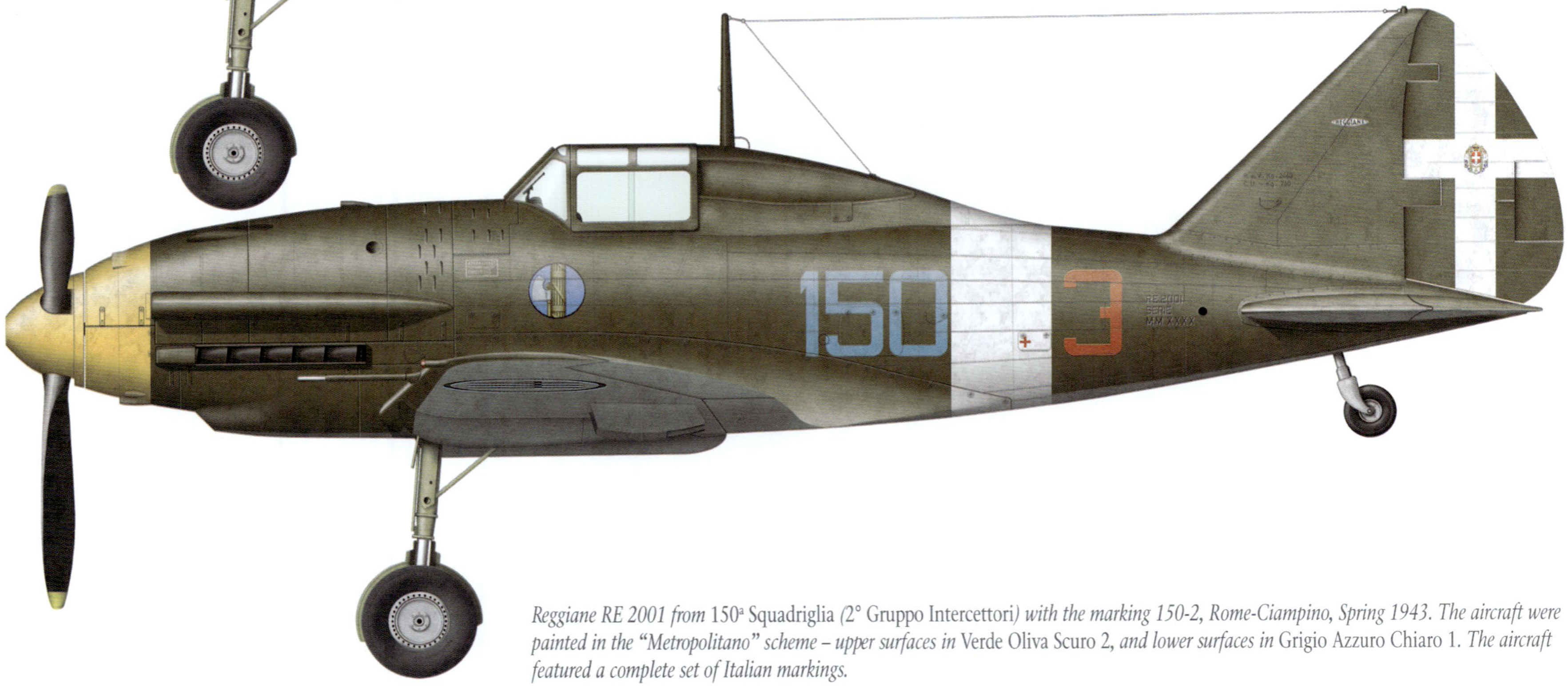

Reggiane RE 2001 from 150ª Squadriglia *(*2° Gruppo Intercettori*) with the marking 150-2, Rome-Ciampino, Spring 1943. The aircraft were painted in the "Metropolitano" scheme – upper surfaces in* Verde Oliva Scuro 2, *and lower surfaces in* Grigio Azzuro Chiaro 1. *The aircraft featured a complete set of Italian markings.*

Reggiane RE 2001 Serie II *(M.M.7209)*, 150ª Squadriglia *(*2° Gruppo Autonomo C.T.*), Santo Pietro di Caltagirone, June 1942. The aircraft, marked as 150-1, was piloted by* Tenente *Remo Cazzolli. The aircraft were painted in the "Metropolitano" scheme, which involved painting the upper surfaces with* Verde Oliva Scuro 2, *while the lower surfaces were* Grigio Azzuro Chiaro 1. *The aircraft featured a complete set of Italian markings. The group's emblem was on the tail, and the pilot's emblem – the coat of arms of Trento (Trent) – was on the engine cover.*

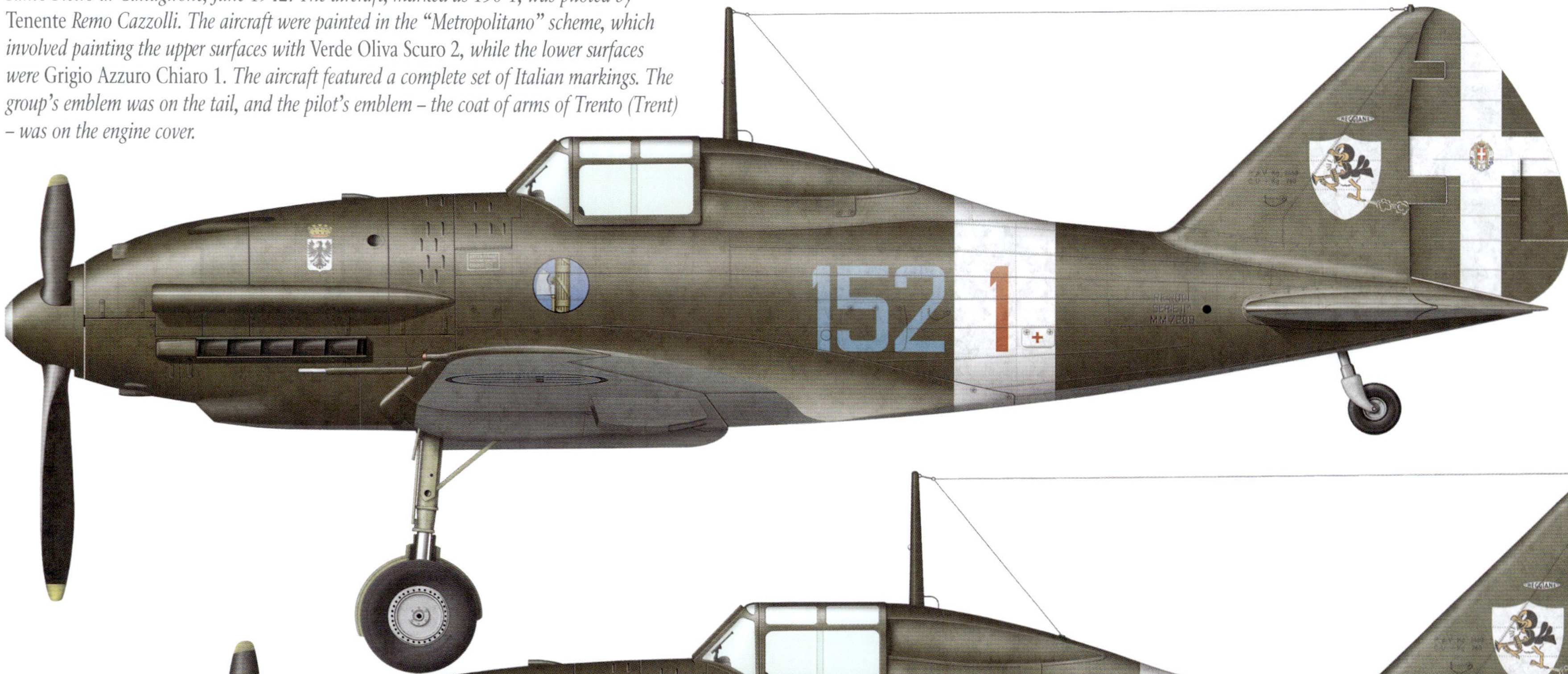

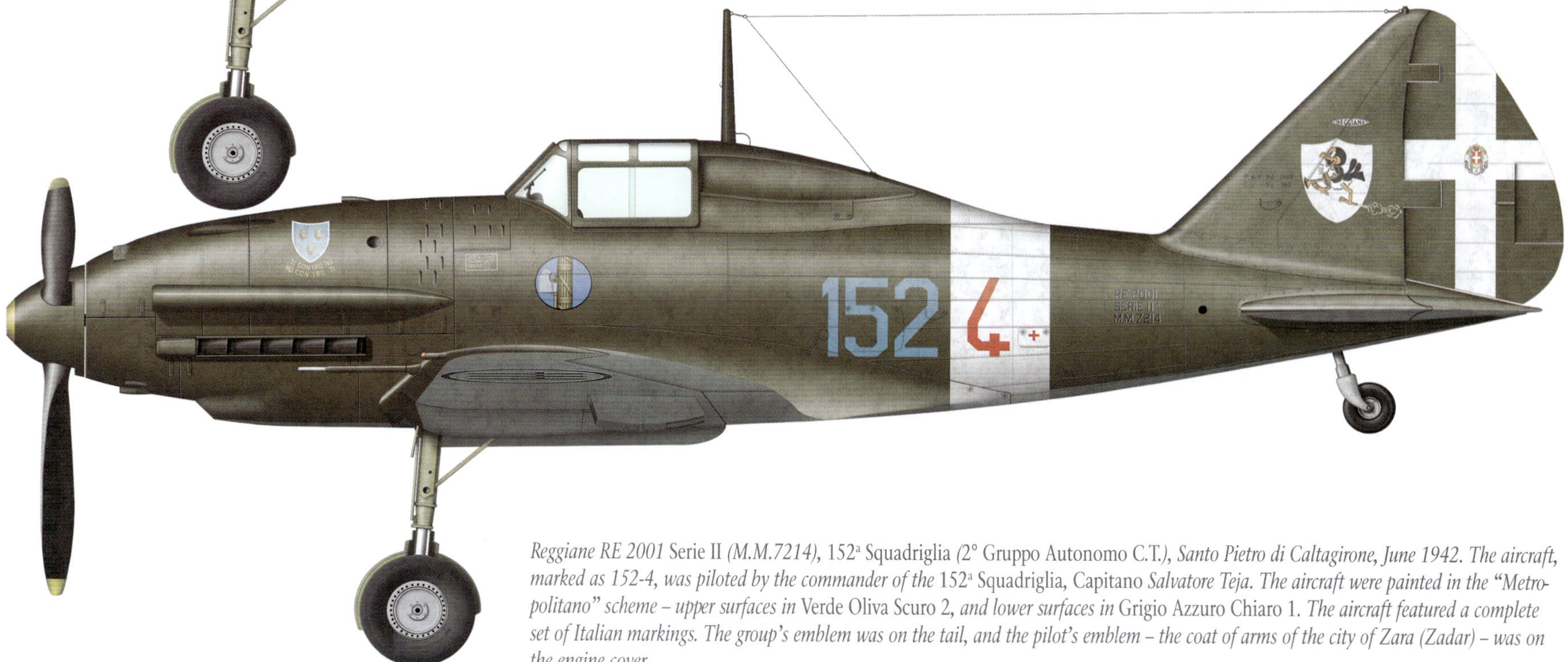

Reggiane RE 2001 Serie II *(M.M.7214)*, 152ª Squadriglia *(*2° Gruppo Autonomo C.T.*), Santo Pietro di Caltagirone, June 1942. The aircraft, marked as 152-4, was piloted by the commander of the* 152ª Squadriglia, Capitano *Salvatore Teja. The aircraft were painted in the "Metropolitano" scheme – upper surfaces in* Verde Oliva Scuro 2, *and lower surfaces in* Grigio Azzuro Chiaro 1. *The aircraft featured a complete set of Italian markings. The group's emblem was on the tail, and the pilot's emblem – the coat of arms of the city of Zara (Zadar) – was on the engine cover.*

Reggiane RE 2001 Serie II *(M.M.7235),* 150ª Squadriglia *(*2° Gruppo Autonomo C.T.*),* *Santo Pietro di Caltagirone, June 1942. The aircraft, marked as 150-10, was piloted by* Tenente *Arnaldo de Merich. The aircraft were painted in the "Metropolitano" scheme – upper surfaces in* Verde Oliva Scuro 2, *and lower surfaces in* Grigio Azzuro Chiaro 1. *The aircraft featured a complete set of Italian markings. The group's emblem was on the tail, and the pilot's emblem on the engine cover was the "Joker".*

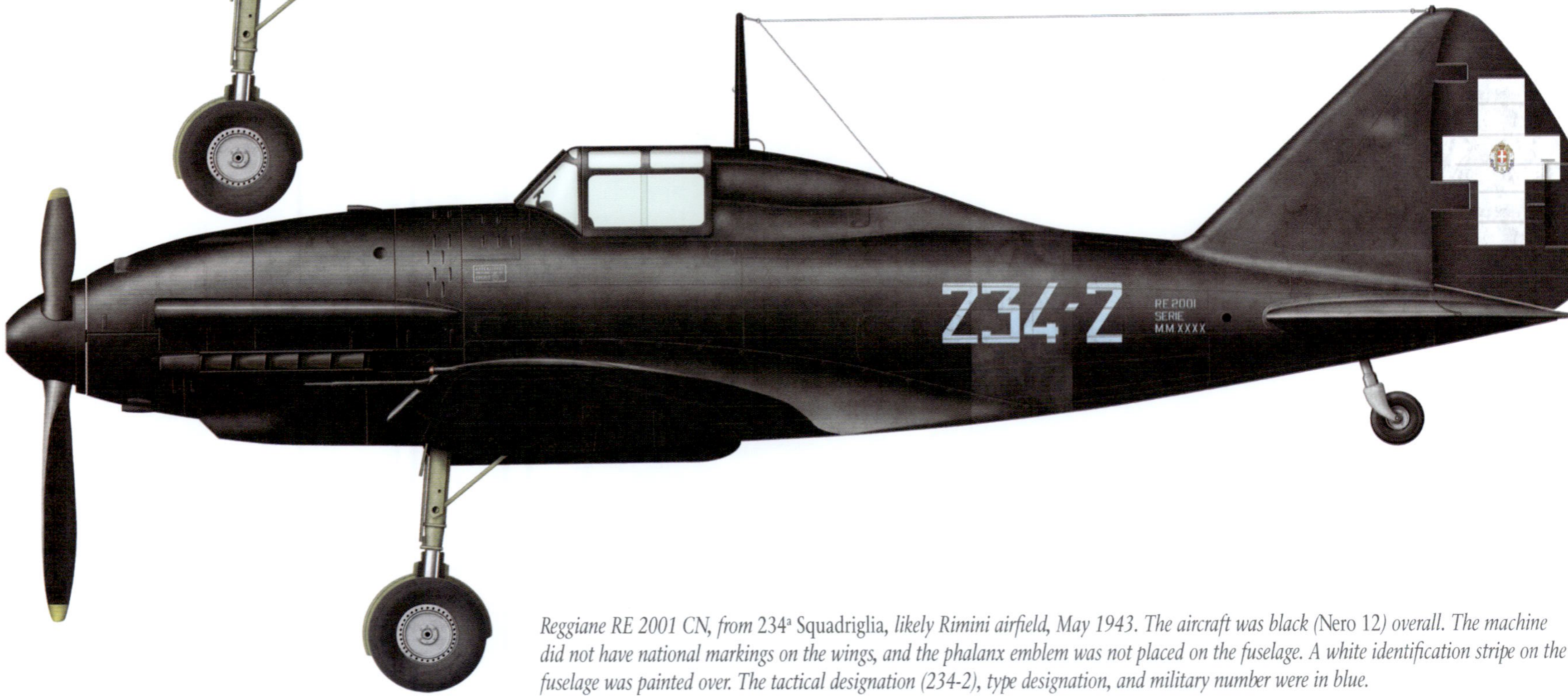

Reggiane RE 2001 CN, from 234ª Squadriglia, *likely Rimini airfield, May 1943. The aircraft was black (*Nero 12*) overall. The machine did not have national markings on the wings, and the phalanx emblem was not placed on the fuselage. A white identification stripe on the fuselage was painted over. The tactical designation (234-2), type designation, and military number were in blue.*

Reggiane RE 2001 with the designation "303-5" from 303ª Squadriglia, *Rome-Ciampino, December 1942. The aircraft were in the "Metropolitano" paint scheme – upper surfaces in* Verde Oliva Scuro 2, *and lower surfaces in* Grigio Azzuro Chiaro 1. *The aircraft featured a complete set of Italian markings.*

Reggiane RE 2001 with the designation "359-4" from 359ª Squadriglia *(22°* Gruppo Autonomo C.T.*), late 1942. The aircraft were in the "Metropolitano" paint scheme – upper surfaces in* Verde Oliva Scuro 2, *and lower surfaces in* Grigio Azzuro Chiaro 1. *The aircraft featured a complete set of Italian markings. A white triangle under the cockpit was prepared for the painting of the unit's emblem.*

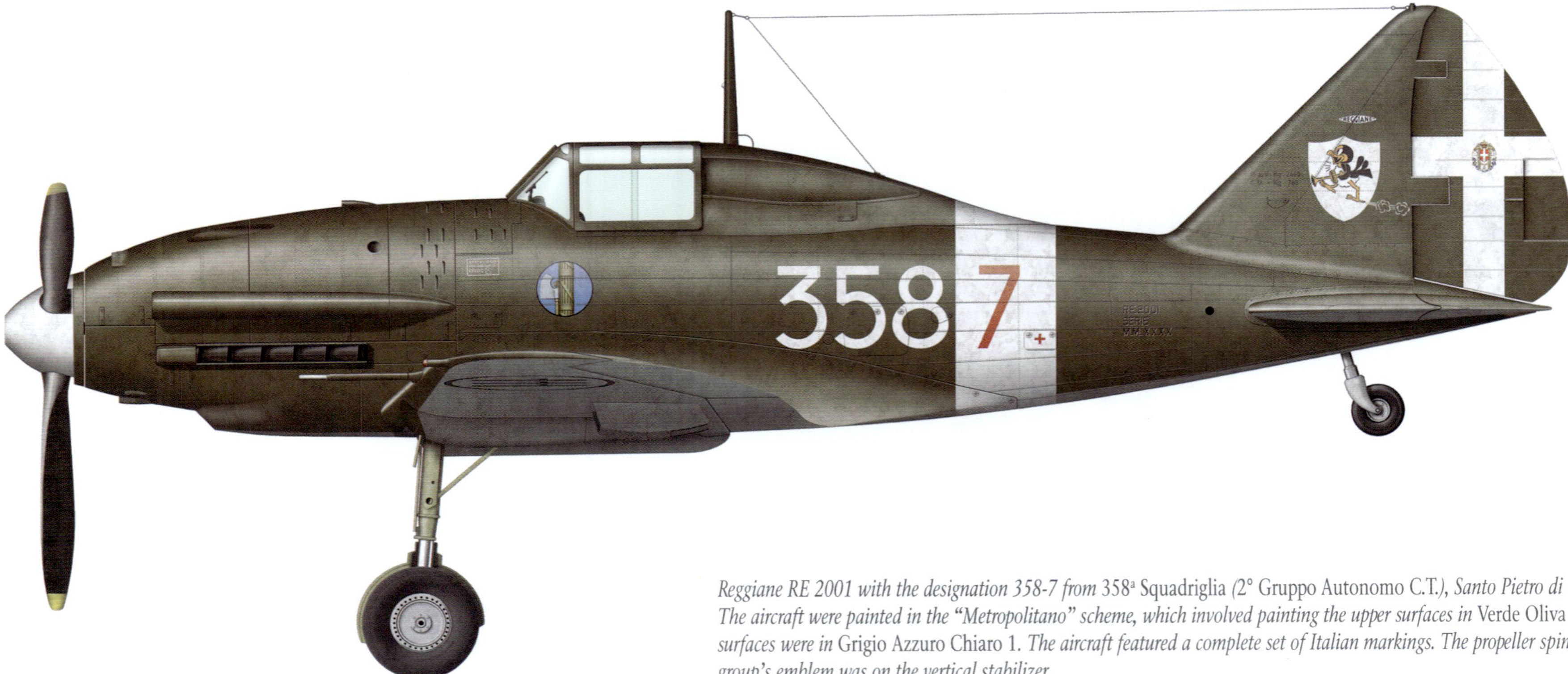

Reggiane RE 2001 with the designation 358-7 from 358ª Squadriglia *(*2° Gruppo Autonomo C.T.*), Santo Pietro di Caltagirone, May 1942. The aircraft were painted in the "Metropolitano" scheme, which involved painting the upper surfaces in* Verde Oliva Scuro 2*, while the lower surfaces were in* Grigio Azzuro Chiaro 1*. The aircraft featured a complete set of Italian markings. The propeller spinner was white, and the group's emblem was on the vertical stabilizer.*

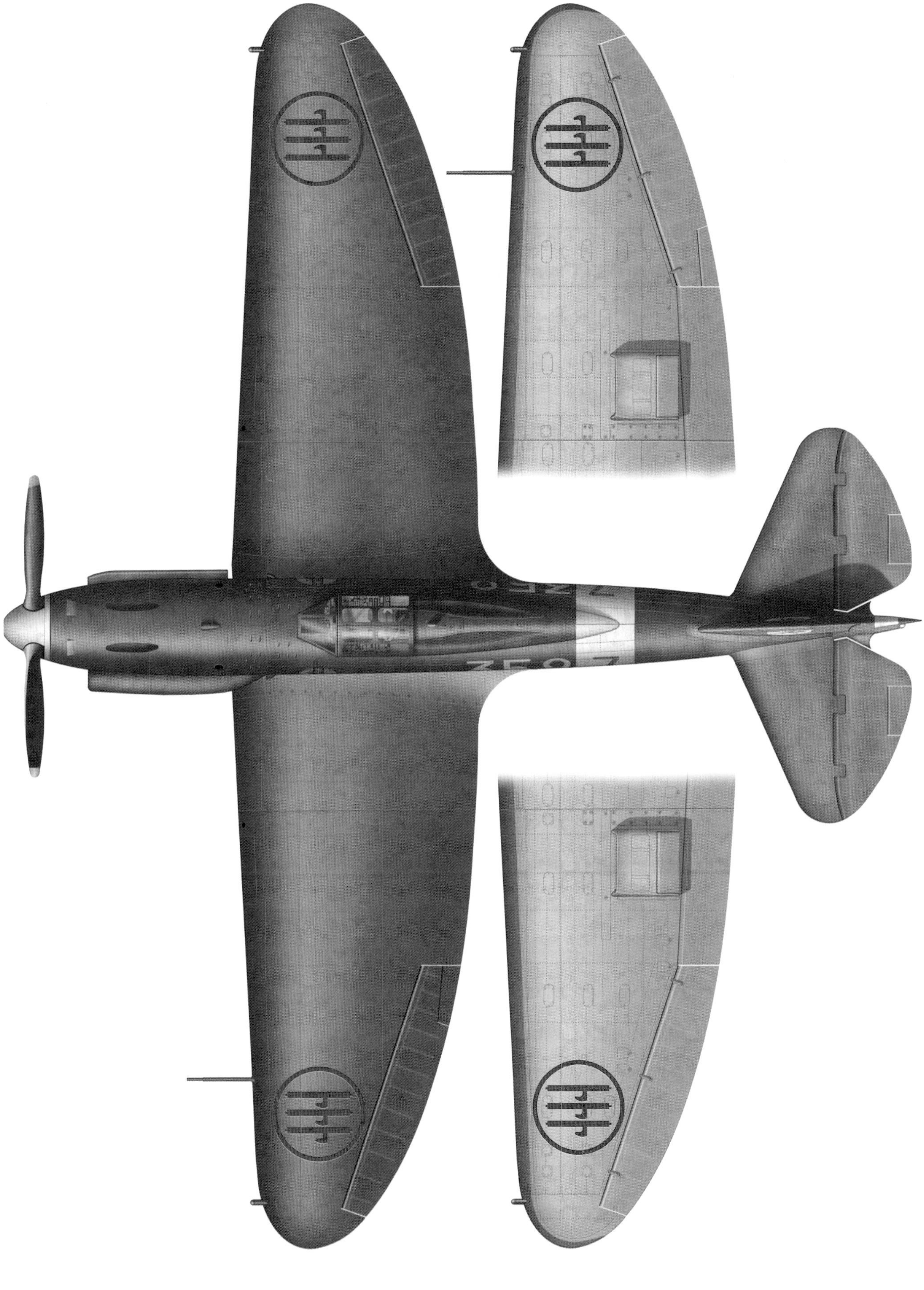

Reggiane RE 2001 Serie II *(M.M.7303) from* 362ª Squadriglia *(*22° Gruppo Autonomo C.T.*), second half of 1942. The aircraft were in the "Metropolitano" paint scheme – upper surfaces in* Verde Oliva Scuro 2, *and lower surfaces in* Grigio Azzuro Chiaro 1. *The central part of the fuselage was very much faded. The aircraft featured a complete set of Italian markings.*

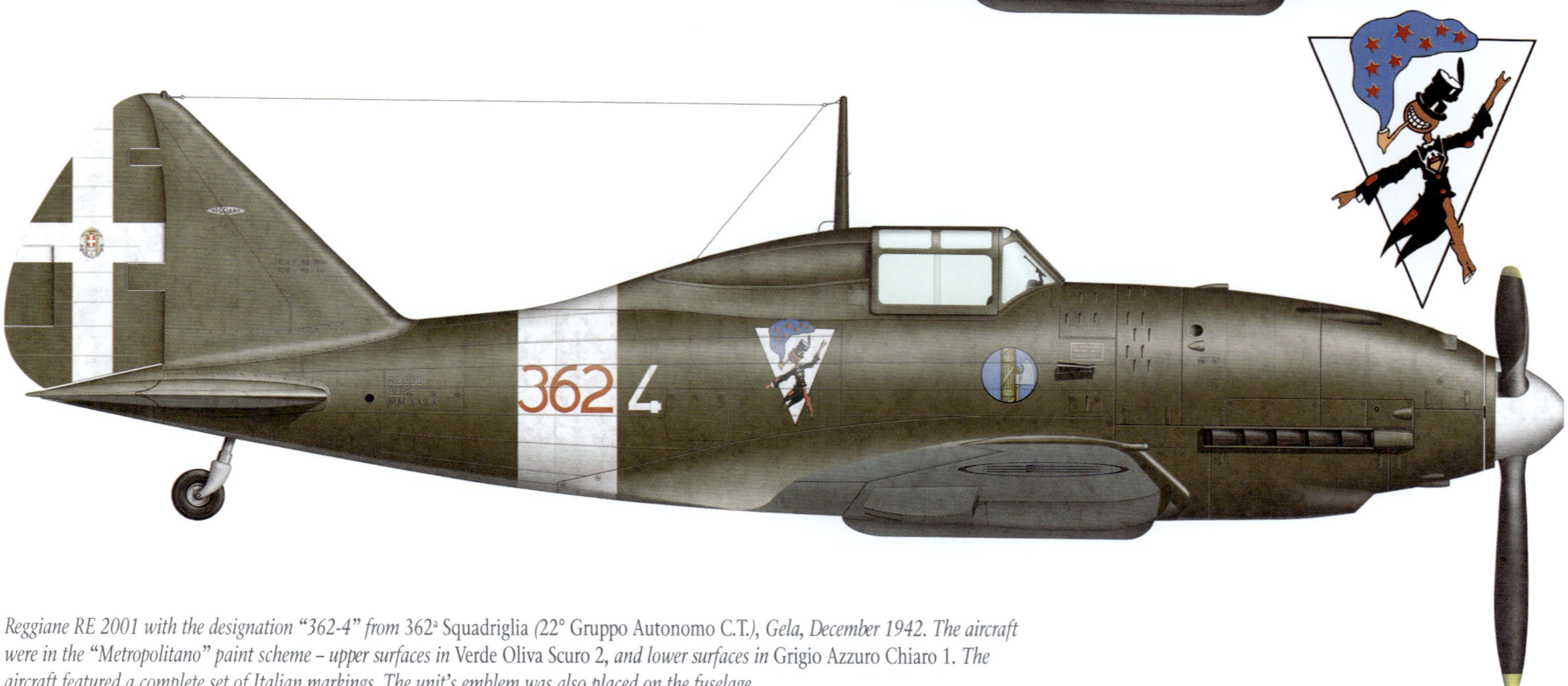

Reggiane RE 2001 with the designation "362-4" from 362ª Squadriglia *(*22° Gruppo Autonomo C.T.*), Gela, December 1942. The aircraft were in the "Metropolitano" paint scheme – upper surfaces in* Verde Oliva Scuro 2, *and lower surfaces in* Grigio Azzuro Chiaro 1. *The aircraft featured a complete set of Italian markings. The unit's emblem was also placed on the fuselage.*

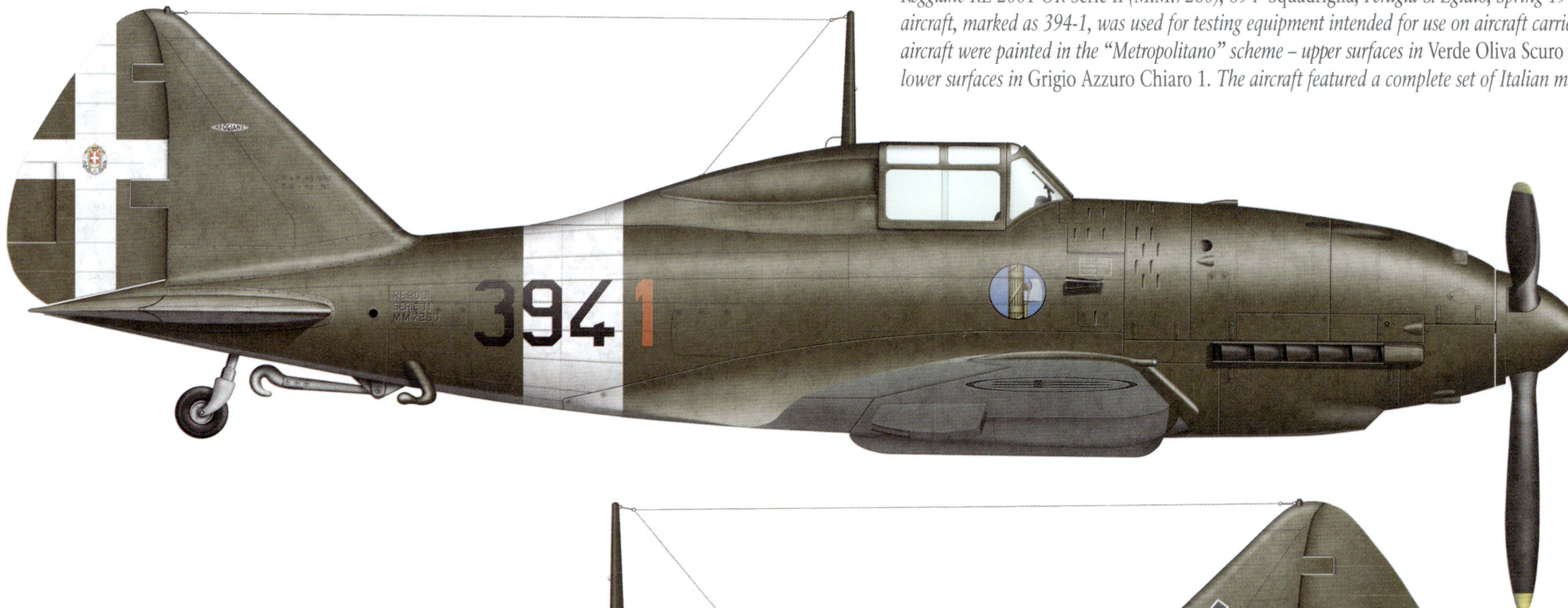

Reggiane RE 2001 OR Serie II *(M.M.7260),* 394ª Squadriglia, *Perugia-S. Egidio, Spring 1943. The aircraft, marked as 394-1, was used for testing equipment intended for use on aircraft carriers. The aircraft were painted in the "Metropolitano" scheme – upper surfaces in* Verde Oliva Scuro 2, *and lower surfaces in* Grigio Azzuro Chiaro 1. *The aircraft featured a complete set of Italian markings.*

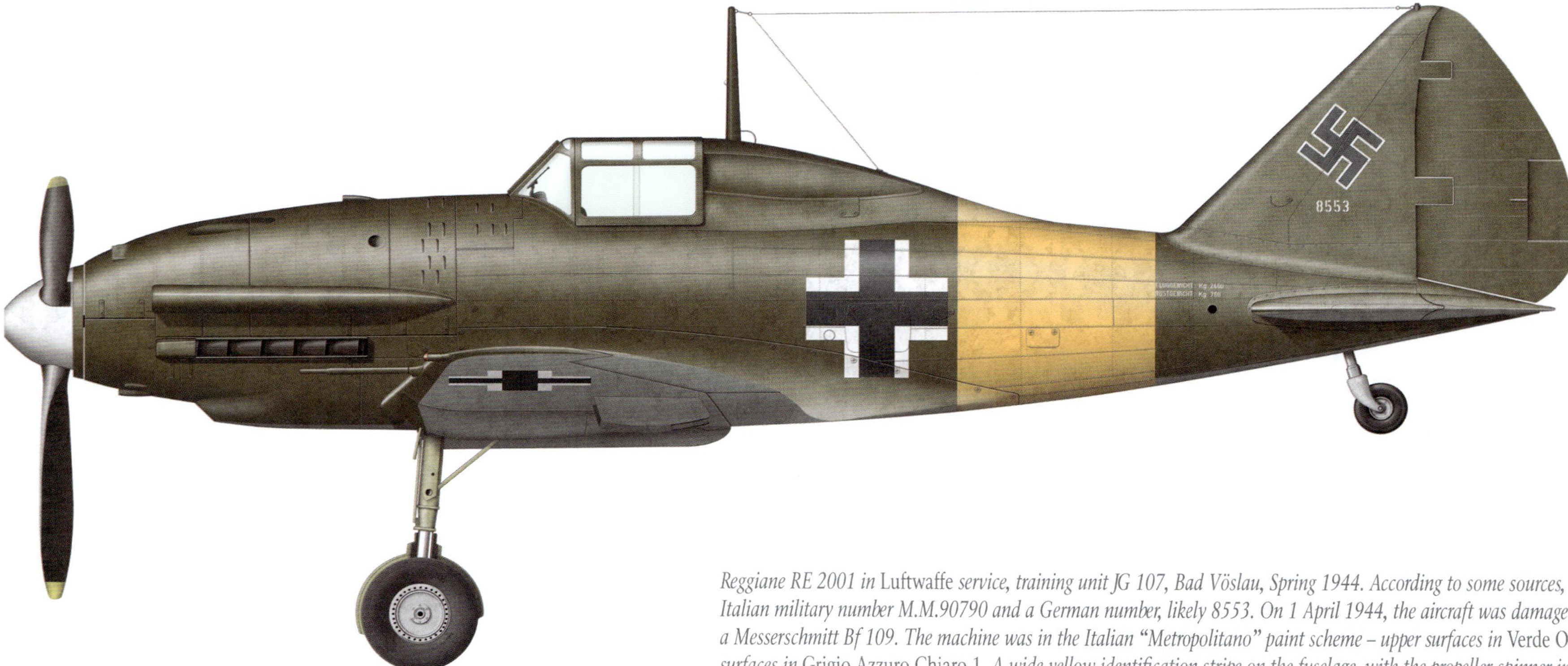

Reggiane RE 2001 in Luftwaffe *service, training unit JG 107, Bad Vöslau, Spring 1944. According to some sources, the aircraft had the Italian military number M.M.90790 and a German number, likely 8553. On 1 April 1944, the aircraft was damaged after a collision with a Messerschmitt Bf 109. The machine was in the Italian "Metropolitano" paint scheme – upper surfaces in* Verde Oliva Scuro 2, *and lower surfaces in* Grigio Azzuro Chiaro 1. *A wide yellow identification stripe on the fuselage, with the propeller spinner in white.*

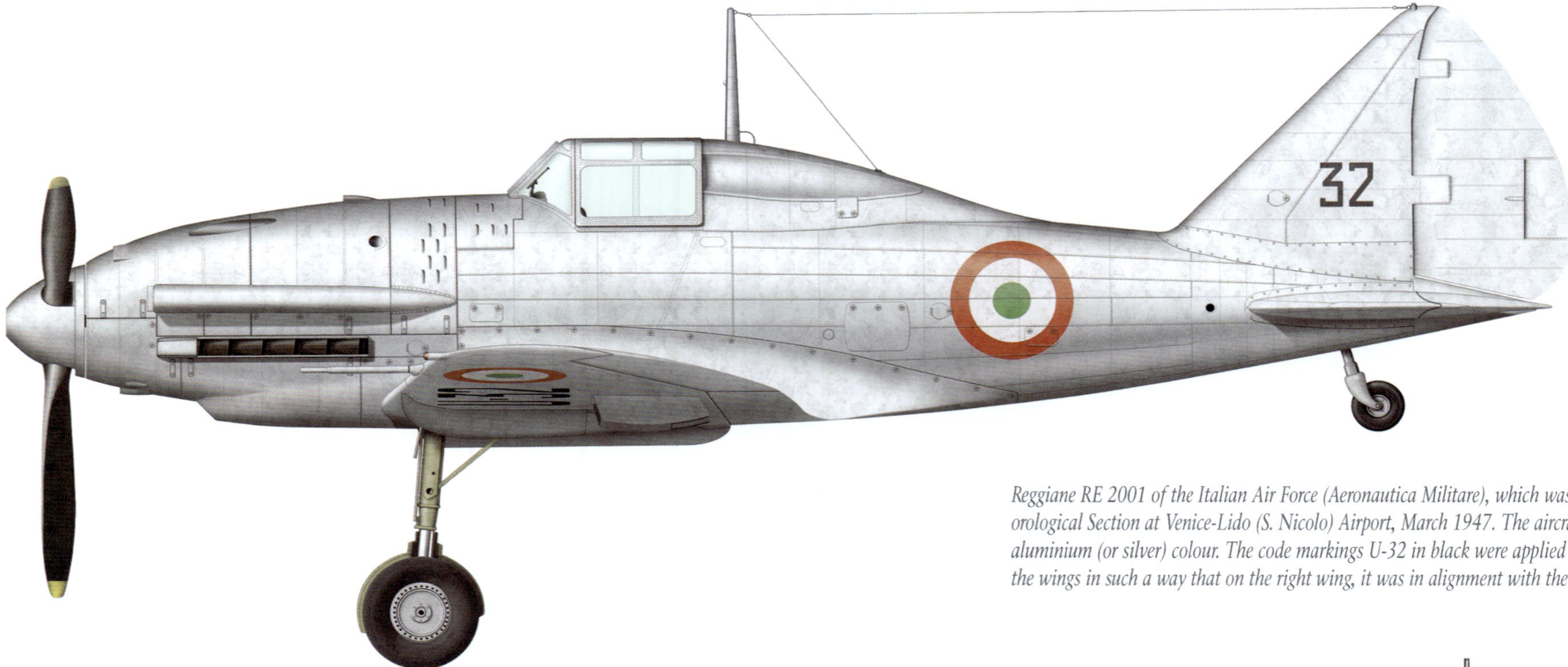

Reggiane RE 2001 of the Italian Air Force (Aeronautica Militare), which was located in the Meteorological Section at Venice-Lido (S. Nicolo) Airport, March 1947. The aircraft was in a natural aluminium (or silver) colour. The code markings U-32 in black were applied to the lower surfaces of the wings in such a way that on the right wing, it was in alignment with the direction of flight.

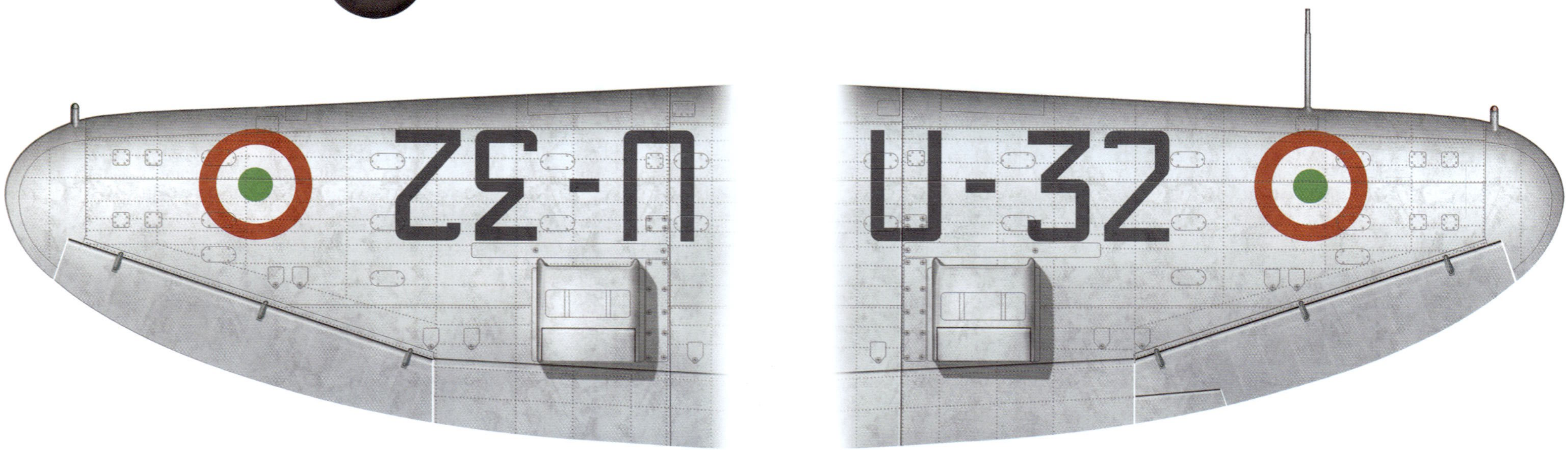

RE 2001 CN Serie VI *(likely M.M.90075), Italian Co-Belligerent Air Force, "white 1", which initially served in the* 82ª Squadriglia *(*155° Gruppo*), and was later transferred to the* 101° Gruppo *(*5° Stormo*). The aircraft was in an unconventional paint scheme – the upper surfaces were sandy with green camouflage spots. The lower surfaces were light grey-blue. The propeller spinner was red.*

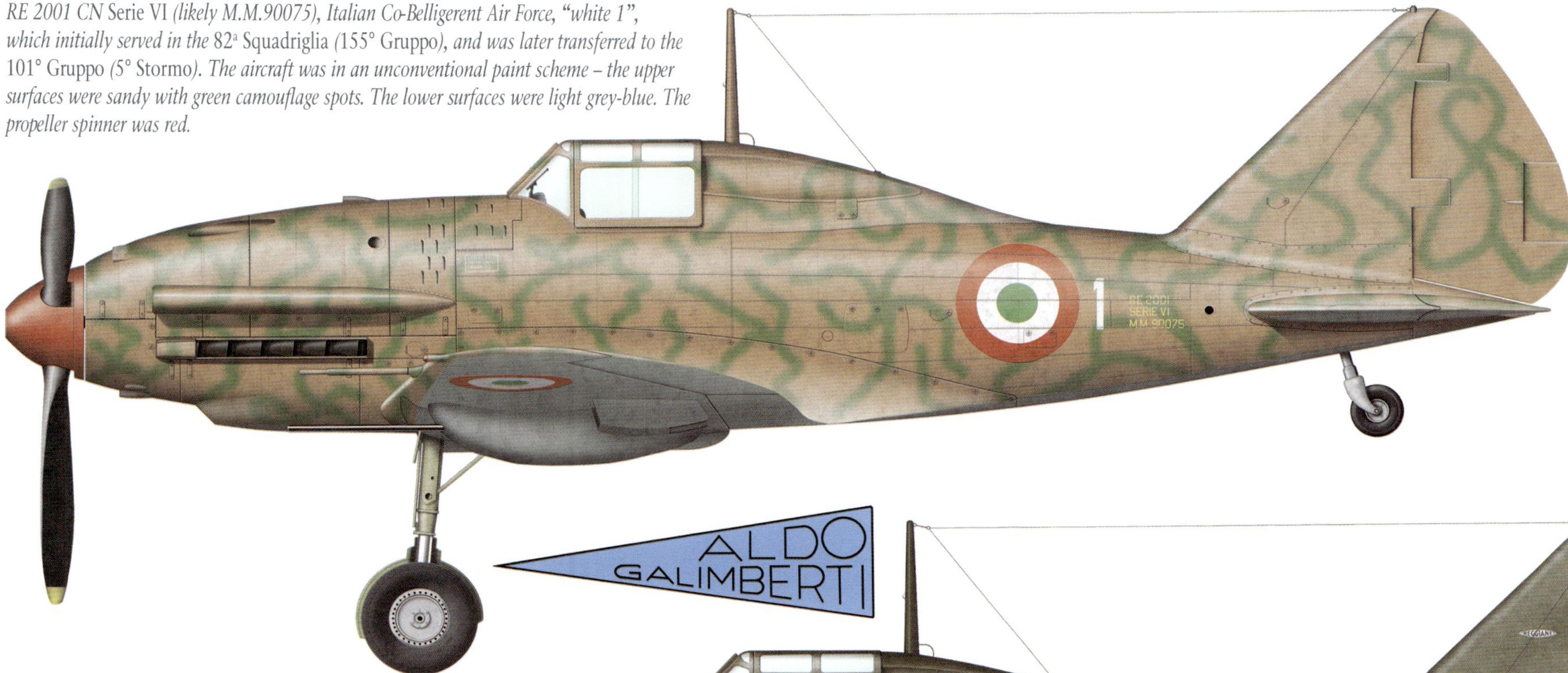

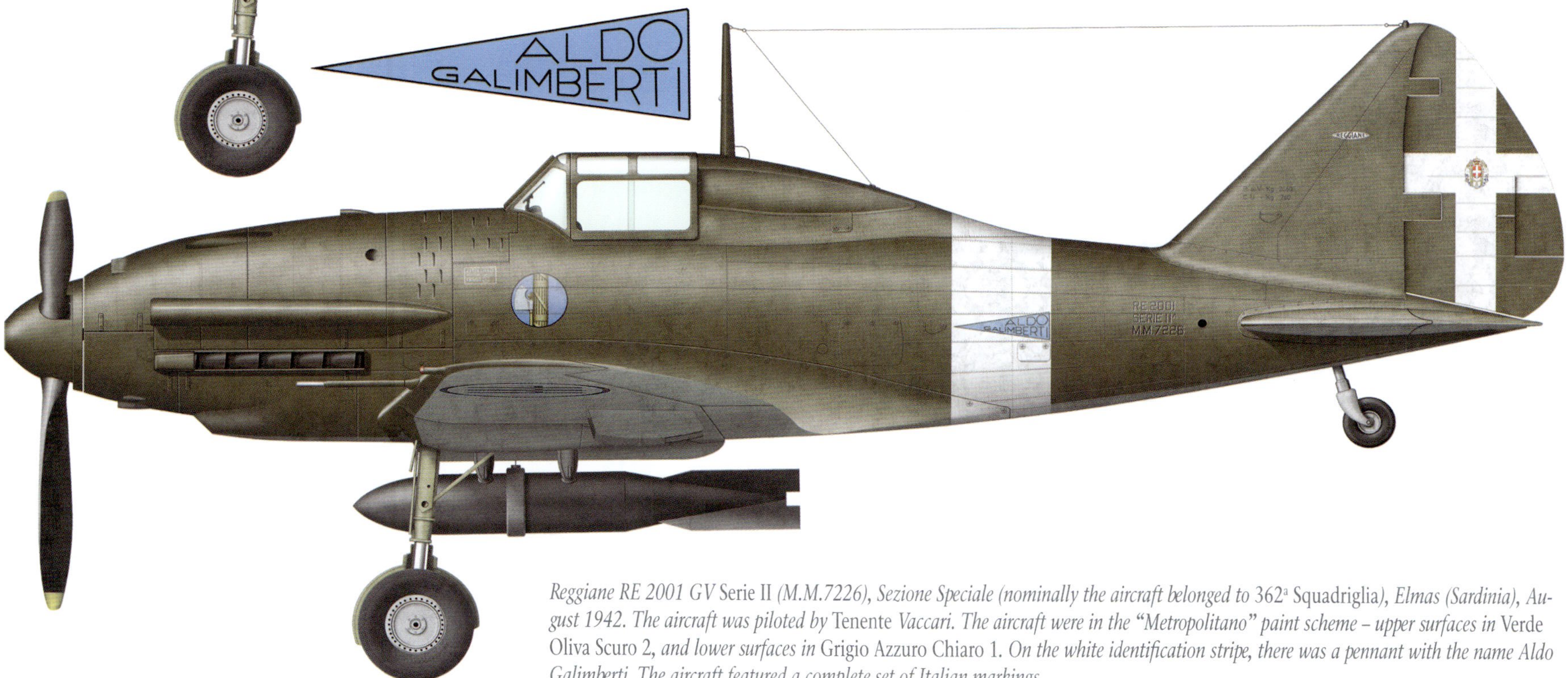

Reggiane RE 2001 GV Serie II *(M.M.7226), Sezione Speciale (nominally the aircraft belonged to* 362ª Squadriglia*), Elmas (Sardinia), August 1942. The aircraft was piloted by* Tenente *Vaccari. The aircraft were in the "Metropolitano" paint scheme – upper surfaces in* Verde Oliva Scuro 2*, and lower surfaces in* Grigio Azzuro Chiaro 1*. On the white identification stripe, there was a pennant with the name Aldo Galimberti. The aircraft featured a complete set of Italian markings.*

RE 2005 *Sagittario*

Conceptual work on the aircraft, which was to be the successor to the RE 2001 *Ariete I*, began at the end of 1940 when the Ufficio Tecnico created a team led by Giuseppe Maraschini for this purpose. The team also included Franco Antonietti, Gino Billi (systems), Giuseppe Giovanardi (landing gear), Serchiani (fuselage), Dondi (wings), and Antonio Longo. Initially, it was assumed that the new machine would be a modification of the RE 2001, on which a more powerful inline engine would be installed. In practice, an entirely new aircraft was constructed, encountering many problems along the way. The biggest challenge was finding a strong and reliable inline engine. The attempt to implement into serial production a domestic power unit, the 1200 hp FIAT A.38 engine, ended in failure. In this situation, efforts began in the summer of 1941 to purchase from Germany the 12-cylinder Daimler-Benz DB 605A-1 engines with a maximum power of 1475 hp and a license for their production. This was not an easy task as this engine was just starting production in Germany. The issue was resolved, and soon in Italy, licensed production of this power unit began under the designation FIAT R.A.1050 R.C. 58-I "Tifone". This was of great significance for the Italian aviation industry as the engine was intended for installation in all "Serie V" fighters, i.e., projects prepared by the Macchi, FIAT, and Reggiane companies.

The first stage of work on the new Reggiane fighter involved aerodynamic tunnel testing at Caproni. The results of these tests significantly influenced the final design of the aircraft. The aircraft, designated RE 2005, was to have new, three-spar (main spar and two auxiliary spars) wings with a semi-elliptical

A wooden mock-up of the RE 2005 during construction, completed in early 1942. Noteworthy are the barrels of three 12.7 mm Breda-SAFAT machine guns.

The first prototype of the RE 2005 (M.M.494) photographed before its first flight at the Reggiane factory. The photos were likely taken on 9 or 10 May 1942.

outline, incorporating four self-sealing fuel tanks – two with a capacity of 160 litres and two of 108 litters. These were located between the spars in the fuselage-adjacent section. Both wings were mounted to the fuselage without a centre wing. The oil and engine coolant radiators were planned to be placed next to each other, forming a single block located under the aircraft's fuselage. Unlike earlier Reggiane family fighters, the widely spaced main landing gear was to be folded in a conventional manner – sideways, towards the wingtips. The tail wheel was also intended to be retractable. Strong pilot protection was planned – the front was to be shielded by a 50 mm thick armoured glass placed in the windscreen. The pilot's seat was to be protected by 8 mm thick armoured plates, and the headrest by 6 mm thick plates.

In October 1941, construction of a wooden mock-up of the aircraft began, which was completed in January 1942. In the same month, construction of two prototypes designated with the military numbers M.M.494 and M.M.495 also started.

The first prototype, M.M.494, was rapidly constructed and by February 1942, it was ready for engine installation. A legend associated with the RE 2005 claims that further work was stalled due to the lack of the original DB 605A-1 engine, which was supposed to be delivered from Germany. Roberto Longhi even suspected hostile actions from competitors, which resulted in the engine being delivered to the Medional-Greco railway station instead of Reggio Emilia. However, this conspiracy theory is not confirmed by existing documents. At the beginning of 1942, the DB 605 engine was indeed at the Reggiane plants. It is a fact, though, that the work on the aircraft was delayed, mainly due to problems encountered during the refinement of the aircraft. Perhaps the most serious issue was the infiltration of exhaust gases into the pilot's cockpit.

A series of photos of the first RE 2005 prototype (M.M.494) after a forced landing on 10 May 1942.

The armament of the prototype consisted of one German 20 mm Mauser MG 151/20 cannon firing through the propeller shaft and four 12.7 mm Breda-SAFAT machine guns. Two of these were installed in the fuselage above the engine, and the other two in the wings. Compared to earlier Reggiane fighters (RE 2000 and RE 2001), this represented a significant advancement.

After solving the design problems, on 7 May 1942, Tullio de Prato, the chief test pilot of the Reggiane factories, performed a trial taxiing. Two days later, on 9 May, he conducted a five-minute flight with the landing gear extended. It is notable that from the start of work on the aircraft to its first flight, approximately 10 months had passed, which was an outstanding accomplishment. On 10 May, at 10:20, de Prato undertook another flight, which was regarded as the official maiden flight of the aircraft. During the approach to landing, it was discovered that the left main landing gear leg had not extended, necessitating a belly landing. The tests resumed on 1 June and by 20 July 1942, the aircraft had completed 14 flights totalling 6 hours and 18 minutes. With the experience gained, modifications were made to the landing gear, fuselage machine gun covers, and the cockpit (the right-tilting cockpit canopy was shortened by 19 cm). An antenna mast was installed behind the pilot's cabin. On 23 September 1942, an engine failure occurred on the prototype piloted by Angelo Tondi, resulting in the aircraft's second belly landing. The damage was not severe, but the aircraft was temporarily grounded from flying.

On 28 September 1942, the second prototype (M.M.495) was flown, allowing the continuation of tests. The most significant change introduced in the second prototype compared to M.M.494 was the strengthened armament – instead of wing-mounted machine guns, German 20 mm Mauser MG 151/20 cannons were installed. Fitting such armament required some modifications, including an increase in the efficiency of the pneumatic weapon reloading system. It should be added that this change was most likely implemented on M.M.495 towards the end of October 1942. Thus, for the first month, the aircraft had the same armament as the first prototype. It's worth noting that at the beginning of 1943, the wing-mounted machine guns were also replaced with cannons in the first prototype, M.M.494. The second prototype also had a modified (shorter) cockpit canopy and an extended air intake to the compressor on the left side of the engine cover. Interestingly, this aircraft had a very fascinating history. In the spring of 1943, M.M.495 received a German VDM propeller and a spinner from a Messerschmitt Bf 109G fighter. The engine cover was also slightly modified. The machine was tested with the original German DB 605AM engine (serial number 48014) equipped with the MW 50 injection system. The maximum speed of the modified aircraft increased to over 650 km/h. According to some sources, German pilots also flew the aircraft in this configuration. After a series of tests, the machine returned to its original configuration and was assigned to the *362ª Squadriglia*. On 20 July 1943, the aircraft was completely destroyed during a forced landing near Aversa following an engine failure.

During the prototype tests of the RE 2005 conducted at the Reggiane facilities and the experimental centres in Guidonia and Furbara, there were ongoing issues with the landing gear deployment (likely caused by the design of the gear doors) and jamming of the gun armament. Efforts were made to eliminate these faults through modifications introduced at the end of 1942. However, the problems with the landing gear were probably not entirely resolved, as this issue also occurred in the production models. Additional holes appeared in the panels covering the fuselage machine guns, providing better cooling. Other changes included strengthening certain elements in the construction of the wings and the rear part of the fuselage (covering and spars), resulting from vibrations in the tail section during dives. However, generally, both the performance and behaviour of the aircraft during factory tests were positively evaluated by the test pilots. It seemed that the aircraft could be quickly directed to serial production. In reality, the future of the RE 2005 depended on the outcome of confrontations with aircraft prepared by two competing manufacturers – FIAT and Macchi.

At the turn of October and November 1942, comparative trials of the prototype M.M.495 and the first prototype of FIAT G.55 were conducted at the Centro Sperimentale Aeronautico in Guidonia. Both aircraft were piloted by *Capitano* Mario de Gasperi. In early December, the same pilot performed a demonstration of the prototype RE 2005 for German aviation specialists. Contrary to some opinions, the new Italian fighter did not make a profound impression on the Germans, especially as the MG 151/20 cannon jammed during the demonstration. The information about sending the prototype RE 2005 to Germany for tests, and then using the aircraft for the defense of Berlin and Romanian oil fields, is another legend surrounding this design.

In many publications about the RE 2005, it is often stated that the RE 2005 was the best aircraft in the "Serie V", surpassing its competitors, the Macchi C.205V *Veltro* and FIAT G.55 *Centauro*. However, the results of the competition for a modern fighter for the *Regia Aeronautica*, held from 18 to 23 December 1942 at the experimental centre in Guidonia, do not confirm this. The competition procedure evaluated many varied parameters of the aircraft, but also took into account production conditions and applied technologies. In terms of performance, the Macchi design took first place, FIAT's was second, and the Reggiane RE 2005 came in last. In terms of ease of piloting, the C.205 triumphed, with the other aircraft tying for second place. A similar outcome was seen in the evaluation of the aircraft's equip-

The first RE 2005 prototype (M.M.494) in standard military paint (the "Metropolitano" scheme) photographed at the Guidonia research centre.

The first prototype of the RE 2003 (M.M.494) after a belly landing on 23 September 1942. The pilot was Ten.Col. *Angelo Tondi, and the landing was caused by an engine failure. Visible are modifications introduced during testing – a shortened canopy, antenna mast, and altered engine and fuselage machine gun covers.*

A photo of the first prototype (M.M.494) taken in early July 1942.

The second prototype of the RE 2005 (M.M.495), on which a German VDM propeller was tested. The aircraft was fitted with a German DB 605A-1 engine with the MW 50 system.

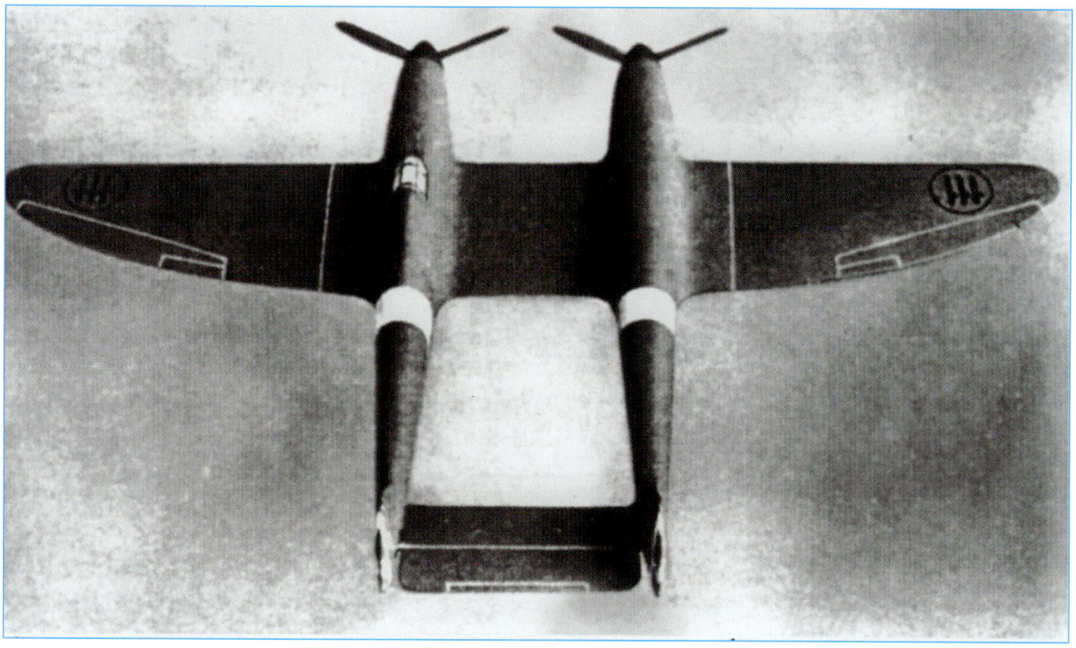

A wooden model of the Reggiane RE 2005 Bifusoliera *aircraft.*

ment. In terms of design and its resilience, the C.205 and G.55 tied for first place, with the RE 2005 in third. Only in terms of ease of production did the *Sagittario* surpass the *Veltro*, but it was still inferior to the *Centauro*. The RE 2005's undeniable advantage was its armament. The prototype *Veltro* was armed only with two 12.7 mm machine guns above the engine and two 7.7 mm machine guns in the wings. The *Centauro*, on the other hand, had four 12.7 mm machine guns (two in the fuselage and two in the wings) and a 20 mm Mauser MG 151/20 cannon in the fuselage. However, the serial production aircraft of the competitors were to have strengthened armaments. The wing-mounted machine guns in the C.205V were replaced with 20 mm MG 151/20 cannons (though the first series of 100 aircraft retained the prototype's armament). The same was true for the FIAT G.55 – after completing 3 prototypes and 17 serial examples, 20 mm Mauser MG 151/20 cannons replaced the wing-mounted machine guns, giving it a firepower equal to the RE 2005.

Considering the test results and the threat posed by high-altitude bombing raids conducted by USAAF and RAF heavy bombers, the *Centauro*, with its superior high-altitude performance, was selected for production. In December 1942, FIAT received an order for 1,800 aircraft. This meant that the G.55 would become the primary fighter of the *Regia Aeronautica* in the future. The C.205V also went into production, as it could be immediately produced due to its nearly identical airframe to the C.202 Folgore, and it performed very well at low altitudes. Macchi also developed the heavily armed high-altitude fighter prototype C.205N Orione, and at the end of January 1943, an order for 1,200 of these aircraft was placed. At the turn of 1942/1943, only the Reggiane factories were left without large orders for the *Sagittario*. However, the future turned out to be favourable for the company from Reggio Emilia – orders soon appeared, but the problem was their fulfilment.

Mass Production

On 27 October 1942, the Reggiane factories received an order for 16 *Serie 0* aircraft (M.M. 092343 – M.M. 092358). These machines featured strengthened armament, similar to the second prototype, consisting of two 12.7 mm Breda-SAFAT machine guns (with a reserve of 350 rounds per barrel) installed in the fuselage above the engine, and three 20 mm Mauser MG 151/20 cannons. The fuselage cannon had an ammunition reserve of 150 rounds, while the two wing-mounted cannons had 200 rounds per barrel.

The contract was so small that by the end of 1942, Giuliano Ventimiglia, a representative of the Consorzio Eksportazioni Aeronautiche, tried to interest the Swedish Air Force command in the new Reggiane fighter. There was hope for the sale of 50 aircraft to Sweden. This country had a license purchased from Germany for the production of DB 605A engines, which could facilitate the transaction. There was also consideration of granting the Swedes a license to build aircraft at the SAAB Trolhättan plants. On 19 January 1943, permission was obtained to demonstrate the aircraft to the representatives of the customer, but on 2 February, it was revoked. The permission to sell 50 aircraft and the license was also withdrawn. Although on 9 June 1943, the Minister of Aviation, who was Benito Mussolini, unblocked the transaction, the military and political situation in Italy meant that the export contract was not realized.

RE 2005 (M.M.092352) photographed at the factory airport in Regia Emilia in 1943. It was probably the most extensively photographed mass produced Sagittario. Note the asymmetrically mounted under-fuselage bomb rack with a maximum weight of 640 kilograms.

RE 2005 (M.M 092352) with a damaged wing tip in August 1943, Castiglione del Lago airport. Attention is drawn to the partially painted-over national markings on the wing and the painted-over phalanx signs on the fuselage. This was a standard change introduced after the overthrow of Mussolini in July 1943.

The Reggiane RE 103 R.C. 40/50 engine with a power of 1500–1700 HP, which was to be an alternative power unit for the RE 2004. This engine, however, was not sufficiently developed and did not enter production.

As previously mentioned, the dreaded scenario of a lack of larger orders, which was a major concern at Reggiane, ultimately did not materialize. In January 1943, the Ministerio dell'Aeronautica placed an order for 100 RE 2005 *Serie I* aircraft (M.M.092359–092458) to be produced at the Reggiane plants. In the same month, an additional order for 500 aircraft was placed, with 300 to be manufactured by Reggiane and 200 by Caproni Aeronautica Bergamasca. These aircraft, forming *Serie II*, were assigned military numbers M.M.095419–095918. Reality showed that these orders were completely unrealistic, far beyond the production capabilities of the Caproni group's facilities. Of the 600 aircraft ordered, it's likely that only one – M.M.092359, the prototype for the *Serie I* aircraft – was actually built.

Interestingly, when in spring 1943 the equipment situation of the Italian Air Force became dire, and every aircraft counted, another order was placed. On 18 April 1943, 18 *Serie 0* aircraft (M.M. 096100 – M.M. 096117) were ordered. This order likely aimed at producing aircraft as quickly as possible without any modifications. Only 13 machines from this contract were built (including 9 by the time of Italy's capitulation in September 1943). The remaining 5 aircraft were at various stages of assembly but were never completed.

It was planned that starting from the 24th aircraft, a bomb ejector would be standardly mounted on the RE 2005. Like the RE 2001, it was believed that the *Sagittario* could be effectively used as a fighter-bomber. The Reggiane factories received the order to modify the aircraft and conduct tests on 5 March 1943. A bomb ejector capable of carrying a maximum load of 640 kg was installed under the fuselage of the prototype RE 2005 (it seems that this was M.M.494, as at that time M.M.495 was being tested with German propellers), but not centrally, rather asymmetrically – to the right side of the coolant and oil radiator. A different placement of the ejector was not possible as it would have obstructed the air intake to the radiator. There is information suggesting the intention to install two ejectors under the wings for bombs with a maximum weight of 160 kg each. However, it seems that this idea was not implemented. The tests of the ejector conducted at the Furbara range did not yield positive results. During the trials, the length of the take-off run increased by 200 meters. Worse, the aircraft was unstable during take-off, veering to the right. The accuracy of the bomb drops in the tests was also unsatisfactory. There was also an incident where *Cap*. Enzo Sant'Andrea had to land with a bomb still suspended under the fuselage.

Summarizing the production aspects of the RE 2005, the Reggiane factories ultimately managed to fulfill only a small portion of the orders for the *Sagittario*. In total, including the prototypes, only 32 machines were produced.

Projects

The RE 2005 served as the basis for developing several intriguing variant designs. However, most of these ideas were not realized and remained only as conceptual "paper projects".

RE 2005 *Bifusoliera*

Towards the end of 1942, a design was prepared for the RE 2005 Bifusoliera, a twin-fuselage multi-role aircraft. This aircraft was characterized by strong armament – six 20 mm Mauser MG 151/20 cannons and two 12.7 mm Breda-SAFAT machine guns. A universal attachment allowed for carrying a 500-kilogram bomb or a 930-kilogram torpedo. The oil and coolant radiators were to be located in the wings, similar to the RE 2001bis. The aircraft's take-off weight was estimated to be 6100 kilograms, with a maximum speed of 680 km/h and a range of 1500–1700 kilometres. The project reached the stage of a wooden model for wind tunnel testing.

RE 2005 *Lignea*

In early 1942, Pier Luigi Nardi presented a design for the RE 2005 with wooden-structured wings, utilizing technology similar to that of the British DH 98 Mosquito. In the spring of 1942, the Direzione Generale delle Construzioni Aeronautiche ordered two sets of wings, and soon after, two wooden fuselages. However, producing these components proved unfeasible due to the lack of appropriate technology and specialists. Ultimately, the project was terminated in April 1943.

RE 2005 *Navale*

In 1943, there was an idea to adapt the Reggiane RE 2005 and FIAT G.55 aircraft for operation from the aircraft carrier "Aquilla", replacing the earlier chosen deck aircraft (FIAT G.50AN and Reggiane RE 2001 G). However, this entire initiative remained merely in the planning stage.

RE 2205 – Combat Deployment

Regia Aeronautica

In the *Regia Aeronautica*, the first unit to receive the RE 2005 fighters was the *362ª Squadriglia* of the *22° Gruppo Autonomo C.T.*, stationed at the Naples-Capodichino airfield. In March 1943, the group's commander, *Magg.* Vittorio Minguzzi (an Italian ace with 5 victories in World War II and 3 in Spain), had the opportunity to perform several familiarization flights in the first prototype *Sagittario* at the research centres in Guidonia and Furbara. He assessed the aircraft as performing excellently in the air, and the experienced Italian pilot had high hopes for this design, seeing it as a strongly armed aircraft capable of effectively combating Allied aviation. The choice of Minguzzi for familiarization flights with the RE 2005 was not coincidental, as at the beginning of 1943, it had been decided that the *22° Gruppo* would be the first unit to be re-equipped with the new fighters. This was intended to enhance the combat capabilities of the unit, which had until then been armed with RE 2001, C.202, and D.520C fighters. On 22 March, the prototype RE 2005 (M.M.494) was assigned to the *362ª Squadriglia*, and two days later, *Magg.* Minguzzi flew its first patrol flight. In April, the squadron's inventory was increased by four *Sagittario* from *Serie 0* (M.M.092343 – M.M.092346).

On the evening of 2 April 1943, *Magg.* Minguzzi, flying on M.M.494 as part of a group of twenty aircraft sent to intercept B-24D Liberator bombers from the 98th Bomber Group (9th USAAF), reported one of the two claimed victories of heavy bombers near Naples. In his report, the pilot emphasized the excellent flying characteristics of the aircraft at an altitude of 7,000 meters, which enabled him to conduct two attacks while the C.202s were only able to make one approach to the enemy. It is worth noting, however, that in this engagement, the Americans did not lose any bombers (there weren't even any damaged aircraft). On 10 April, *Cap.* Germano La Ferla and *Ten.* Giulio Torresi (credited with a total of 10 victories during the war) reported success against the Liberators. They claimed to have downed a B-24D, but American losses were limited to just one damaged bomber. The following day, in another engagement near Naples, *Serg.* Marcello Baccara and *Ten.* Armando Moresi each claimed to have shot down a Liberator. However, the latter had to bail out of his hit RE 2005 (M.M.092343) and was rescued by an Italian trawler.

The subsequent days witnessed several unsuccessful attempts to intercept American bombers. However, a significant success was achieved on 28 April 1943, when a mixed formation of 16 aircraft from the *22° Gruppo*, consisting of four RE 2005s, 11 C.202s, and one D.520, intercepted about 30 B-24 Liberators from the 376th Bomber Group at an altitude of 7,000 meters. *Magg.* Vittorio Minguzzi, flying the prototype *Sagittario*, recorded a confirmed kill of a Liberator, which crashed into the sea in flames. The downed aircraft was likely the B-24D named "Pizzonia" with the serial number 41-24270 from the 512th Bomber Squadron. Although Minguzzi's aircraft was hit in the cooling system, he managed to land safely at Capodichino. Other pilots of the *22° Gruppo* reported an additional five probable vic-

A retouched, propaganda photo of an RE 2005 in flight.

A photo taken during the visit of King Victor Emmanuel III and high Italian commanders to the Furbara air base in March 1943, on the occasion of the 20th anniversary of the founding of the Regia Aeronautica. The aircraft in the photo is most likely a Serie 0 *machine with the military number M.M.092352. The presence of two windows in the upper panel of the canopy indicates that it is not the second prototype (M.M.495).*

tories. Later, one of these, claimed by *Serg*. Donati flying a C.202, was confirmed by ground witnesses and awarded to him as a confirmed kill. In May 1943, RE 2005 pilots carried out 10 interception flights against Allied aircraft but did not record further successes.

On 1 June 1943, during the bombing of the Naples-Capodichino airfield, two RE 2005s were damaged, leading to the temporary relocation of the *Sagittarios* to Capua airfield. On 21 June, pilots of the *22° Gruppo* claimed the shooting down of two B-17s for certain and one "Flying Fortress" as probable, southwest of Ischia – Ventotene. This probable success was achieved by an RE 2005 pilot – *Ten*. Dino Signorini-Gremigni. In this engagement, the Americans indeed suffered a loss – the B-17F (42-29605) "Huney Bun" from the 429 Squadron (2nd Bomber Group) crashed into the sea near Ischia. Nine crew members were captured, and one was killed. On 26 June 1943, the RE 2005 (M.M.092345) was damaged on the ground during an enemy raid on the Naples-Capodichino airfield and required repairs at the Reggiane factory. By the end of June, the unit had 8 operational RE 2005s. It was planned that the aircraft would be relocated to Littoria airfield, with the task of defending Rome. However, plans changed subsequently.

On 2 July 1943, the unit was relocated to Sicily, to the Catania-Fontanarossa airfield. Following the commencement of Operation "Huskey," the *362ª Squadriglia* was moved to the Comiso airfield. On the first day of combat, 11 July, in the morning hours, four RE 2005s attacked a formation of A-20G Bostons escorted by Spitfires. In this engagement, *Cap*. La Ferla, *Ten*. Vaghi, and *Serg*. Arduini each reported shooting down a Spitfire (another version of the story says they collectively shot down one Spitfire). Additionally, *Cap*. Giulio Torresi claimed one confirmed and one probable Spitfire downed near Catania. The only confirmed Allied loss, however, was an American Spitfire Vc ES340 from the 307th Fighter Squadron (31st Fighter Group) piloted by 2nd Lt. August Goldenberg, who was declared missing in action. It is difficult to determine which Italian pilot was responsible for this downing. In the afternoon,

An RE 2005 marked as 362-9 photographed in the summer of 1943 at the Littoria airfield (now Latina).

five RE 2005s escorted FIAT G.50 fighter-bombers from the *158° Gruppo* attacking enemy ships in the bay near Syracuse. During this mission, they engaged with Spitfires from No. 111 Squadron RAF, resulting in the loss of *Ten.* Luigi Nitoglia, who was on his first combat flight. Additionally, *Ten.* Enrico Salvi returned to the airfield in a heavily damaged aircraft and had to perform an emergency landing.

The next day, a flight led by *Cap.* Torresi, including *Ten.* Salvi and *Ten.* Vaghi, ambushed a pair of reconnaissance Spitfire IXs from No. 40 Squadron SAAF. Torresi shot down the aircraft flown by F/L K. Robinson, who was captured after parachuting out. The second Spitfire, piloted by P/O. B.V. Clarence, managed to return to Malta despite sustaining damage. That day, the RE 2005s suffered another loss – *S.Ten.* Traiano Dilissano did not return from a reconnaissance flight and was officially declared missing.

On 13 July over Catania, Torresi once again demonstrated his effectiveness by shooting down a Spitfire Vc from No. 93 Squadron RAF that was attacking *Ten.* Vaghi's aircraft. The British pilot, Sgt. F.W. Bridger, was captured but managed to escape.

On 14 July 1943, due to the destruction of airfields in Sicily, the squadron began withdrawing from the island. According to some sources, the operational aircraft were relocated to Reggio di Calabria airfield, where they were taken over by the *371ª Squadriglia*. However, these aircraft were soon lost during enemy air raids on the airfield. Another version suggests that the aircraft flew to Naples-Capodichino airfield. Considering the fact that the pilots of the *22° Gruppo* were engaged in combat with the USAAF over Naples the next day, this latter version seems more likely.

On 15 July, pilots of the 22° Gruppo repelled an attack on Naples by 72 B-17 bombers from the 5th Bomber Wing. Among the pilots who reported successes were two flying RE 2005s. *Ten.* Dino Signorini-Gremigni reported a probable B-17 downing, while *M.llo* Guerrino Prodi was credited with participating in the team downing of another "Fortress." However, his aircraft was shot down by American gunners and crashed into the sea. Guerrino Prodi was declared missing. Interestingly, he was formally a pilot of the *150ª Squadriglia*, which was still flying RE 2001s. This suggests that the *Sagittario* might have also been in service with this squadron, although it's more likely that there was some confusion in the assignment of pilots to squadrons after the relocation from Sicily.

On 18 July 1943, the *362ª Squadriglia* received four new RE 2005s as reinforcements. On 20 July, six of these aircraft were sent into action but did not achieve any success. Two fighters had to make emergency landings, one of them piloted by Vittorio Minguzzi. During ascent, the engine of his RE 2005 (M.M.495) caught fire. He managed to extinguish the flames in a dive, but the forced landing resulted in the aircraft breaking apart (the fuselage split into two) and his hospitalization. *Cap.* Enzo Sant'Andrea succeeded him as the commander of the *22° Gruppo.*

On 29 July around 14:30, during an attack on the Aquino airfield, P-38 Lightning pilot Capt. Carl F. Rudder from the 14th Fighter Group engaged in combat with a pair of RE 2005s. Rudder identified the enemy aircraft as C.202s and reported damaging both machines. However, *Cap.* La Ferla claimed in his report that he shot down one Lightning individually and another in conjunction with *Ten.* Salvi. This claim, however, is not corroborated by American losses – the 14th Fighter Group did not lose any aircraft that day. On the Italian side, *Ten.* Salvi's aircraft sustained damage.

Ground crew with an RE 2005 from 362ª Squadriglia *at the Capua airfield (or, according to other sources, Littoria), in June 1943.*

On 11 August 1943, just after noon near Rome, *Ten.* Augusto Minstruzzi (nominally from the *369ª Squadriglia*), flying an RE 2005, claimed the shooting down of a Boeing B-17F. That day, the Americans did lose a bomber of this type near the Italian capital, but it was most likely downed by Col. Angelo Tondi, piloting a captured P-38G. The next day, near Ventotene, three RE 2005 pilots claimed a probable victory over a P-38. In this area, the Americans lost two aircraft from the 1st Fighter Group, but in addition to the Italians, four *Luftwaffe* pilots (from JG 53) also claimed these successes.

On 17 August, during a fight over Sparvimento, a formation of German and Italian fighters clashed with Lightning aircraft from the 48th Fighter Squadron (14th Fighter Group), claiming three American planes shot down. One of these victories was credited to an RE 2005 pilot – *Serg.M.* Lucio Biagini (*359ª Squadriglia*). On 19 August, *Ten.* Edgaro Vaghi participated in the team downing of a B-17. Verifying this success is very difficult, if not impossible. The Americans lost 5 "Fortresses" that day, but only two were acknowledged as victims of enemy fighters. *Luftwaffe* pilots claimed the downing of 13 B-17s, and the Italians added two more to the tally.

On 21 August 1943, of the three RE 2005s scrambled, one returned with severe fuselage damage, and *Serg.* Ugo Ibello was forced to make a belly landing. His aircraft was ultimately "written off" after being hit by a German Bf 109G from JG 53. Another success was recorded by *Ten.* Dino Signorini-Gremigni, who claimed the downing of an American P-38 near Naples, one of 7 Lightnings supposedly downed by Italian fighters. In reality, 3 P-38s from the 1st Fighter Group were damaged in this engagement. In August, *Cap.* Giulio Torresi left the unit to become a test pilot at the FIAT factories and later commanded the *3ª Squadriglia* (*1° Gruppo Caccia*) of the ANR. He was killed in combat with American P-47 Thunderbolts on 1 July 1944.

On 25 August, four aircraft were launched, but due to vibrations in the tail section, Lieutenant Dario Signorini-Germigni was forced to bail out of the *Sagittario* M.M.092356 using a parachute. Following this incident, flights on the RE 2005 were suspended, partly because the problem had occurred on other aircraft, and similar situations had arisen before. Tests conducted in Guidonia and Reggio Emilia by Tulio de Prato revealed that vibrations occurred in a dive when exceeding speeds of 660 km/h. A remedy for this dangerous phenomenon was to adjust the trimmers in the horizontal stabiliser. After making this modification, the aircraft were deemed combat-ready. However, it was noted that during aggressive manoeuvres in aerial combat, the situation could recur. Undoubtedly, solving the problem required deeper analysis and more radical actions. This was hindered by the armistice signed between Italy and the Allies on 8 September 1943. Regarding the tests conducted by Tulio de Prato in the summer of 1943, it is worth noting that in one dive, he reportedly reached a speed of 988 km/h! However, there is no unequivocal evidence for this, as it is based solely on the pilot's account.

At the time of Italy's surrender, seven RE 2005 aircraft (according to some sources, five) were stationed with the *22° Gruppo* at Capua and Naples-Capodichino airports. The Italian Air Force command had planned for the aircraft to fly north and provide cover for the Regia Marina ships. However, they were ultimately destroyed at the airports to prevent their capture by the Germans.

Photos of the tail of an RE 2005 Sagittario *(M.M.092344), in the spring of 1943, at the Naples-Capodichino airfield.*

It's challenging to precisely determine the wartime record of the RE 2005 aircraft. Between 22 July and 8 September 1943, pilots of the *22° Gruppo* took part in 21 air battles and claimed 24 confirmed and 17 probable enemy aircraft shot down. They also reported damaging 13 Allied aircraft. Not all of these declared successes involved *Sagittario* pilots – the group also operated other aircraft types. Additionally, several victories were recorded before 22 July 1943. It's estimated that the RE 2005 contributed to approximately 16–17 of these shootdowns and a few Allied aircraft damages.

As for losses, a total of 12 RE 2005s were lost. Four were destroyed in combat actions (with 3 pilots killed). Two aircraft were lost due to accidents (engine failure, deformation of the tail section of the fuselage). During its short service with the *Regia Aeronautica*, there were also frequent malfunctions (engine, landing gear, deformation of the tail section of the fuselage), indicating that this interesting aircraft was not fully refined and prepared for operational service.

Today, only a fragment of the tail section of RE 2005 M.M.092351 survives, which is displayed at the Museo dell'Aeronautica Gianni Caproni in Trento (Tyden).

An RE 2005 with the marking of 362ª Squadriglia, *demonstrating how the pilot's canopy cover opens.*

Italian mechanics displaying a shield with the emblem of 362ª Squadriglia. *In the background is a RE 2005* Sagittario Serie 0.

A photo of an RE 2005 after a combat flight taken in the summer of 1943 at the Littoria airfield (now Latina).

Aeronautica Cobelligerante Italiana and Aeronautica Militare

In October 1943, due to a significant shortage of aircraft, there was an idea to refurbish three RE 2005 planes that were located in Sicily. Considering the limited availability of spare parts, this was quite a risky idea. The plan was abandoned when the *Aeronautica Cobelligerante Italiana* received British Spitfire Vs and American Bell P-39Q Airacobras.

According to some sources, in 1947 there was a plan to assemble several RE 2005s from parts found at the Reggiane factories. These aircraft were supposedly to be offered to the Argentine Air Force. However, there is no certainty that such a plan actually existed. Argentina did purchase FIAT G.55 aircraft from Italy. They were also offered Macchi C.205Vs (for naval aviation), but this transaction ultimately did not occur.

USAAF

Regarding the USAAF, many sources claim that one of the damaged RE 2005 aircraft captured by Allied forces, likely at the Catania-Sigonella airfield, was repaired by the Americans and then tested in the USA, where it reportedly received high ratings. Between 15 and 24 November 1946, the aircraft was supposedly demonstrated during the Aircraft Show in Cleveland. However, to this day, no evidence in the form of a photograph or other document has surfaced to confirm this story.

Aeronautica Nazionale Repubblicana

The *Aeronautica Nazionale Repubblicana* (ANR), which fought alongside Germany, likely had only two or three RE 2005 aircraft in its inventory. Older sources mention up to six aircraft, but these figures are not confirmed. The military numbers of two RE 2005s are known: M.M.092352 and M.M.096111. More information is available about the former, which served as a liaison and training aircraft in the Reparto Aero Collegamento. Photos of this aircraft taken in spring 1944 at the Milan-Bresso airfield are known. *Sagittario* M.M.092353 is often cited as a third aircraft.

*The Reggiane RE 2005 (M.M.092352) with ANR (*Aeronautica Nazionale Repubblicana*) markings and a red tactical number 4, at the Milan-Bresso airfield, in March-April 1944. This aircraft was assigned to the* Reparto Aereo Collegamento del Sottosegretariato Aeronautica *as a liaison and training aircraft.*

*The Reggiane RE 2005 (M.M.092352) with ANR (*Aeronautica Nazionale Repubblicana*) markings and a red tactical number 4, at the Milan-Bresso airfield, in March-April 1944. This aircraft was assigned to the* Reparto Aereo Collegamento del Sottosegretariato Aeronautica *as a liaison and training aircraft.*

Luftwaffe

In the autumn of 1943, the *Luftwaffe* took possession of 8–9 *Sagittario* aircraft (M.M.092345, M.M.096100, 096102, and 095105–096110). Some of these aircraft underwent modifications, including a reversal of the throttle's direction of operation, which in the *Luftwaffe* was opposite to that used on Italian aircraft. Some sources also mention that these planes were equipped with VDM propellers and Bf 109G spinners, but this is not confirmed by photographic documentation, which is very scarce. The RE 2005s were received by the Germans in October 1943, and in January 1944, another aircraft, M.M.096111, which had previously been with the ANR, likely joined them. M.M.096112 might also have ended up in German hands.

Despite the small number of RE 2005s in German service, many myths have developed around their use. One such myth discusses their employment in defending Berlin and the Romanian oil fields near Ploiești. The undocumented transport of one RE 2005 (M.M.096100) to Germany for testing and examination is also part of these legends. It seems most likely that the *Sagittario* did not leave Italy and served within the country as part of *Luftdienst Kommando Italien*, an auxiliary unit formed at Naples-Capodichino airport and moved to Maniago airfield after Italy's capitulation in September 1943. In June 1944, this unit was renamed *Fliegerzielstaffel 20* and moved to Aviano in July, before being dissolved in December 1944.

Information about the RE 2005's service in the German air force is scarce and mainly pertains to accidents and damage from Allied bombings. On 16 March 1944, M.M.096108 sustained 50% damage during an emergency landing at Maniago. Two days later, an American Liberator raid bombed Maniago airfield, completely destroying M.M.096106. Two other aircraft (M.M.096100 and M.M.096110) suffered less severe damage. On 19 April 1944, an aircraft with an unknown number was 40% damaged in an accident, and on 1 June, M.M.96100 was damaged again due to an engine failure.

An RE 2005 aircraft from Luftdienst Kommando Italien *at the Reggiane factory airfield in Reggio Emilia, autumn 1943. The aircraft likely had the military number M.M.096109.*

Possibly the only known photo of an RE 2005 with German markings and a tactical number. Unfortunately, the quality of the photo does not allow for a definitive identification of the military number. Some sources suggest that the aircraft had the number M.M.092345.

Camouflage and Markins

Regia Aeronautica

The first RE 2005 prototype with the serial number M.M.494 was initially in the natural aluminium colour. There are views that the aircraft was uniformly covered in a kind of varnish in a light gray shade. The only exceptions were the canvas-covered control surfaces, which were painted in a dark olive green colour (*Verde Oliva Scuro 2*). The rudder bore a white cross, but without the emblem of the royal house. Additionally, the fuselage featured a white identification stripe. Later, this aircraft was painted according to the scheme that became standard for all subsequent *Sagittarios*. This was the "Metropolitano" scheme, involving painting the upper surfaces in dark olive green (*Verde Oliva Scuro 2*) and the lower surfaces in a light grey-blue (*Grigio Azzuro Chiaro 1*). The fuselage retained the white stripe, a standard identifying feature of Italian aircraft. The rudder displayed a white cross with the royal house emblem in the middle. Typically, the aircraft also featured the fascio (bundle of rods) emblem, positioned on the fuselage beneath the pilot's cabin. The recognition signs were in a reduced visibility version – black fasces in a black circle. On the rear part of the fuselage, just before the horizontal stabilizer, there was a white military serial number (Matricolo Militare), e.g., M.M.092346. The type description was only present on the repainted first prototype. Also, this aircraft was the only *Sagittario* to feature the Reggiane factory logo on the vertical stabilizer. The second prototype (M.M.495) and most of the production aircraft had the name *Sagittario* painted on the stabilizer, usually in white. However, the appearance of this inscription differed slightly on the left and right sides of the stabilizer. Some authors suggest that on some aircraft, the inscription was red with white shading, but this is a subject of debate.

In July 1943, following the overthrow of Benito Mussolini, the fascio symbols and the wing recognition signs were painted over (though sometimes the black outline was left intact).

Tactical markings on RE 2005s from the *362ª Squadriglia* were placed on the fuselage – the unit number (362) was painted in red before the white identification stripe. The individual aircraft number was positioned behind the identification stripe on the fuselage and was in white. Propeller spinners were usually 2/3 olive green and 1/3 white. Some aircraft (e.g., 362-2 and 362-3) had the unit's emblem, "Lo Spauracchio" (scarecrow), painted on the white identification stripe.

Aeronautica Nationale Repubblicana

For the *Aeronautica Nazionale Repubblicana* (ANR), which sided with the Italian Social Republic (RSI), the aircraft retained their original paint schemes. Some sources suggest that the paint was refreshed, which also facilitated the overpainting of old national markings and tactical designations, but this information is not confirmed. The national markings in the form of so-called "postage stamps" were painted on the fuselage and vertical stabilizer, while the wings bore the fasces. The rear part of the fuselage carried the individual aircraft number. Only one tactical number is known – "red 4" (on aircraft M.M.092325). Many sources state that the propeller spinner of this aircraft was painted red, which raises some doubts because this was an identification element of Allied aircraft in the Mediterranean area. Therefore, some authors believe that the spinner could have been olive green.

Luftwaffe

For the *Luftwaffe*, the RE 2005 aircraft captured in September 1943 retained their Italian paint schemes. The recognition signs and identification markings were changed – German crosses appeared on the wings and fuselages, and swastikas (larger than standard on German aircraft) were painted on the tail. White identification stripes were painted on the fuselages. The wingtips were painted yellow (Gelb RLM 04 or RLM 27). The Reggiane RE 2005s in *Luftwaffe* service kept their Italian military numbers, e.g., M.M.096106, M.M. 096109. Due to the very limited number of photographs, it is difficult to make definitive statements about the tactical markings. There is one known photo of an aircraft with a white number 7 on the rudder (possibly M.M.092345). This aircraft had an Italian standard propeller spinner – 2/3 olive green and 1/3 white. Another aircraft, without a tactical number, had a white propeller spinner with a black spiral.

*The first prototype of the RE 2005 with the military number M.M.494, Reggia Emilia airport, May 1942. The aircraft was in the colour of natural aluminium. There are views, however, that the aircraft was overpainted with a coat of light grey paint. Only the control surfaces covered with canvas were painted in olive-green (*Verde Oliva Scuro 2*). A white cross was placed on the rudder, but without the coat of arms of the royal house. Meanwhile, a white identification stripe was located on the fuselage. The type description and M.M. number were in black.*

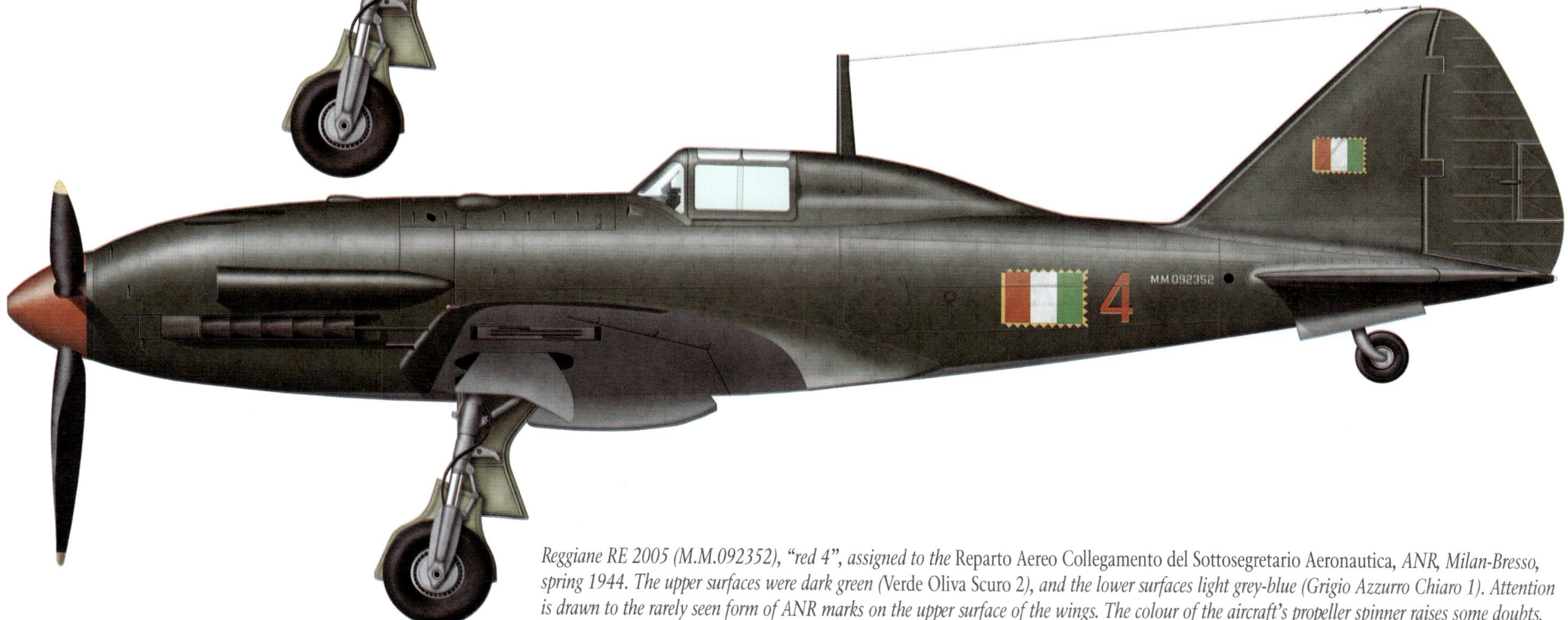

Reggiane RE 2005 (M.M.092352), "red 4", assigned to the Reparto Aereo Collegamento del Sottosegretario Aeronautica, *ANR, Milan-Bresso, spring 1944. The upper surfaces were dark green (*Verde Oliva Scuro 2*), and the lower surfaces light grey-blue (Grigio Azzurro Chiaro 1). Attention is drawn to the rarely seen form of ANR marks on the upper surface of the wings. The colour of the aircraft's propeller spinner raises some doubts. According to many Italian sources, it was painted red. However, this was an identification feature of Allied machines in the Mediterranean area. Probably for this reason, some authors believe that the spinner was olive-green.*

Reggiane RE 2005 (M.M.092352), "red 4", assigned to the Reparto Aereo Collegamento del Sottosegretario Aeronautica, *ANR, Milan-Bresso, spring 1944*

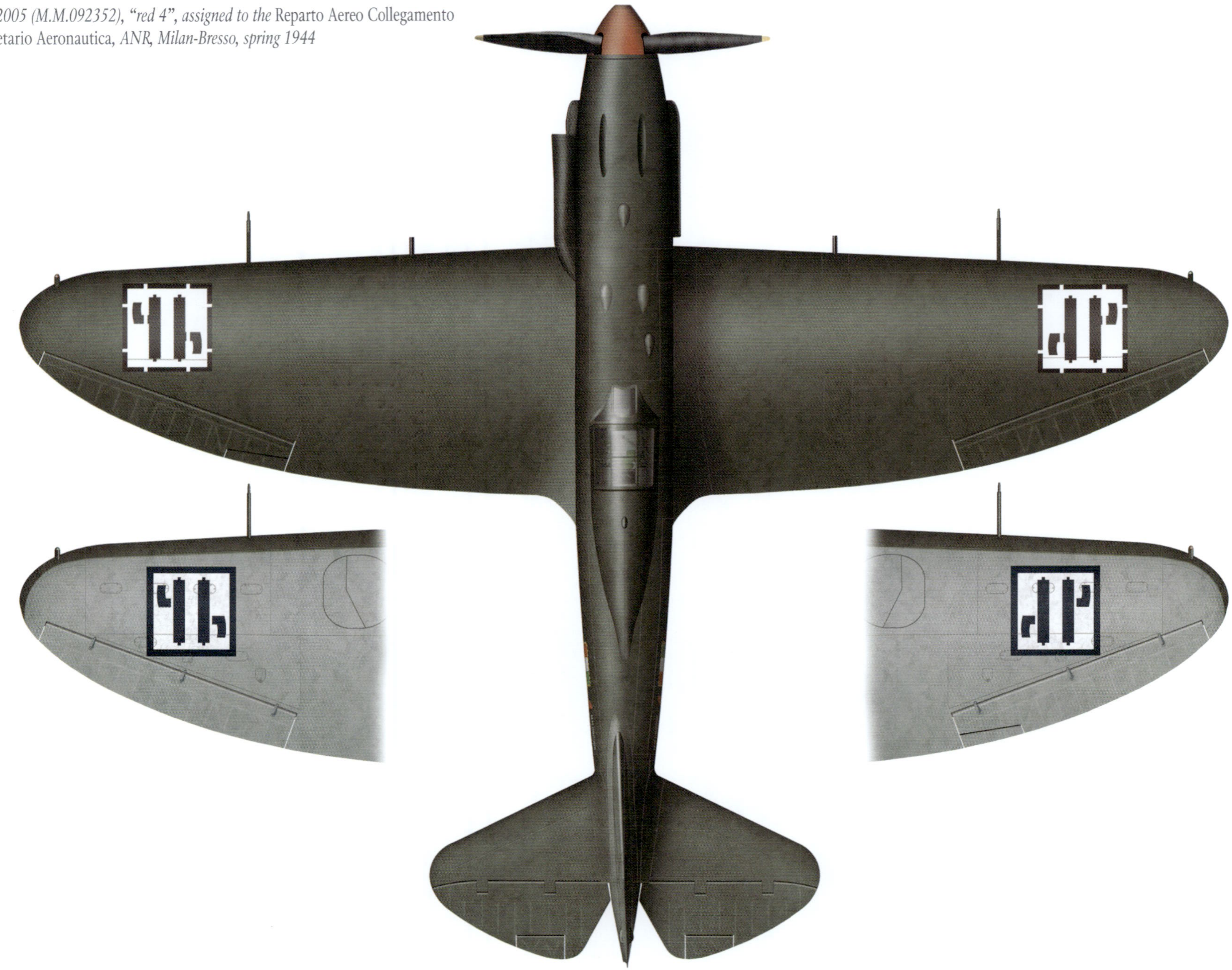

Reggiane RE 2005 (M.M.092351) from the 362ª Squadriglia, *number362-2, Littoria, June 1943. The aircraft were in the "Metropolitano" paint scheme – upper surfaces in* Verde Oliva Scuro 2, *and lower surfaces in* Grigio Azzuro Chiaro 1. *The aircraft featured a complete set of Italian markings.*

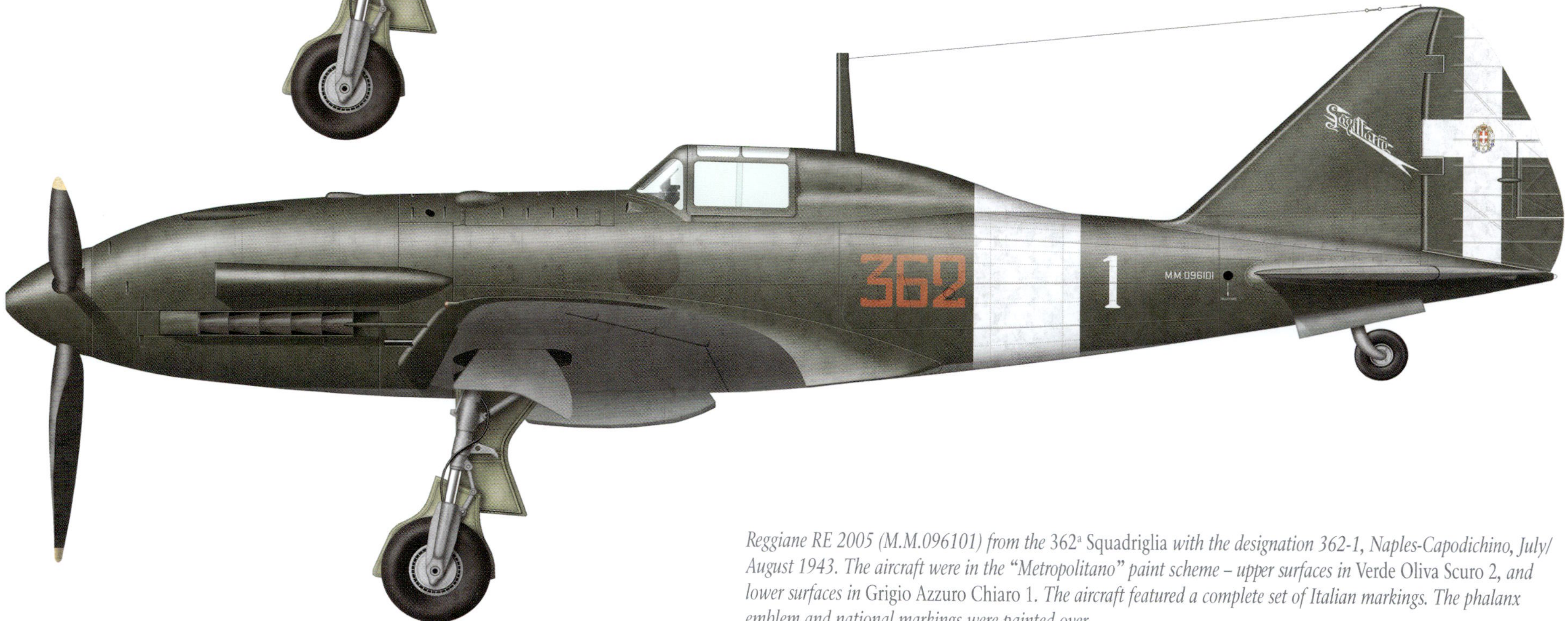

Reggiane RE 2005 (M.M.096101) from the 362ª Squadriglia *with the designation 362-1, Naples-Capodichino, July/August 1943. The aircraft were in the "Metropolitano" paint scheme – upper surfaces in* Verde Oliva Scuro 2, *and lower surfaces in* Grigio Azzuro Chiaro 1. *The aircraft featured a complete set of Italian markings. The phalanx emblem and national markings were painted over.*

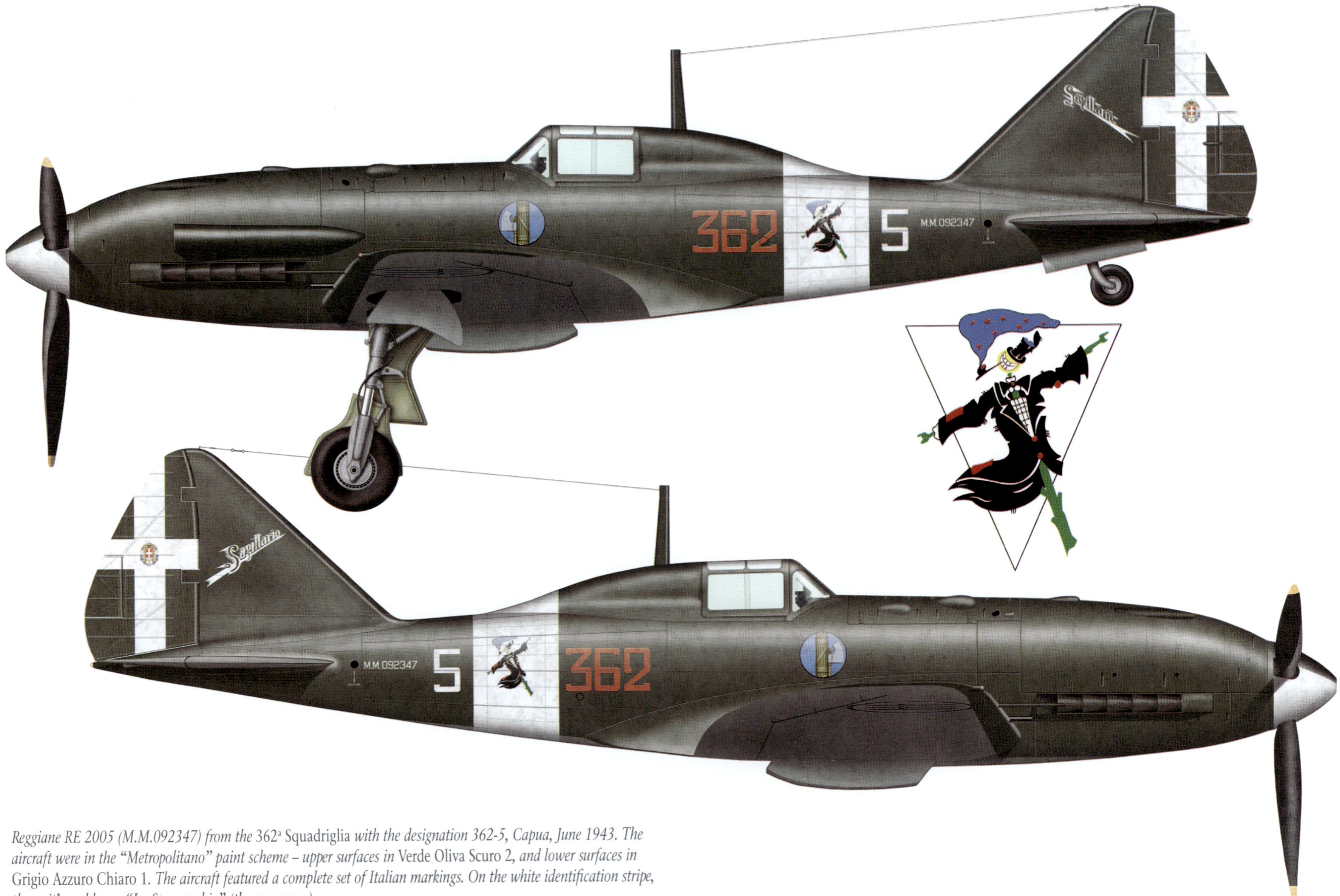

Reggiane RE 2005 (M.M.092347) from the 362ª Squadriglia *with the designation 362-5, Capua, June 1943. The aircraft were in the "Metropolitano" paint scheme – upper surfaces in* Verde Oliva Scuro 2, *and lower surfaces in* Grigio Azzuro Chiaro 1. *The aircraft featured a complete set of Italian markings. On the white identification stripe, the unit's emblem – "Lo Spauracchio" (the scarecrow).*

Reggiane RE 2005 (M.M.0923XX) from the 362ª Squadriglia *with the designation 362-8, Littoria, June 1943. The aircraft were in the "Metropolitano" paint scheme – upper surfaces in* Verde Oliva Scuro 2, *and lower surfaces in* Grigio Azzuro Chiaro 1. *The aircraft featured a complete set of Italian markings.*

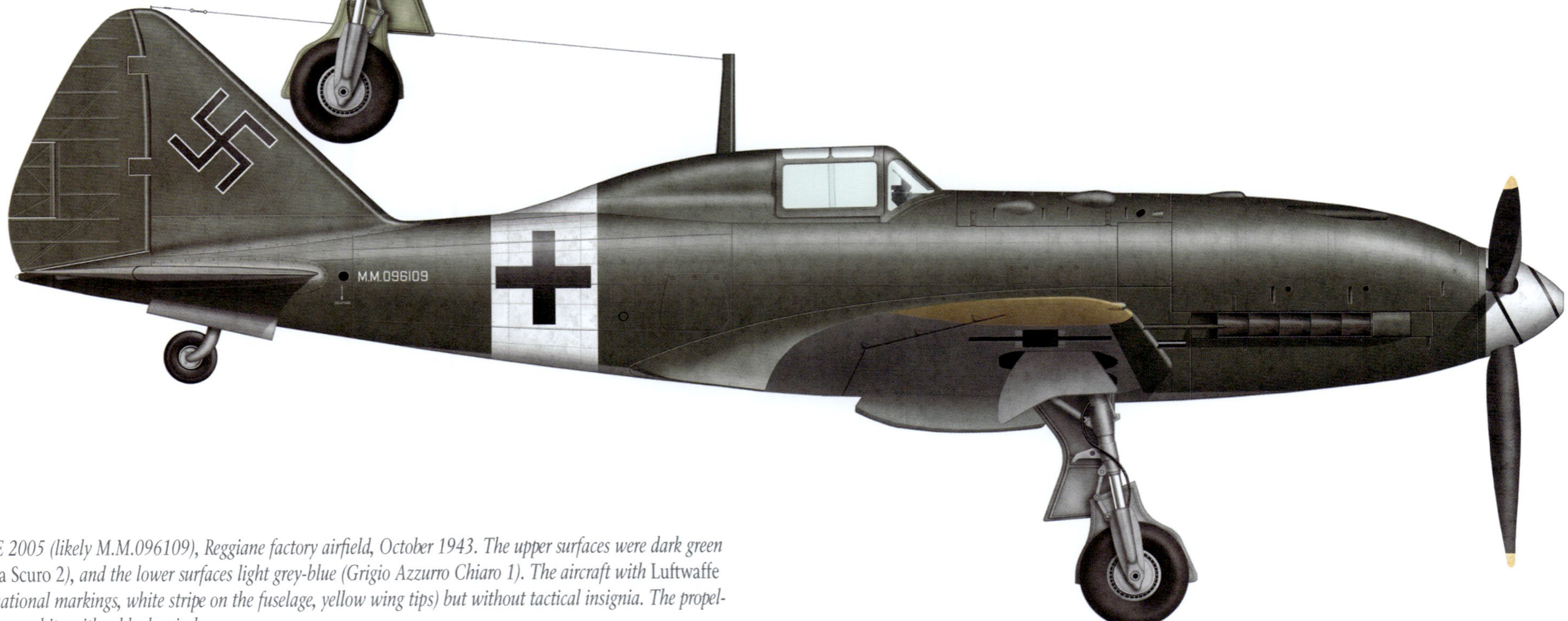

*Reggiane RE 2005 (likely M.M.096109), Reggiane factory airfield, October 1943. The upper surfaces were dark green (*Verde Oliva Scuro 2*), and the lower surfaces light grey-blue (*Grigio Azzurro Chiaro 1*). The aircraft with* Luftwaffe *markings (national markings, white stripe on the fuselage, yellow wing tips) but without tactical insignia. The propeller spinner was white with a black spiral.*

Reggiane RE 2005 (likely M.M.092345), "white 7" assigned to Luftdienst Kommando Italien, *Maniago, end of 1943. The upper surfaces were dark green (*Verde Oliva Scuro 2*), and the lower surfaces light grey-blue (Grigio Azzurro Chiaro 1). The aircraft with* Luftwaffe *markings (national markings, white stripe on the fuselage, yellow wing tips) but without tactical insignia. The propeller spinner was white with a black spiral. The spinner was 2/3 olive-green and 1/3 white.*

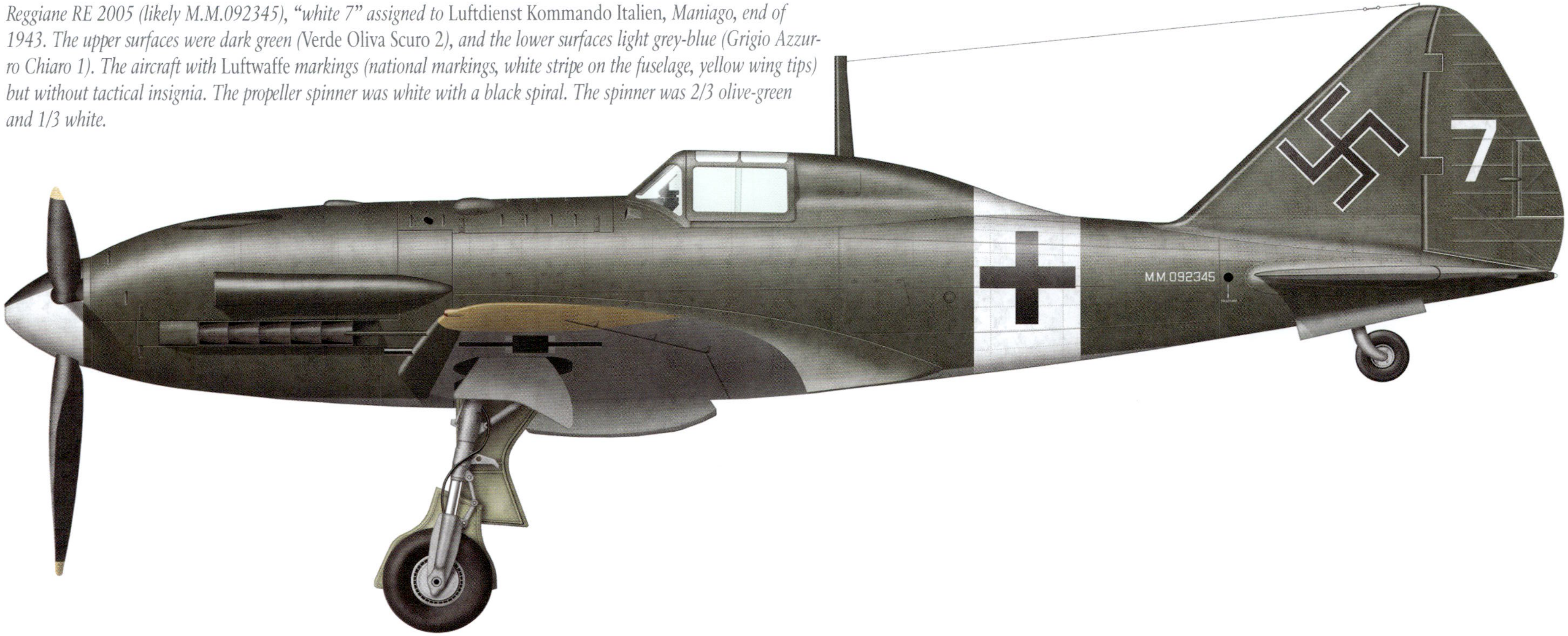

Reggiane's Development Projects

RE 2004

Work on this aircraft at the Officine Meccaniche Reggiane started in 1941, practically simultaneously with the RE 2005. It can be considered as essentially another variant of that design, as the primary difference was the use of a domestic power unit – the X-layout Isotta Fraschini Zeta R.C. 24/60 inline engine with a power of 1250 HP, equipped with a two-stage supercharger. This was a 24-cylinder air-cooled power unit, weighing close to 1000 kilograms. The main issue affecting the success of the entire project was achieving sufficient reliability of the engine. The greatest difficulty was ensuring adequate cooling for the engine, which in practice proved to be a challenging task. This significantly prolonged the development, so that engine trials, mounted on a modified S.79 Sparviero aircraft, only began in May 1943.

Interestingly, despite the engine problems, in June 1942, the Italian Ministry of Aviation ordered the construction of two RE 2004 prototypes (contracts 90.377 and 90.390), which were assigned the military numbers M.M.505 and 506. The aircraft was expected to have strong armament, including two 12.7 mm Breda-SAFAT machine guns in the fuselage and two 20 mm Mauser MG 151/20 cannons in the wings. It was anticipated that the aircraft could reach a maximum speed of 620 km/h, which was less than the RE 2005, indicating that the aircraft was considered a substitute or an emergency solution.

Due to problems with the intended engine, there was consideration of mounting another Italian power unit – the Reggiane RE 103 R.C. 40/50 inline engine with 1500–1700 HP. However, this engine also did not progress beyond the testing phase, and its mass production was not foreseeable in the near future.

In addition to the two prototypes, in November 1942, 12 *Serie 0* aircraft (M.M.09953–09964) were ordered. Later, the order was reduced to 4 aircraft. However, the preparations for the construction of the prototype did not yield any tangible results. According to some sources, the project was closed in September 1943 following the capitulation of Italy, though it's possible that it ended earlier, as suggested by Marco Gueli.

RE 2006

Work on this aircraft began at the end of 1942, led by engineer Alessandro Barteletti. Initially, the machine was to be powered by the same engine as the Reggiane RE 2005, namely the FIAT R.A.1050 R.C.58 "Tifone". However, later the decision regarding the power unit was changed, and it was finally decided to use the German Daimler-Benz DB 603A engine with 1750 HP. With this engine, the aircraft was expected to reach a speed of 750 km/h. Compared to the RE 2005, the aircraft was to have a fuselage 1 meter longer. The vertical stabilizer was to remain the same as in the RE 2005, but the rudder was enlarged. The landing gear was also strengthened. On 9 May 1943, two prototypes were ordered, receiving the military numbers: M.M.540 and M.M.541.

Ultimately, work began on only one machine – M.M.540. After the capitulation of Italy, work on the aircraft continued, and its assembly was conducted in a gymnasium in Corregio. Reports that the aircraft was ready for its maiden flight in the autumn of 1943 are not unequivocally confirmed. In October 1944, the machine was transported in parts to Ponte San Pietro, and then to the Caproni factory in Taliedo. Interestingly, to this day, no photos of the completed machine are known. It is likely that only photographs of wind tunnel models have survived. This has led to much speculation regarding the actual appearance of the RE 2006 and some of its design solutions. For example, the placement of the radiators – under the wings (as in the RE 2005) or in the leading edges of the wings (as in the RE 2001bis). According to some sources, the serial RE 2006 was to have radiators in the wings.

After the war, the RE 2006 was examined by Allied aviation specialists, but they did not show interest in the design. In the spring of 1946, an Allied control commission gave permission for the aircraft to be scrapped. A few months later, fragments of the fuselage, wings, and various components of the RE 2006 were sent to the Instituto d'Aeronautica del Politecnico in Milan, where they were used as teaching aids. Currently, the only surviving part of the aircraft is likely the main landing gear leg.

It is also worth mentioning that the designations RE 2006P and RE 2006PP were used for postal aircraft projects, which had little in common with the fighter aircraft.

Jet-Powered Reggiane

In the autumn of 1942, a project was conceived to equip a modified RE 2005 with an additional jet engine, utilizing the concept known as a "motorjet". This concept involved, in addition to the piston engine, the installation of a jet engine. The creators of this project were Marcello Sarraciano and Antonio Ferri. The project was designated as RE 2005SF or RE 2005R.

The additional jet propulsion was to be provided by an engine designed by engineer Secondo Campini. It consisted of a 12-cylinder inline FIAT A.20 engine with 370 HP, driving two Campini turbochargers. The exhaust nozzle for the jet engine was located at the tail of the aircraft. The total maximum power of the engines installed in the RE 2005 SF/R was 2030 HP. The aircraft was expected to achieve a maximum speed of 730–750 km/h, with a climb time to 8000 meters of about 12 minutes. The project was prepared in at least two variants, differing in the type of compressor used – a centrifugal compressor and an axial compressor.

Upon closer analysis, the "motorjet" concept for the RE 2005 encountered significant problems – an increase in the aircraft's weight, which necessitated the reduction of armament and armour, very high fuel consumption leading to short operational use of the jet propulsion, and a shift in the aircraft's centre of gravity. These drawbacks not only required a significant redesign of the RE 2005 but also raised doubts about the operational capabilities of the planned construction. Opponents of this idea, particularly among the Reggiane designers, included Roberto Longhi who believed that a new aircraft should essentially be built for such a propulsion system ("motorjet"). This led to the cessation of work on the project. A similar concept was also considered for the RE 2006, but this too ended up only as a paper project.

In the summer of 1944, Allied aviation specialists reviewed the RE 2005 SF/R project and the Campini engines. However, they did not generate much interest, which is not surprising. By the final period of World War II, these were archaic concepts with no future.

In the last period of the war, Roberto Longhi also became interested in using jet engines for fighter aircraft propulsion. Considering the economic capabilities of the Italian Social Republic, the potential of the Italian aviation industry, and the development of the situation on the front, the only realistic option was to acquire jet engines from Germany. However, the attempts made by Antonio Alessio and Giovanni Caproni did not yield results. The entire story has not been unequivocally explained to this day, but it is most likely that Germany only provided a wooden mock-up of the Jumo 004 engine for dimensional testing.

Post-War Developments by Longhi

After the war, Longhi aimed to conduct experiments with two Junkers Jumo 004 engines that remained at the airfield in Udine. These engines had been delivered to Italy in 1945 as spare parts for the Arado Ar 234 *Blitz*, used by a reconnaissance unit of the *Luftwaffe*. However, the engines were acquired by another Italian aircraft manufacturer, Angelo Ambrosini.

Years after the war, drawings labelled as RE 2007 emerged, created by Giuseppe Cometti based on guidance from Roberto Longhi. The drawings depicted the aircraft as an advanced jet fighter with swept wings. Claims in some older publications about a partially built airframe, along with technical documentation sent to the United Kingdom and the United States for examination, have no factual confirmation. The situation is further complicated by information about the Caproni-Reggiane Ca.2008, which was supposed to be a developmental version of the RE 2007 developed in 1947–1948 (supposedly with technical support from the Cornell Aeronautical Laboratory, which had a suitable wind tunnel).

The history of jet aircraft developed at the Reggiane and Caproni factories remains unclear, with more conjecture and speculation than verified information. There isn't even certainty that the jet-powered RE 2007 ever existed. This is further questioned by even Tulio de Prato, the chief test pilot at the Reggiane factories, who doubted the existence of the aircraft.

RE 2001 (day fighter) Technical Description

The Reggiane RE 2001 was an Italian all metal, low-wing monoplane, single-seat fighter aircraft. The RE 2001 was also manufactured in night fighter, fighter-bomber, recce and torpedo versions.

Fuselage

The fuselage had a completely metal structure and had high structural resistance qualities combined with a relatively low weight. The fuselage structure consisted of 13 oval bulkheads held by stringers. The first bulkhead was also a firewall and the engine mounts were attached to it. The stressed skin fuselage was highly streamlined, save for the protrusions of the hard-riveted finish. The tail had all metal structure with fabric-covered movable surfaces. The cockpit of the RE 2001 was featured with large, foldable, open on right side canopy.

Wing and control surfaces

The wing had semi-elliptical plan with the leading edge made rectilinear to simplify production process. Wing was divided into centre section, two half-wings and wingtips. The internal structure of which comprised a multi-cell configuration using a total of three spars, stress-skin covering, and two fuel tanks within the centre section. The wing was outfitted with Frise-type ailerons complete with static and aerodynamic balance, along with a split-continuous four-section flaps.

Landing gear

The main undercarriage retracted rearward after being rotated 90 degrees around the leg axis. Landing gear was hydraulically operated and equipped with shock absorbers. The wheels of main undercarriage were produced by Fabbrica Articoli Scientifici e Tecnici (FAST) and had Pirelli Aeroplano tires measured 600x254x170. Fixed steerable tail wheel was retractable and closed by a pair of small doors. The tail wheel (FAST) had Pirelli Aeroplano tire measured 265x100x85.

Fuel and oil system

The fuel system included two tanks in the centre-section of the wing – 264 liters front fuel tank and 200 liters rear fuel tank. In the fuselage behind the cockpit was places the third 80 liters expansion tank. All tanks are fitted with SAMAPE/Sampare protective lining. The oil cooler was placed under the engine, while 29 liters main oil tank was placed at the left wing.

Armament

Armament for aircraft produced in day fighter configuration were two synchronized 12.7 mm Breda-SAFAT machine guns located in the top of the engine cowling with 350 rounds per gun. The rate of fire was 575 rounds per minute. In the wing were placed two non-synchronized 7.7 mm Breda-SAFAT machine guns with 600 rounds per gun. The weapon was cocked and reloaded using the Managhi electro-pneumatic system. The well-proved San Giorgio – Genova Type B reflector gun sight was mounted under the windscreen.

Powerplant

Alfa Romeo R.A. 1000 R.C. 41-I "Monsone" (licence version of Daimler Benz DB 601A-1) in-line engine, which was capable of generating a maximum of 1175 hp. The weight of dry engine was 670 kg. The engine drived a three-blade Alfa Rome R.A. 1000 variable-speed metal propeller (licence version of German VDM propeller) 3100 mm of diameter.

Communication and other equipment

HF radio R.T. Allocchio Bacchini B.30 was mounted in the fuselage. The aircraft was equipped with two Slima type automatic fire extinguisher. On many aircraft provision was also made for wing-mounted gun-camera (on upper surface of the right wing), but this was only installed by special request.

Front of the cockpit of the RE 2001 prototype.

Front of the cockpit of the serial RE 2001.

Elements of the instrument panel.

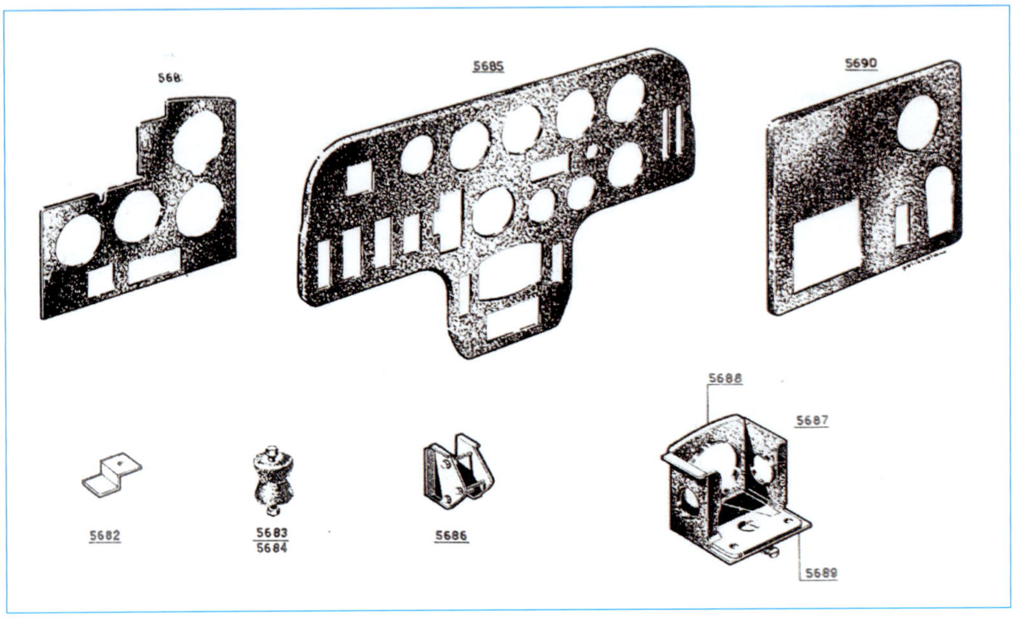

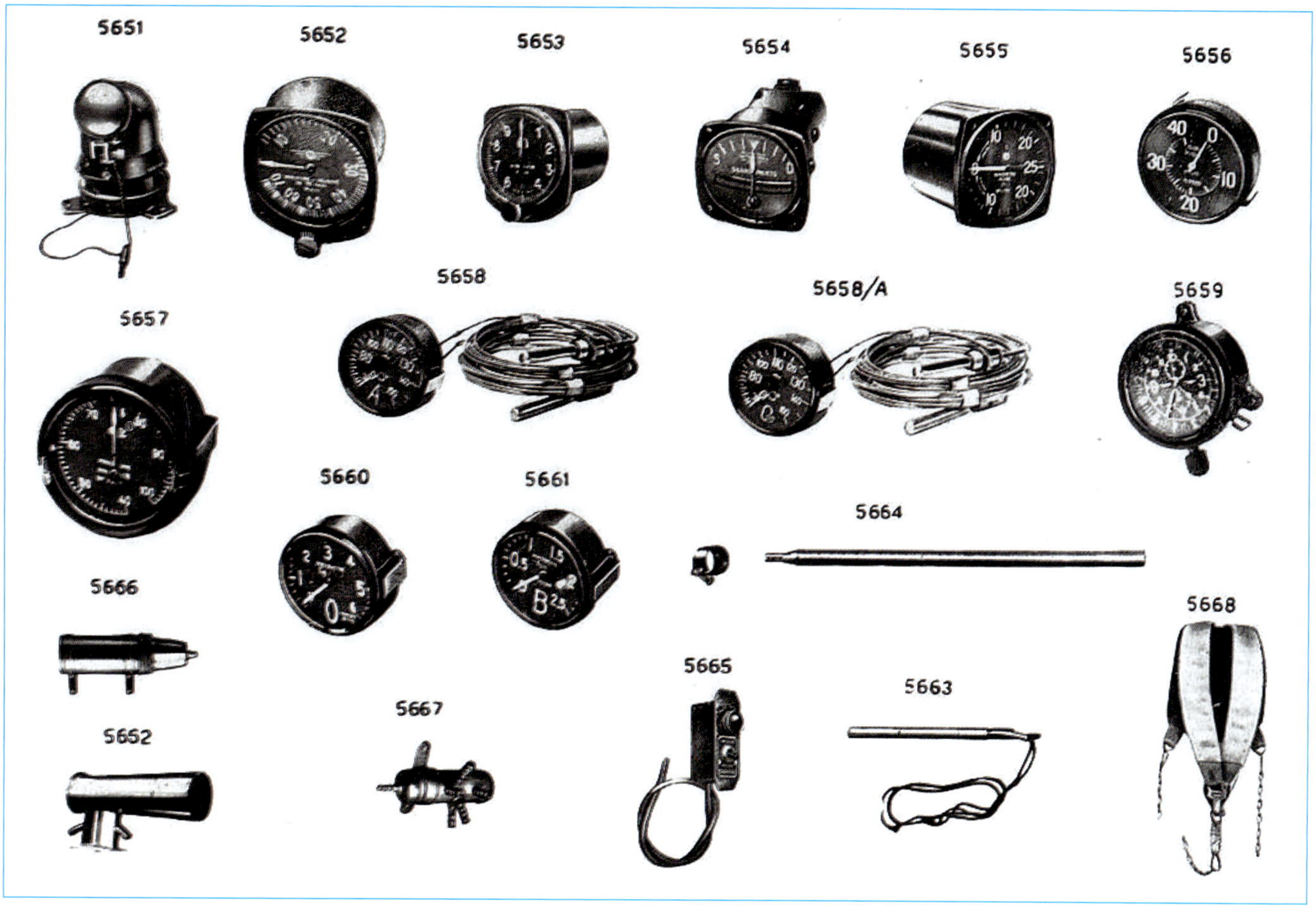

Instruments and some equipment elements.

Right cockpit panel.

Left cockpit panel.

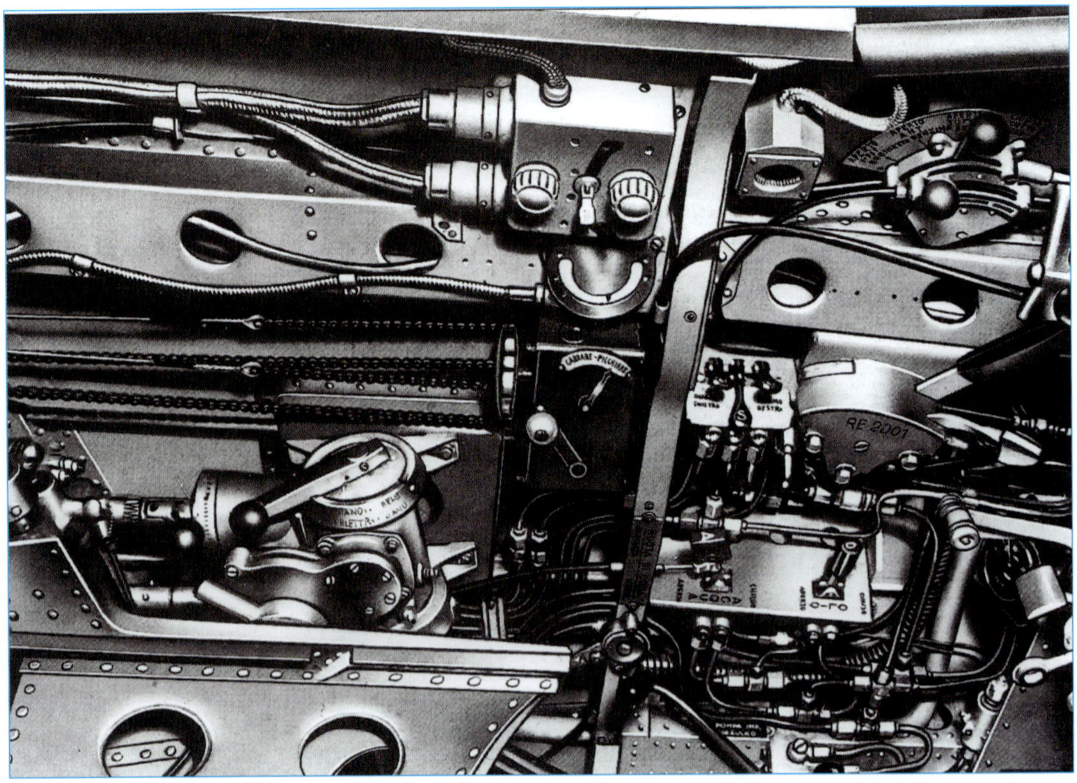

Control stick.

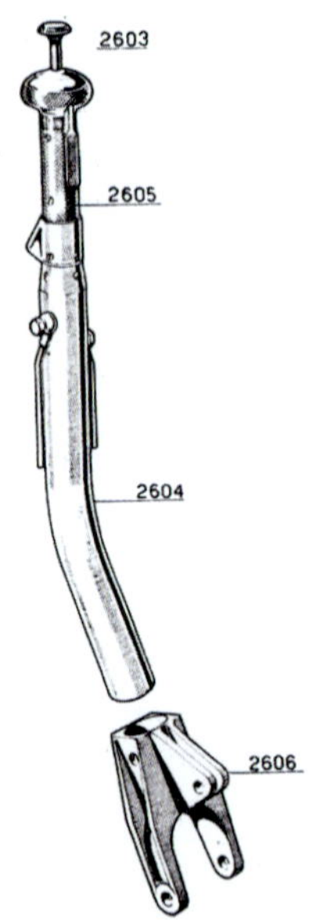

Construction of the rudder pedals.

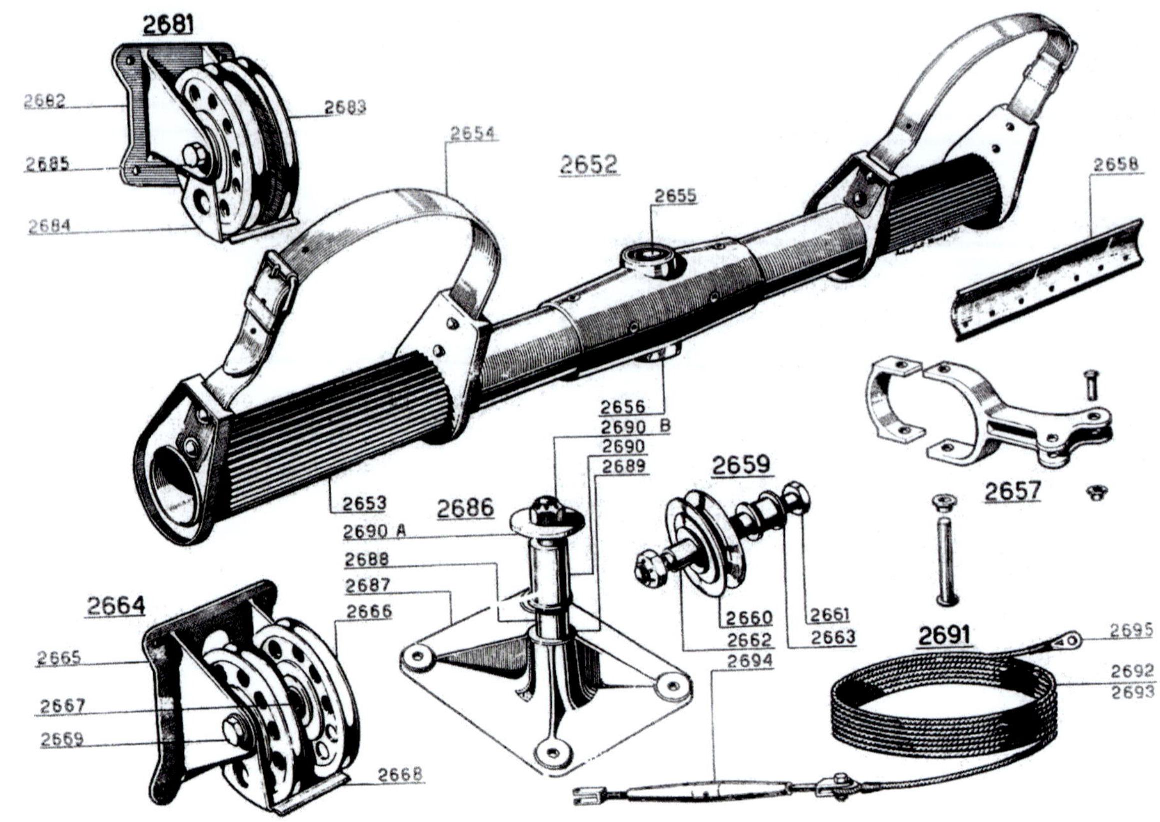

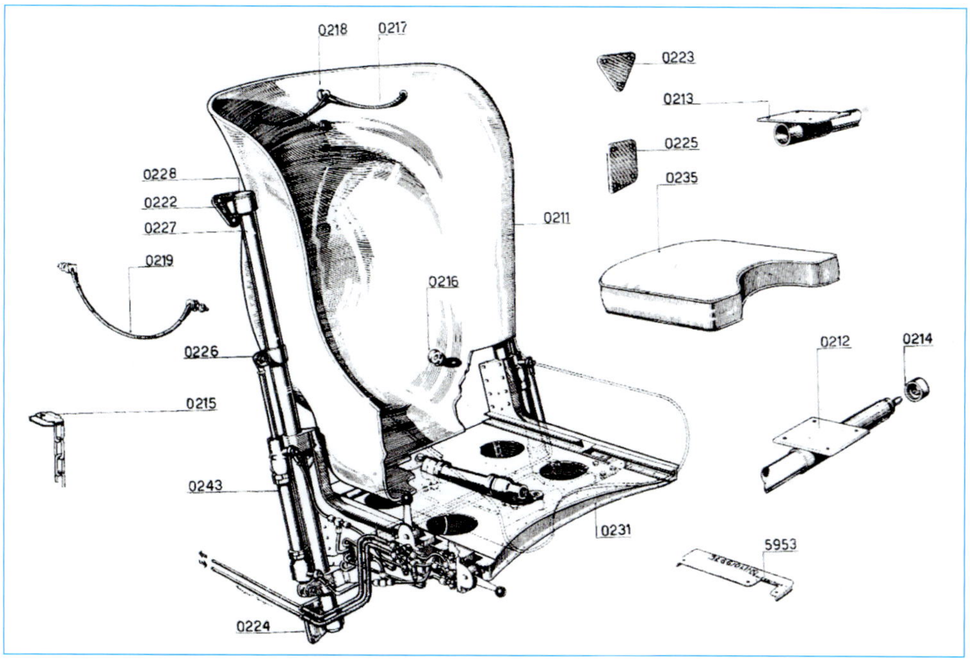

Pilot's seat.

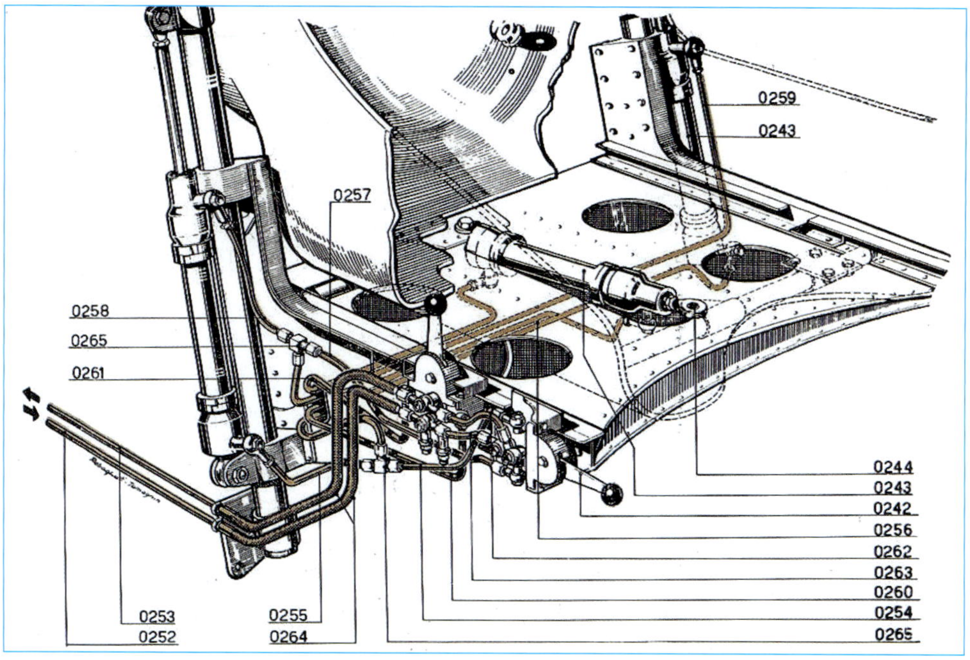

Pilot seat adjustment system.

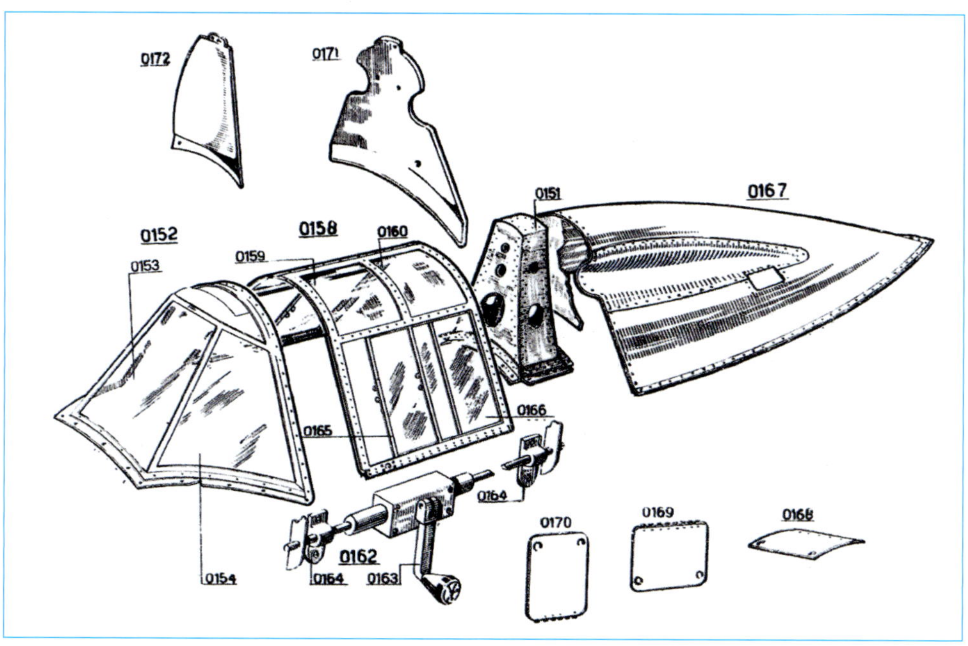

Construction of the cockpit canopy.

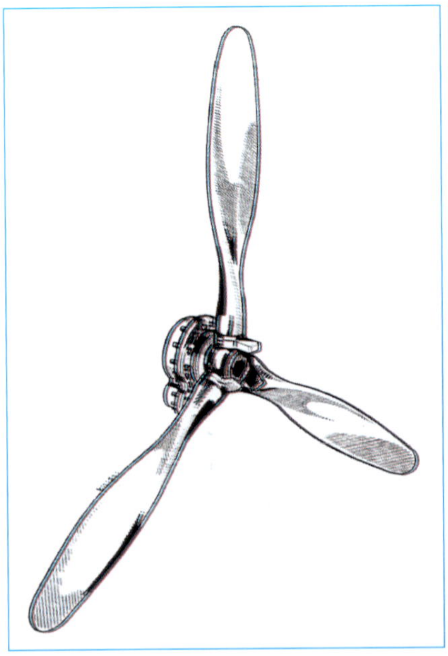

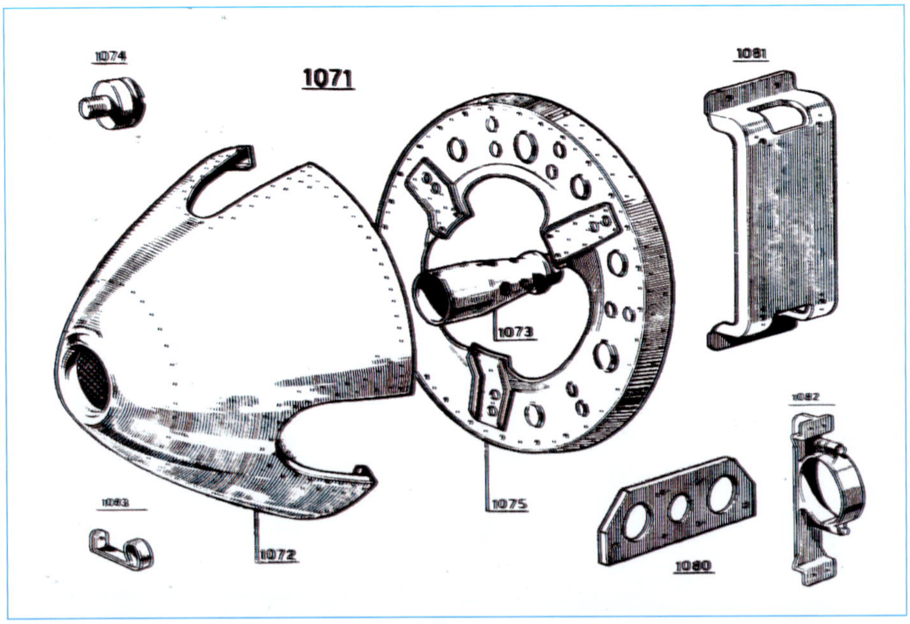

Above: *Alfa Romeo R.A. 1000 propeller.*

Above, right: *Construction of the propeller spinner.*

Front part of the fuselage with the propeller spinner.

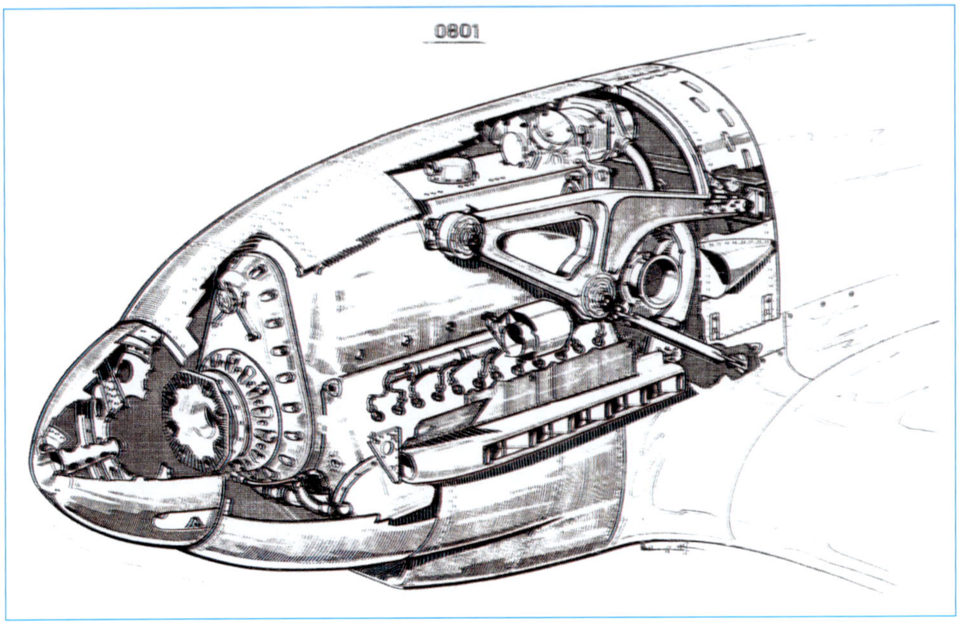

Alfa Romeo R.A. 1000 R.C. 41-I "Monsone" engine.

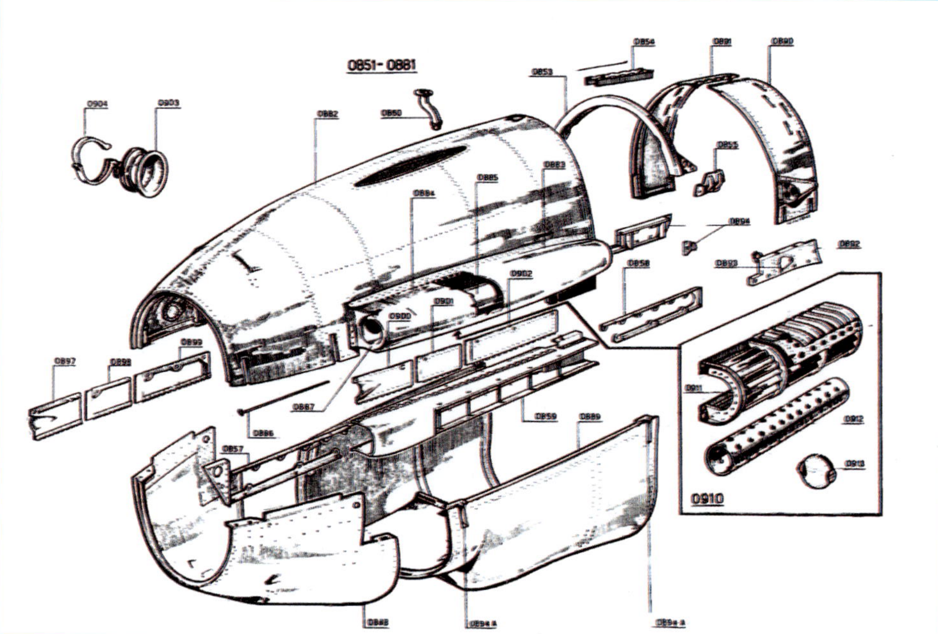

Engine cover components.

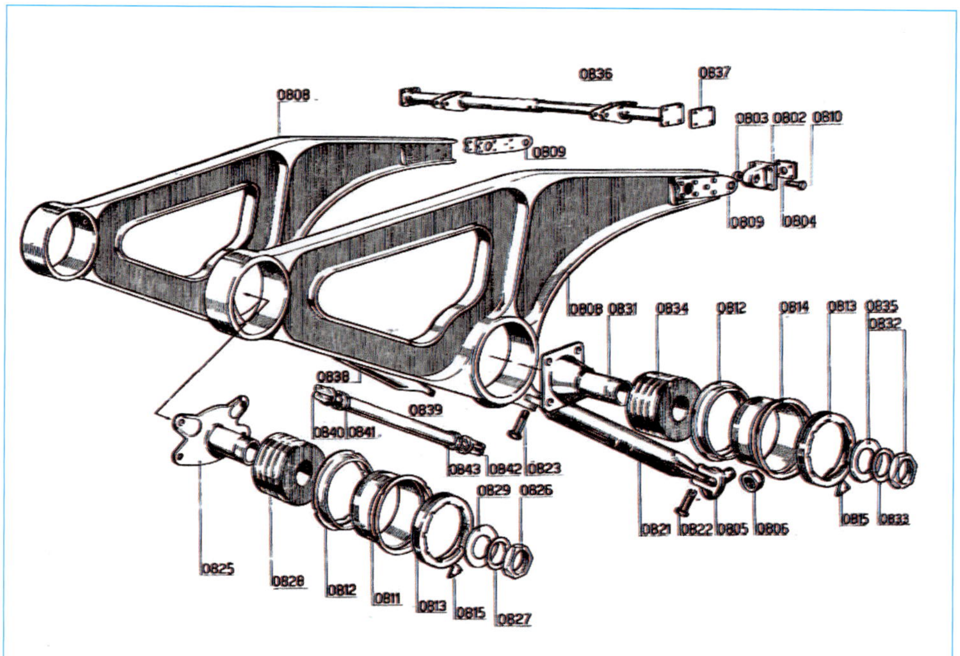

Engine bed of Alfa Romeo R.A. 1000 R.C. 41-I "Monsone".

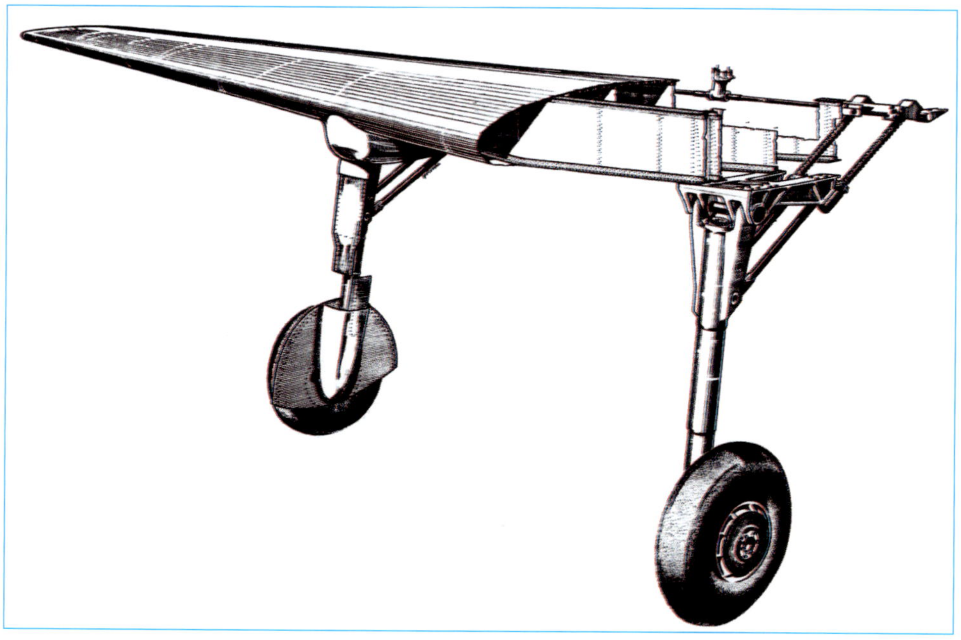

Main landing gear.

Components of the main landing gear.

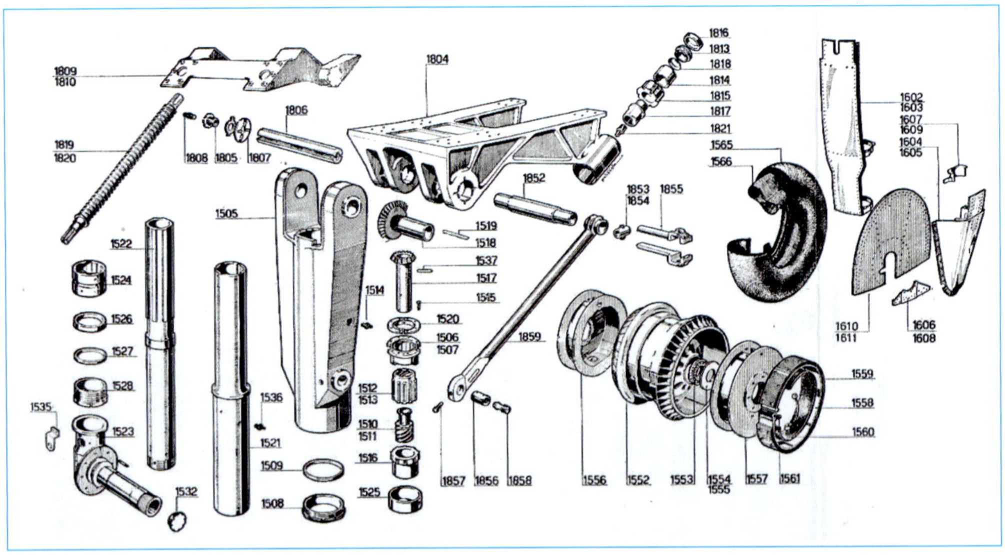

Main landing gear folding mechanism.

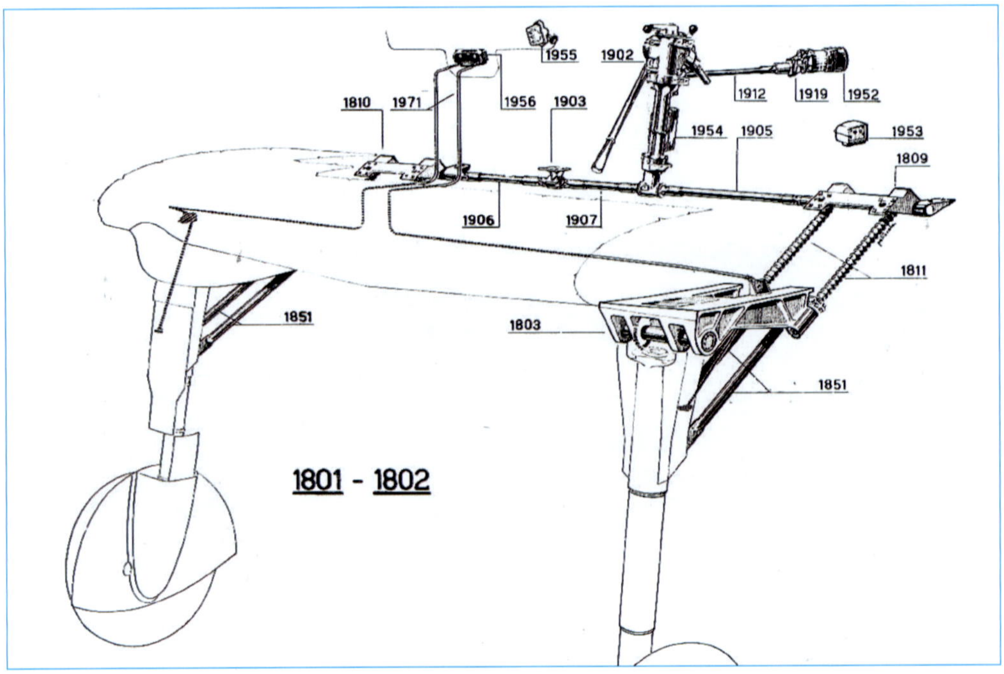

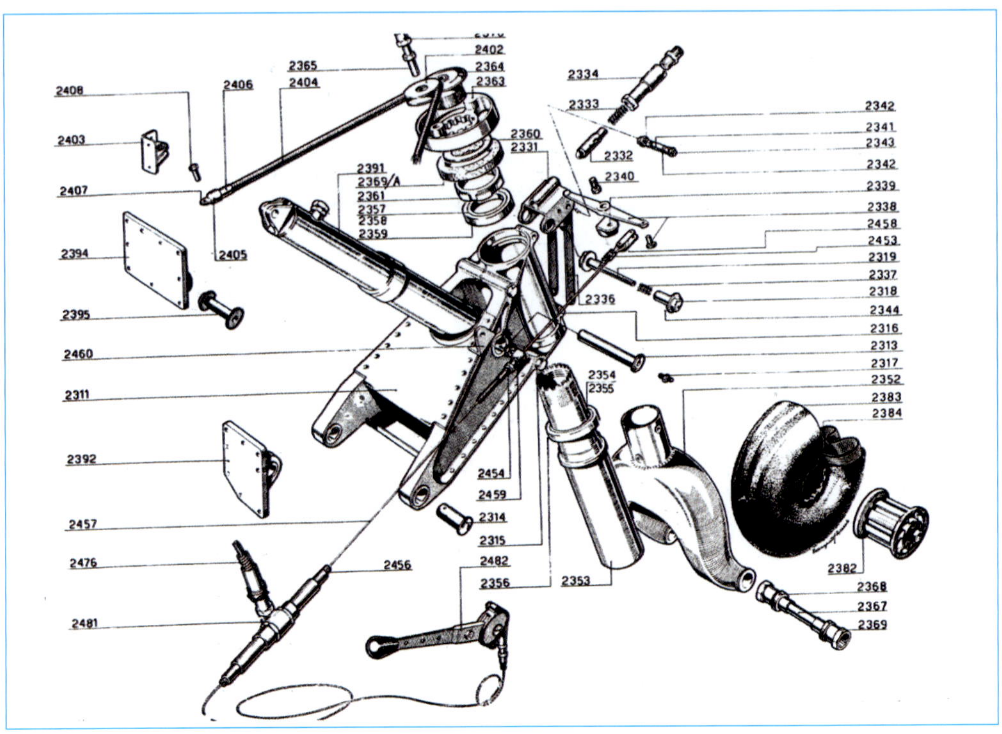

Components of the tail wheel.

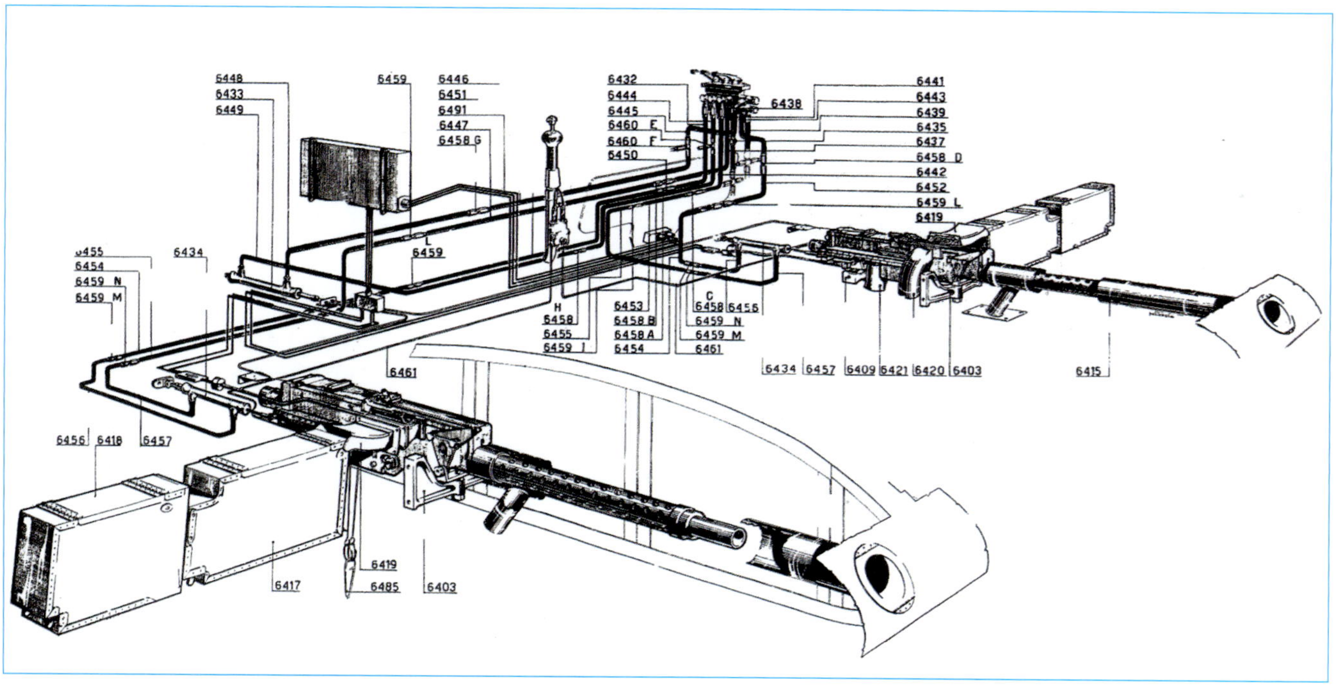

Machine guns.

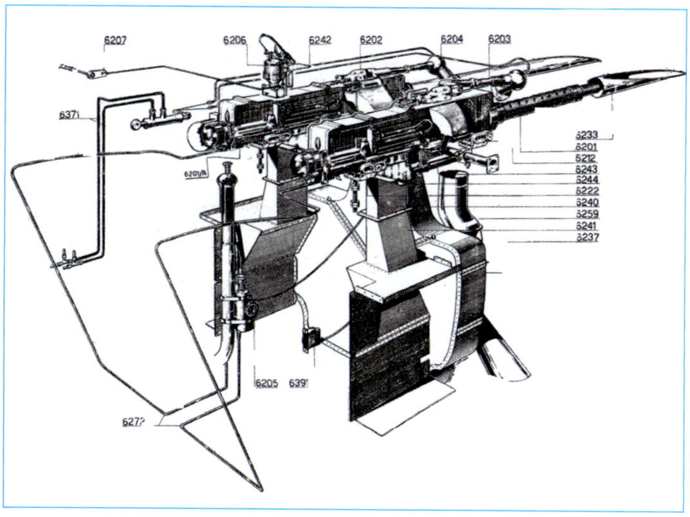

Above: *Fuselage Breda-SAFAT 12.7 mm machine guns.*
Left: *Open wing armament compartment cover.*
Below: *Components of the fuselage armament compartment.*

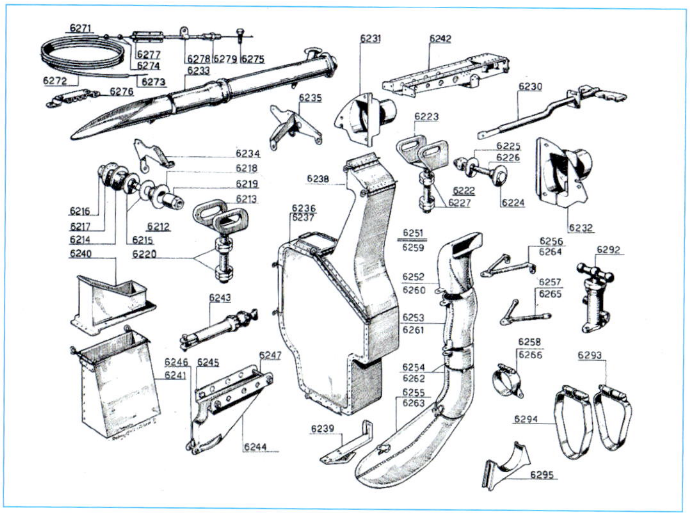

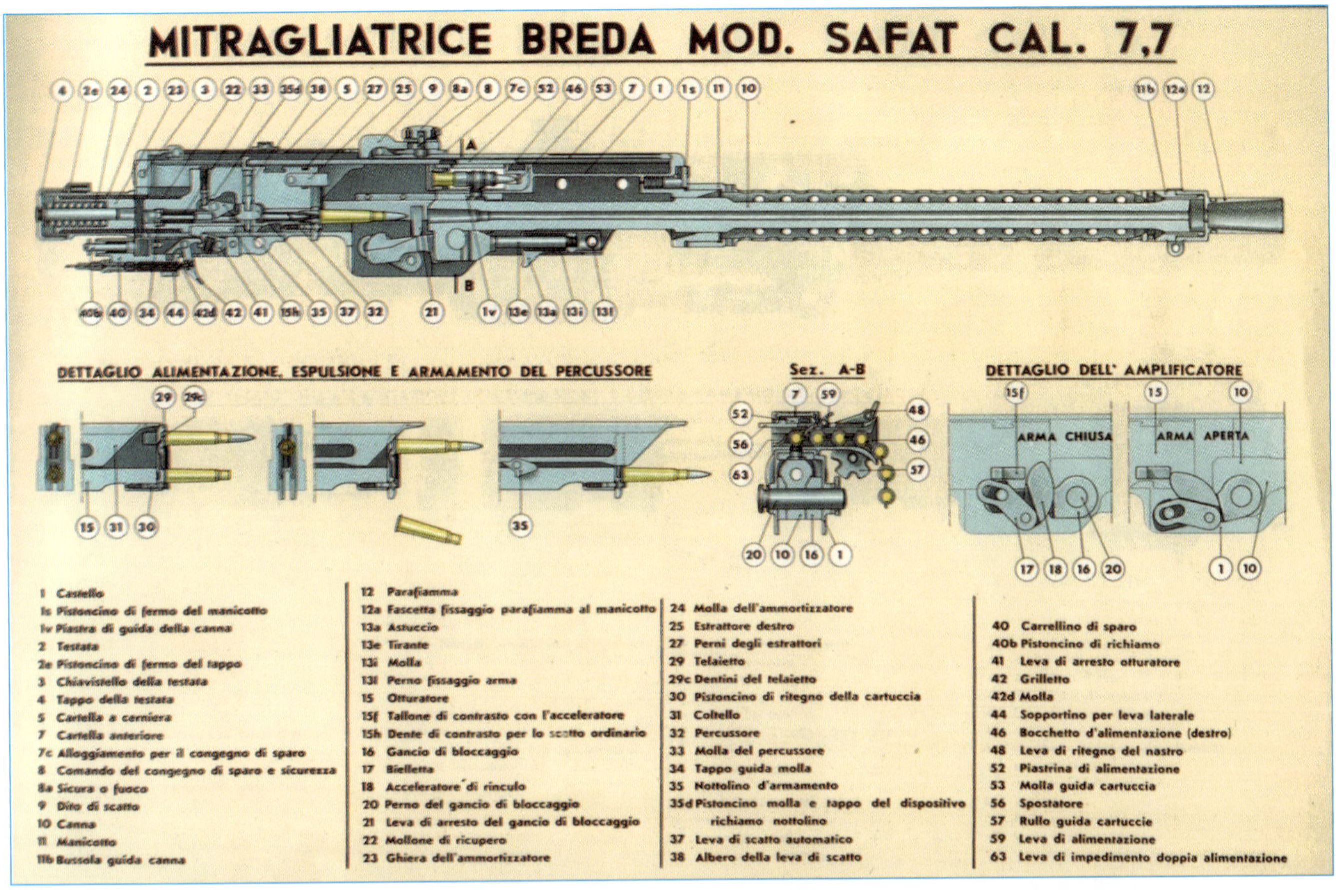

Breda-SAFAT 7.7 mm machine gun.

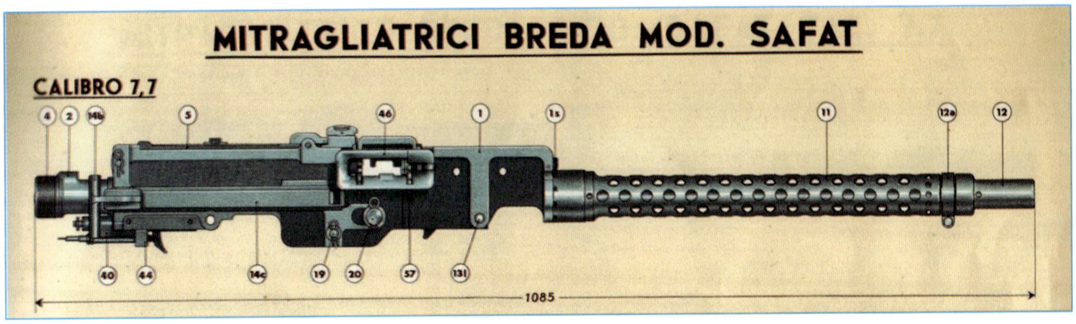

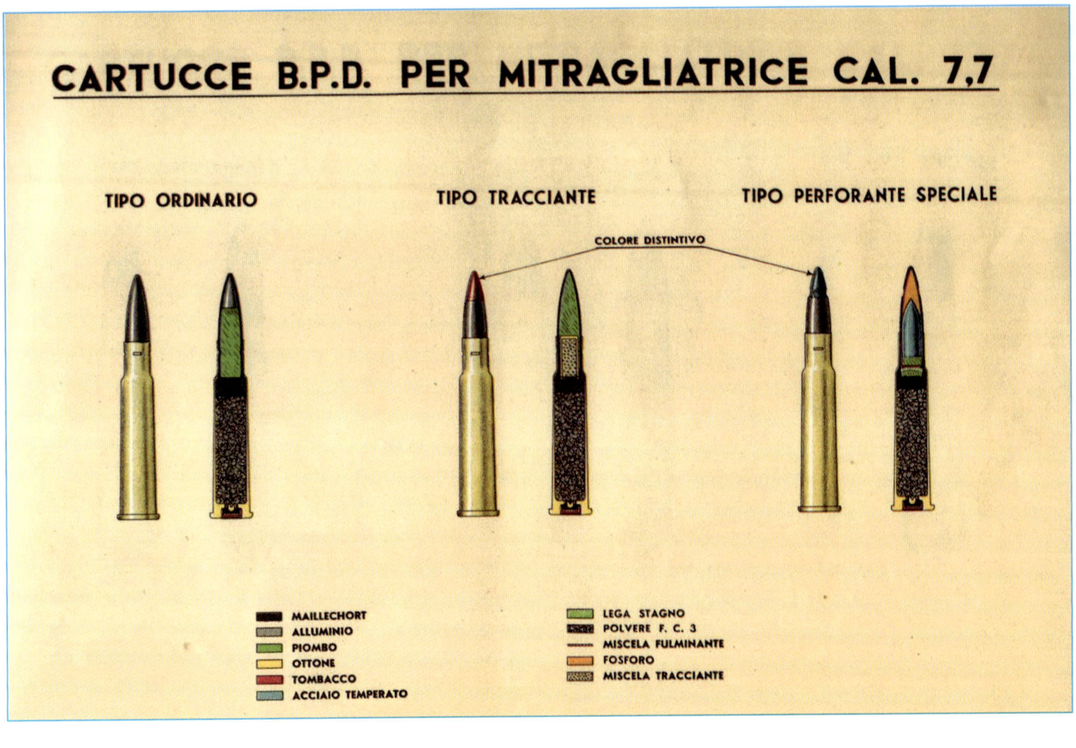

B.P.D. ammunition for the 7.7 mm machine gun. From left to right: standard, tracer, special armour-piercing.

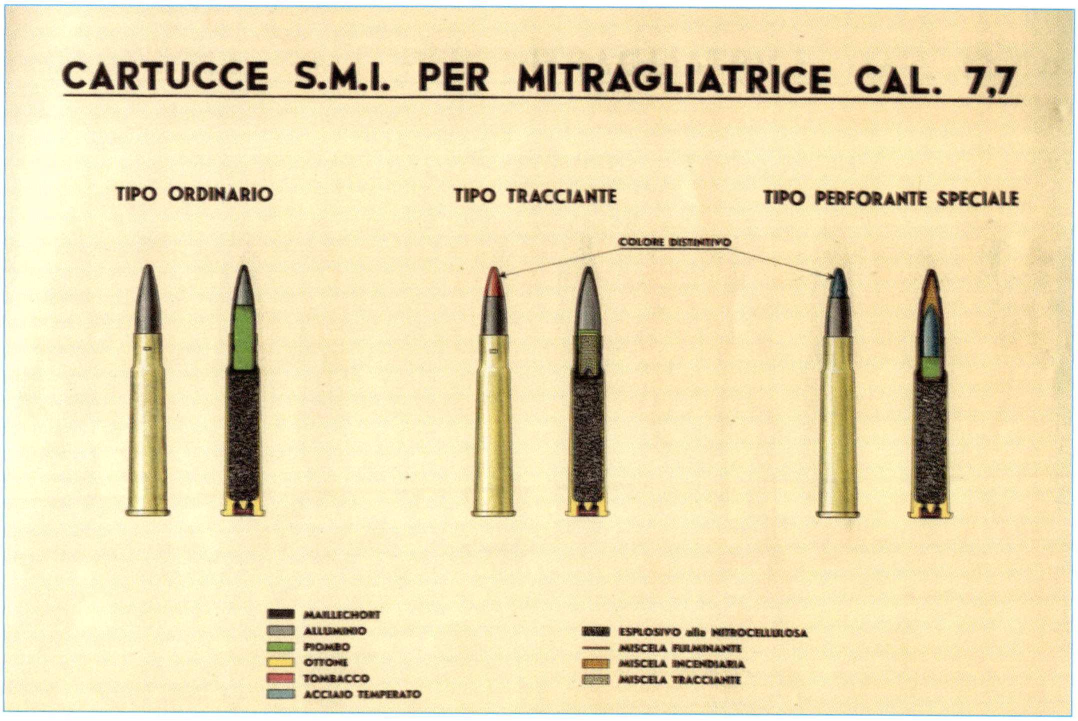

S.M.I. ammunition for the 7.7 mm machine gun. From left to right: standard, tracer, special armour-piercing.

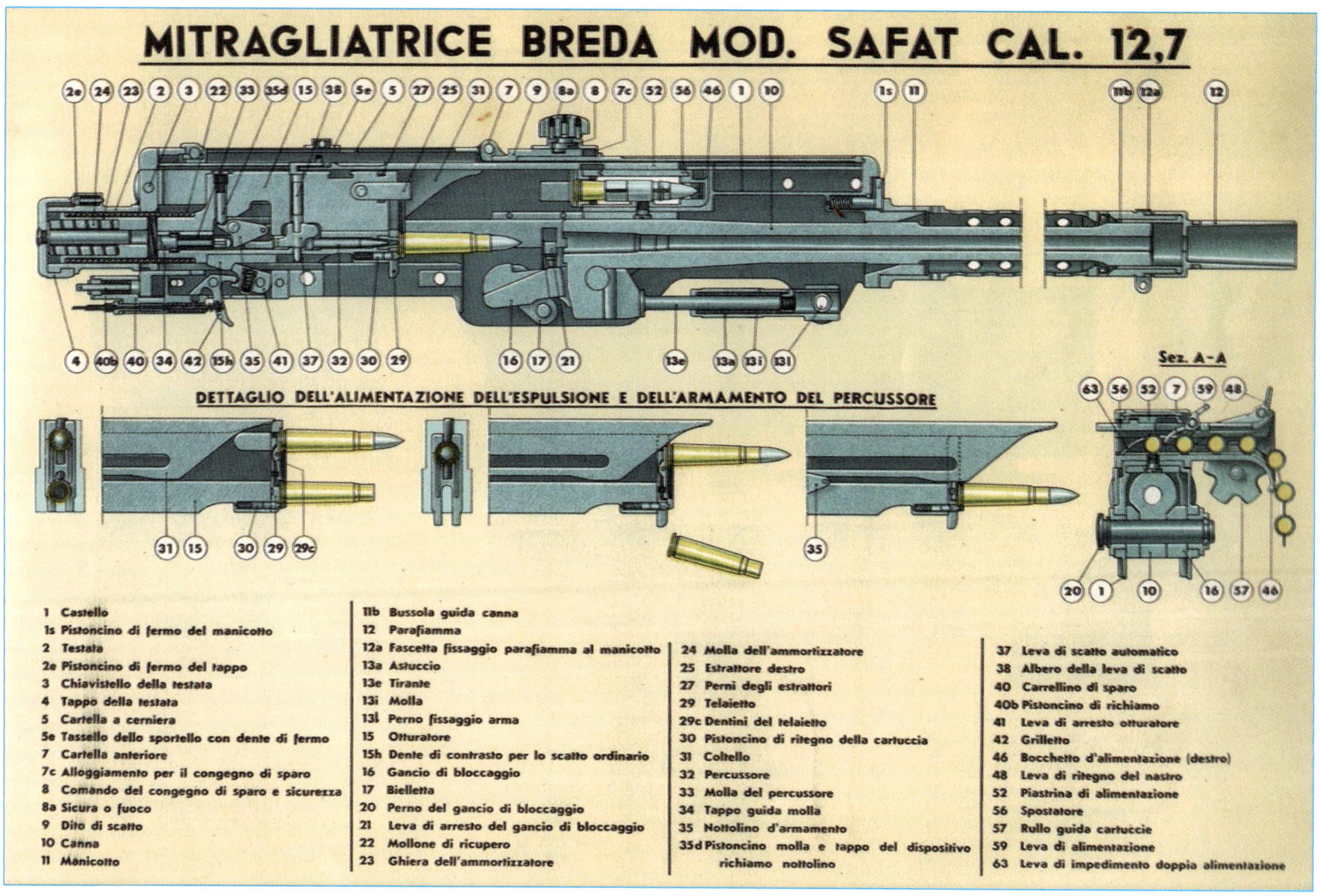

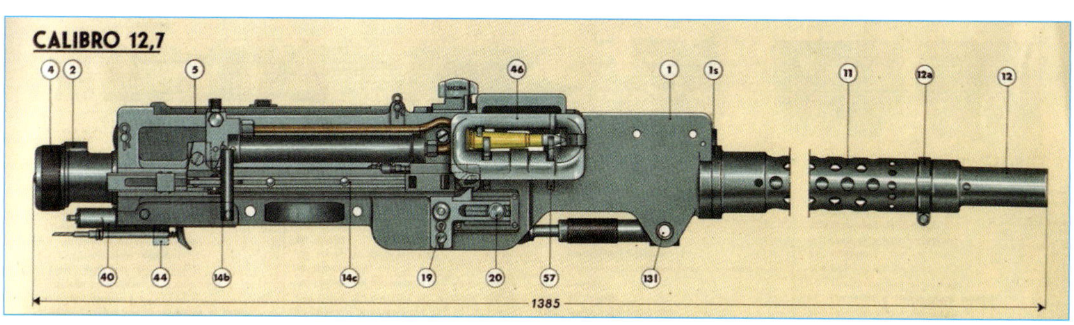

Breda-SAFAT 12.7 mm machine gun.

B.P.D. ammunition for the 12.7 mm machine gun. From left to right: standard, tracer, special.

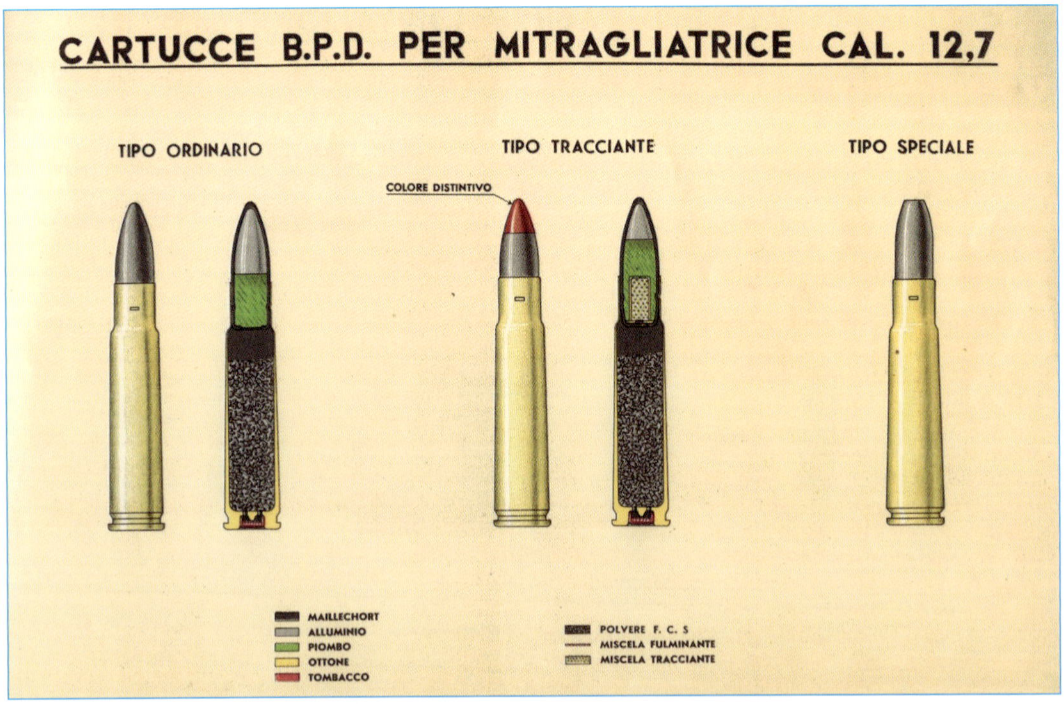

S.M.I. ammunition for the 12.7 mm machine gun. From left to right: standard, tracer, armour-piercing, special, special armour-piercing.

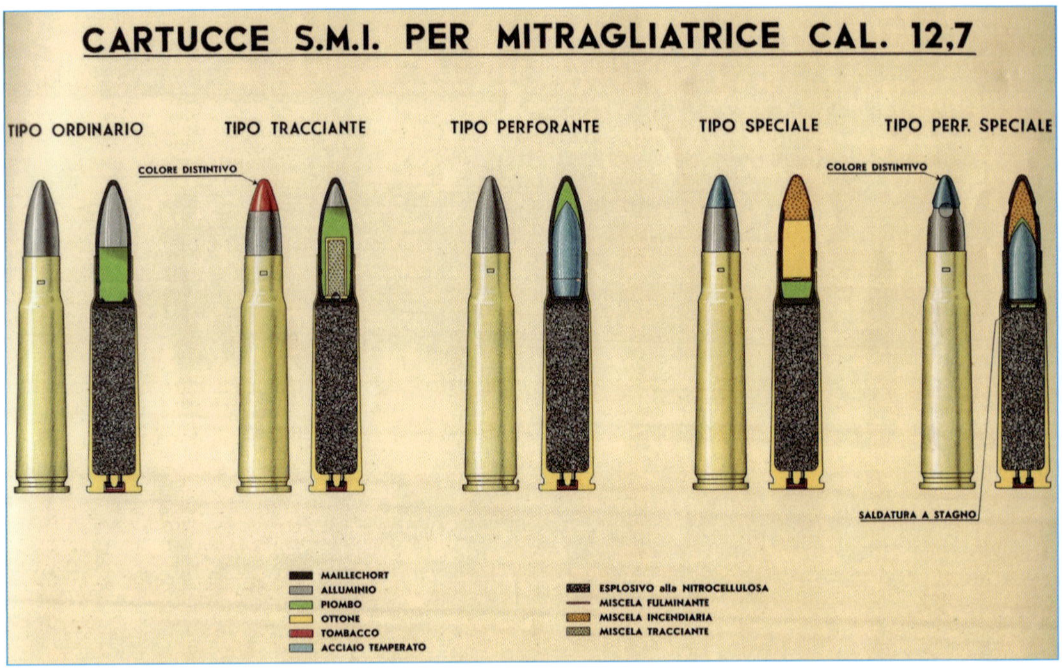

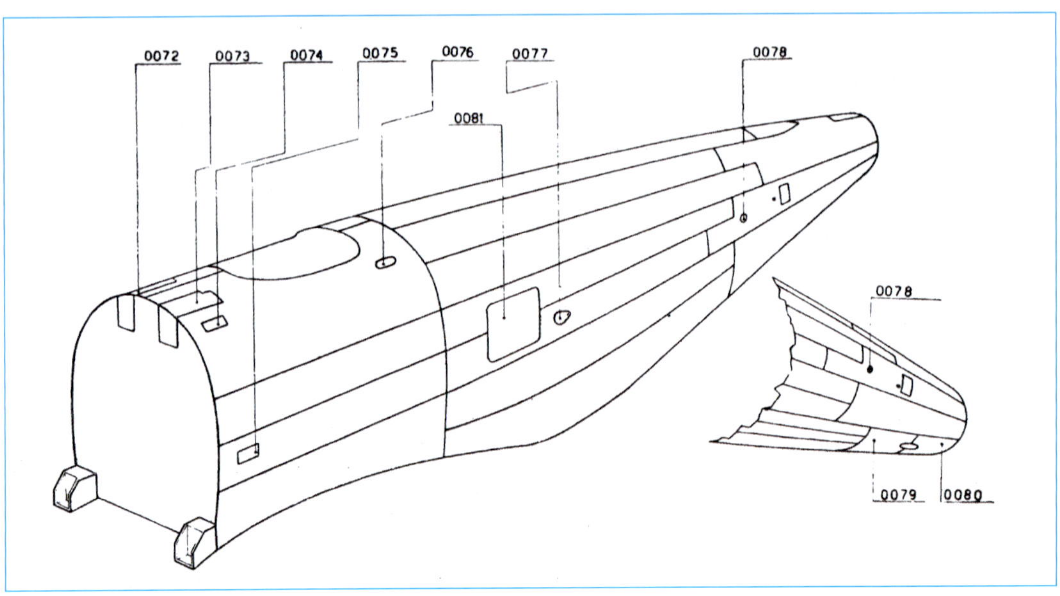

Fuselage construction.

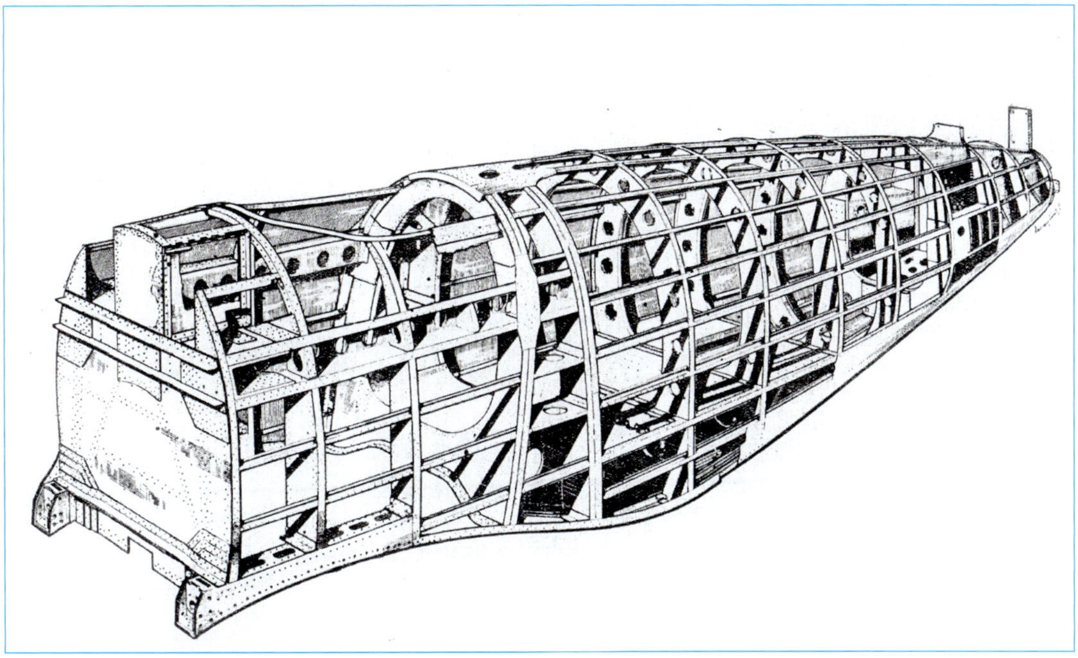

Fuselage structure.

Details of the rear part of the fuselage with a "hump" (anti-turnover) behind the pilot's cockpit. The profiling ensures better rear visibility.

Centre wing structure.

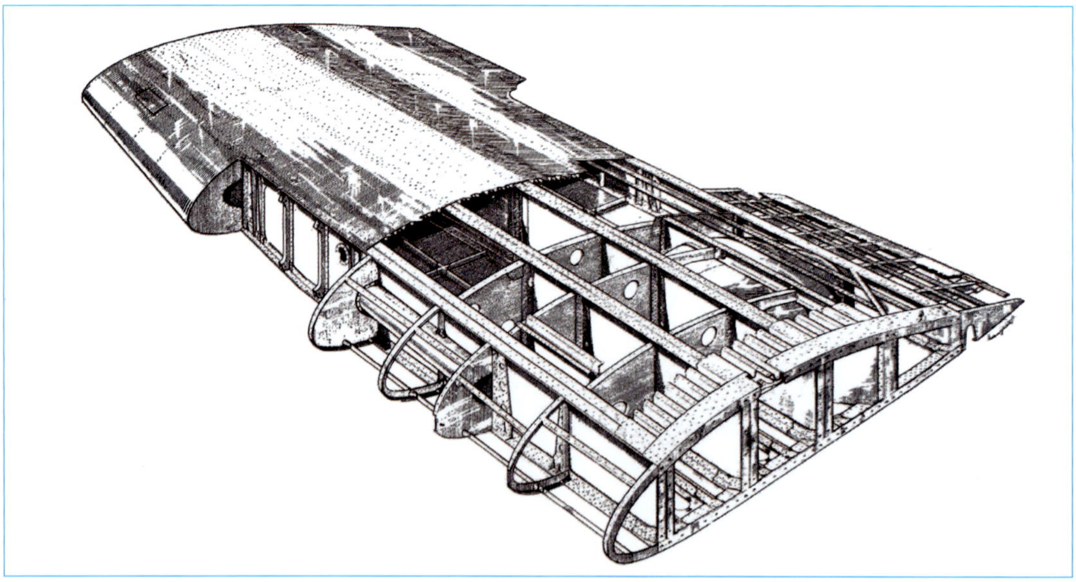

Lower fuel tank cover – internal side view.

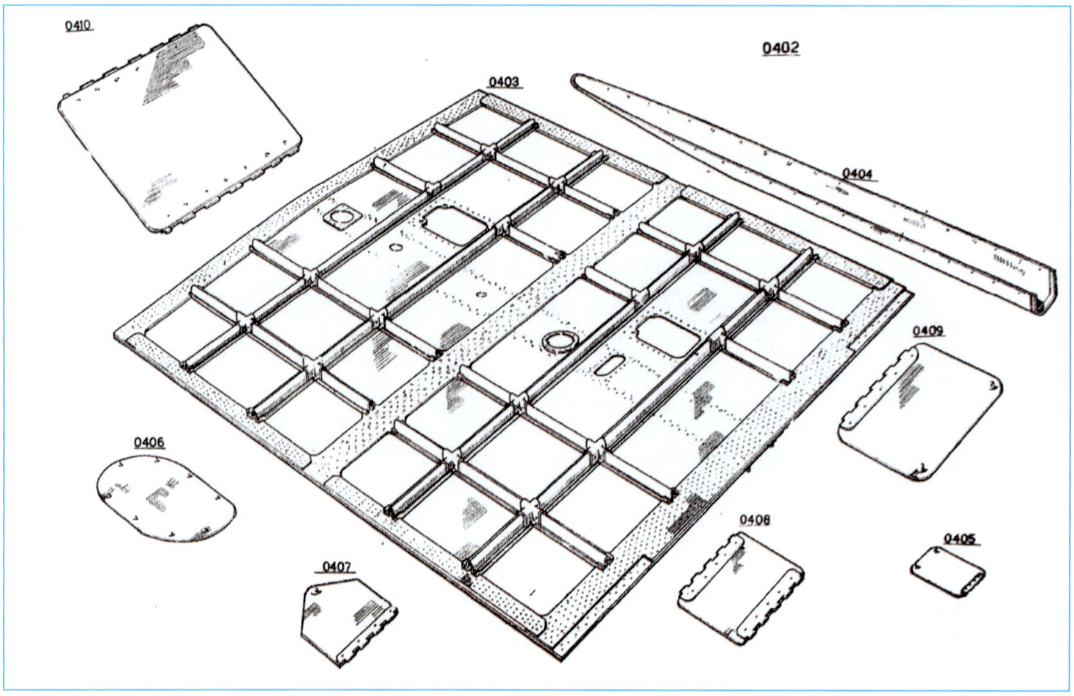

Structure of the right wing.

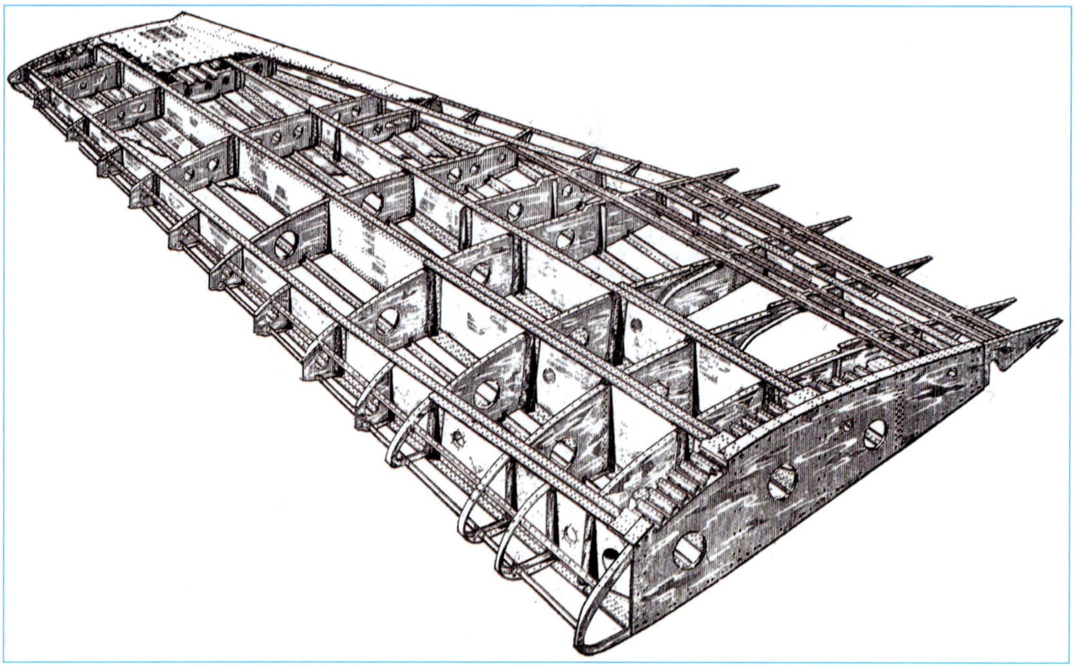

Left wing – view from below.

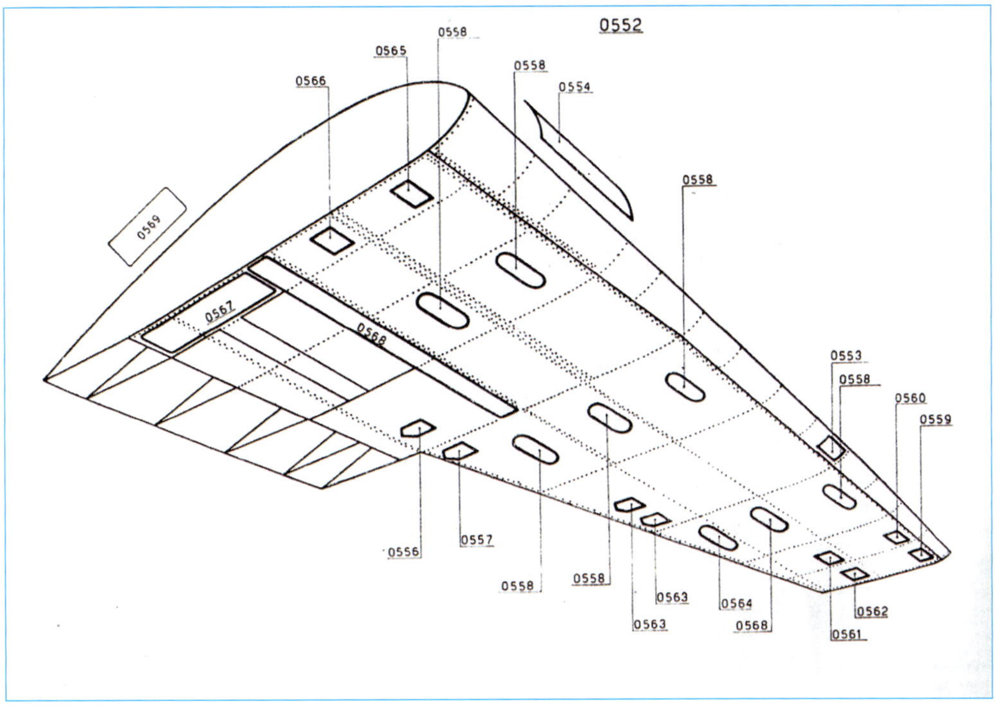

Diagram of the left wing.

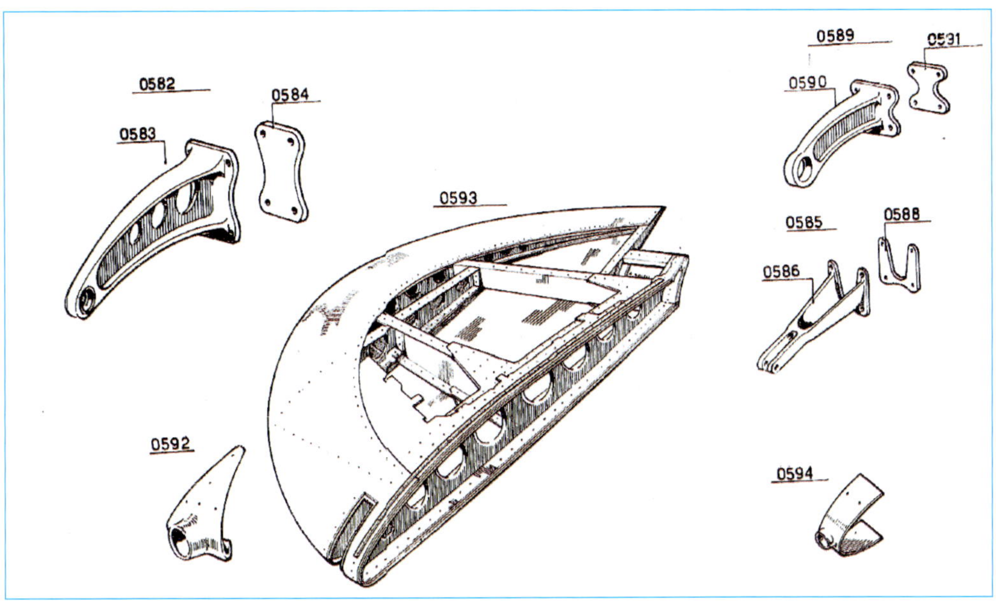

Tip of the right wing.

Ailerons.

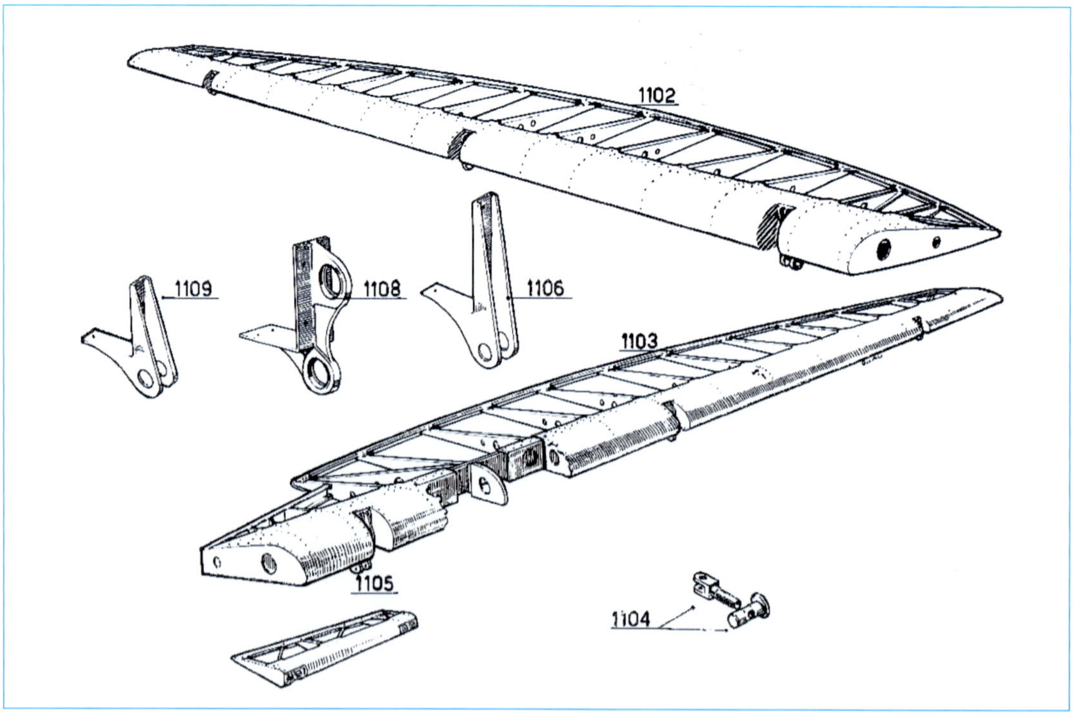

Flaps.

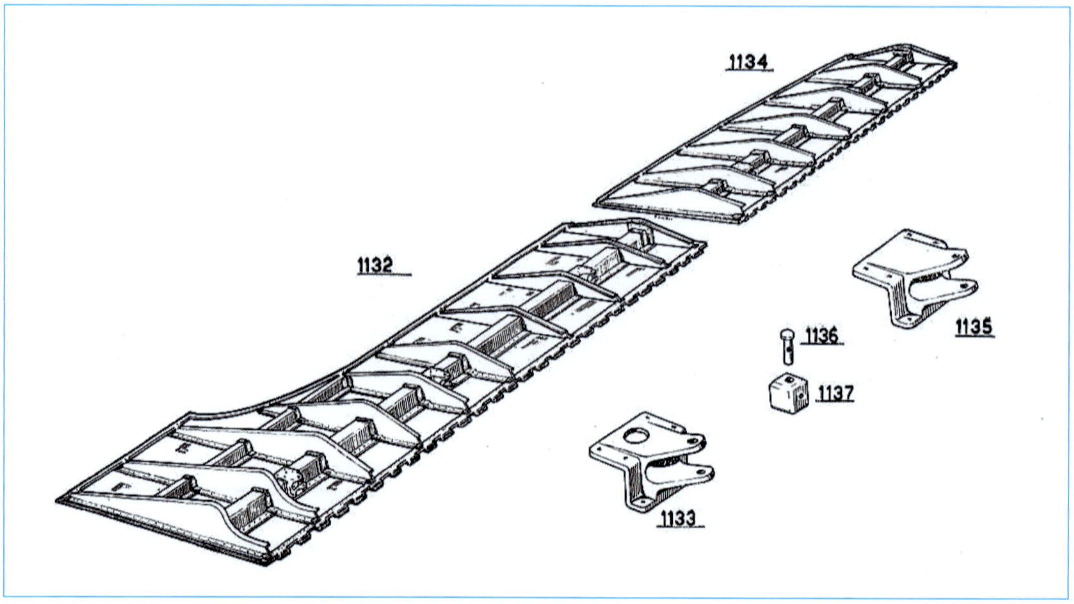

Flap deployment mechanism.

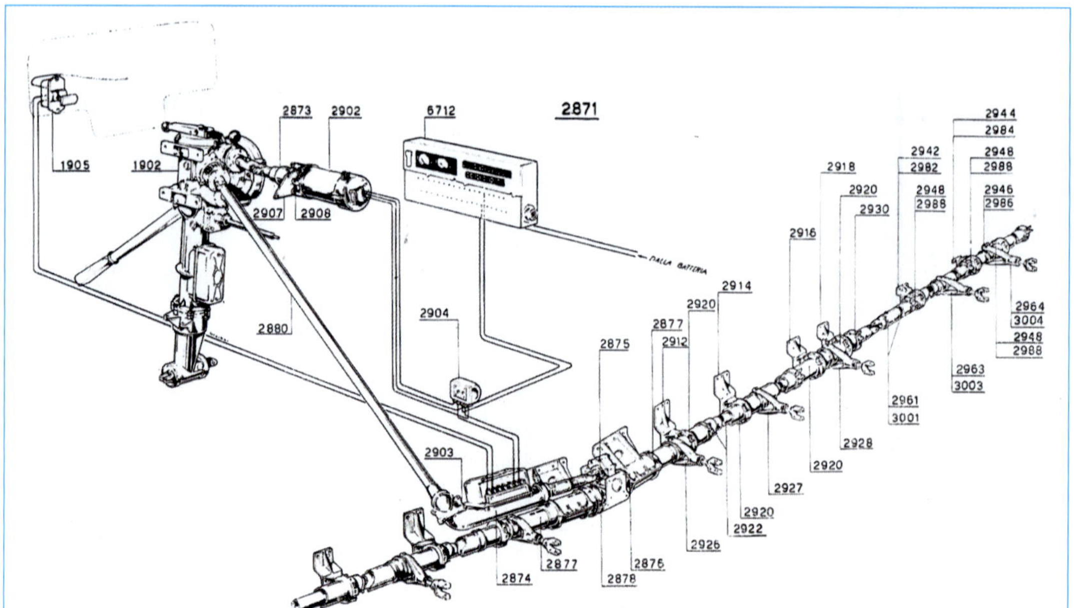

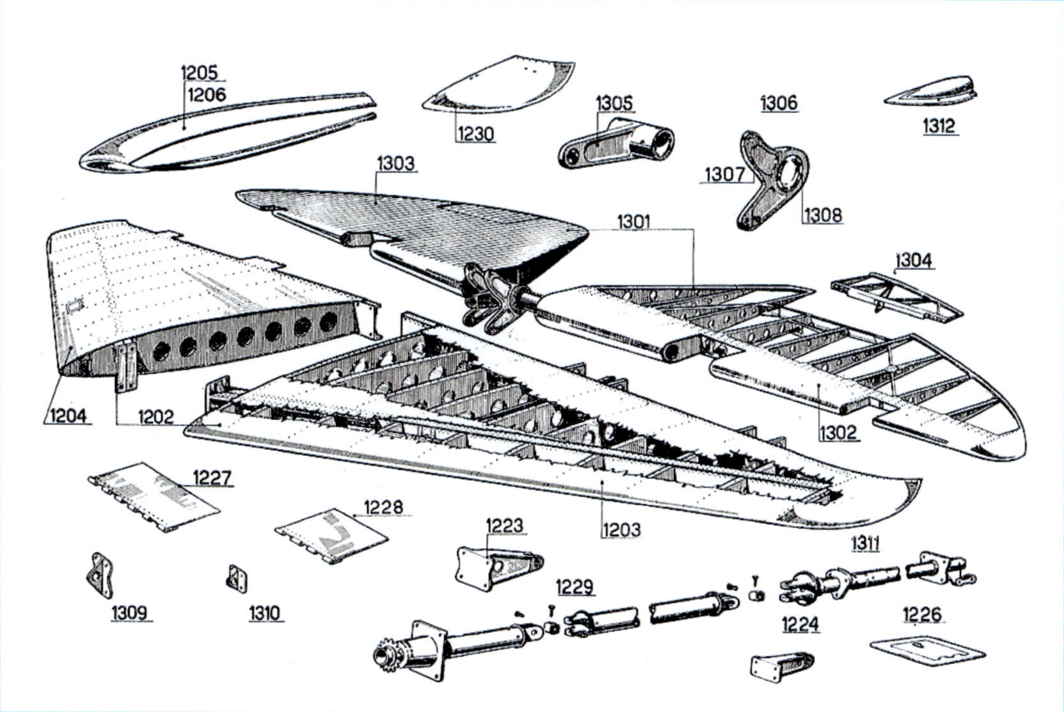

Components of the horizontal stabilizer.

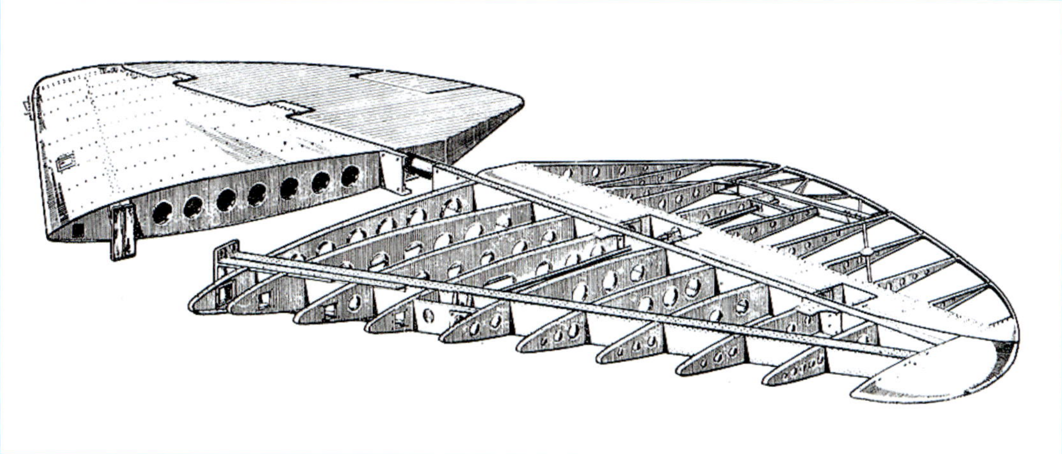

Horizontal stabilizer.

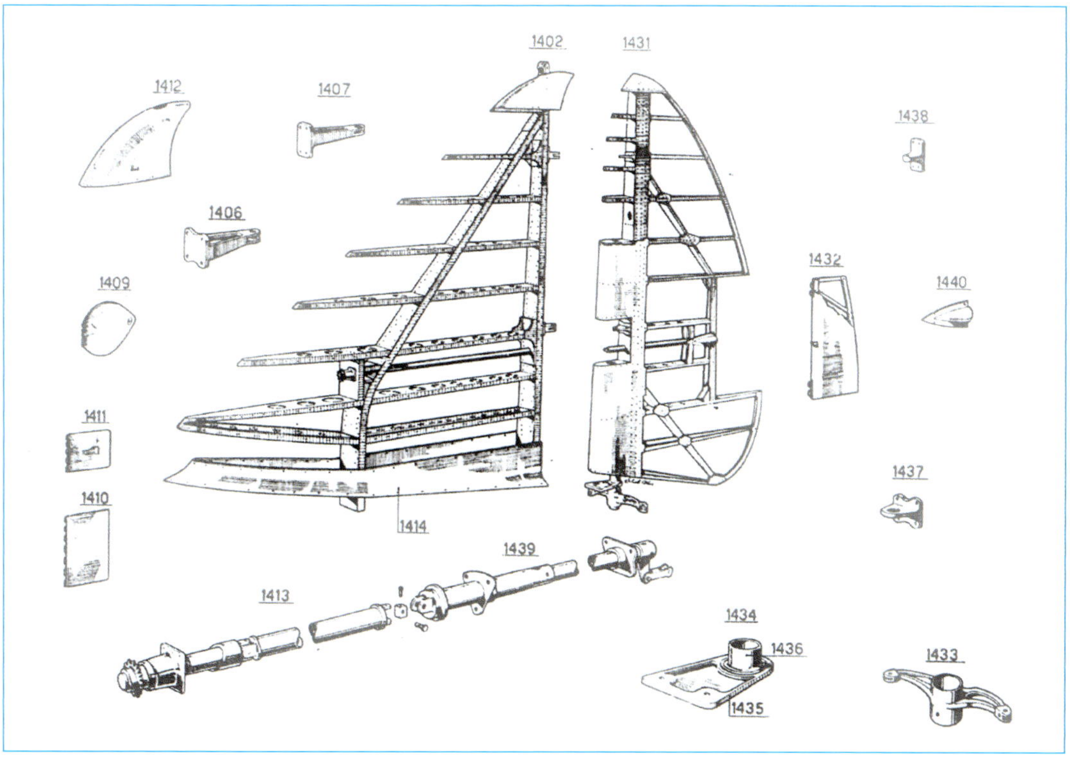

Components of the vertical stabilizer.

Components of the rear part of the fuselage.

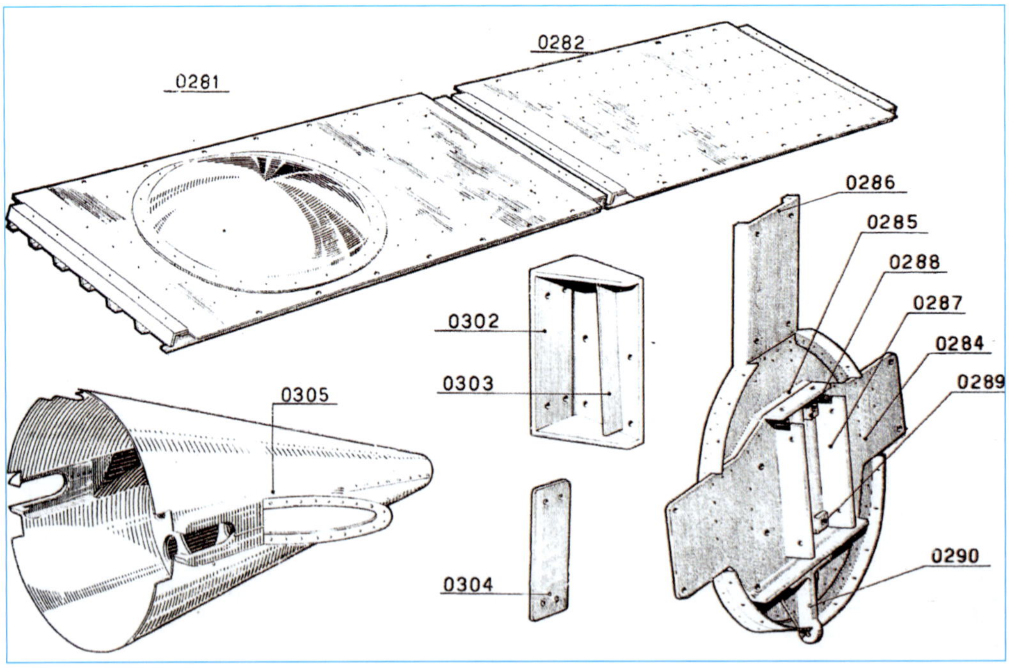

Fuel system diagram.

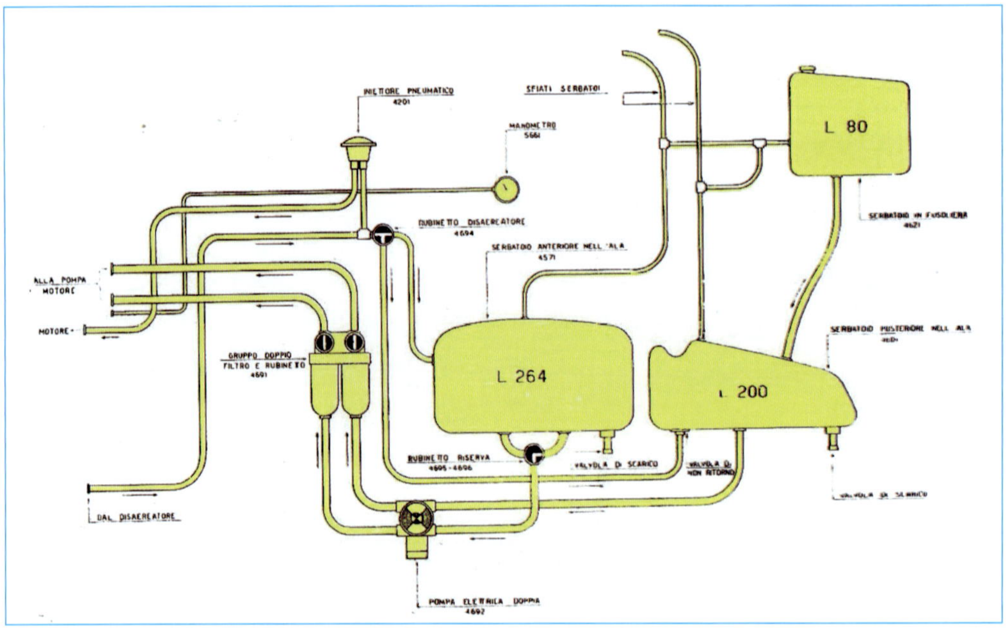

Fuel system components.

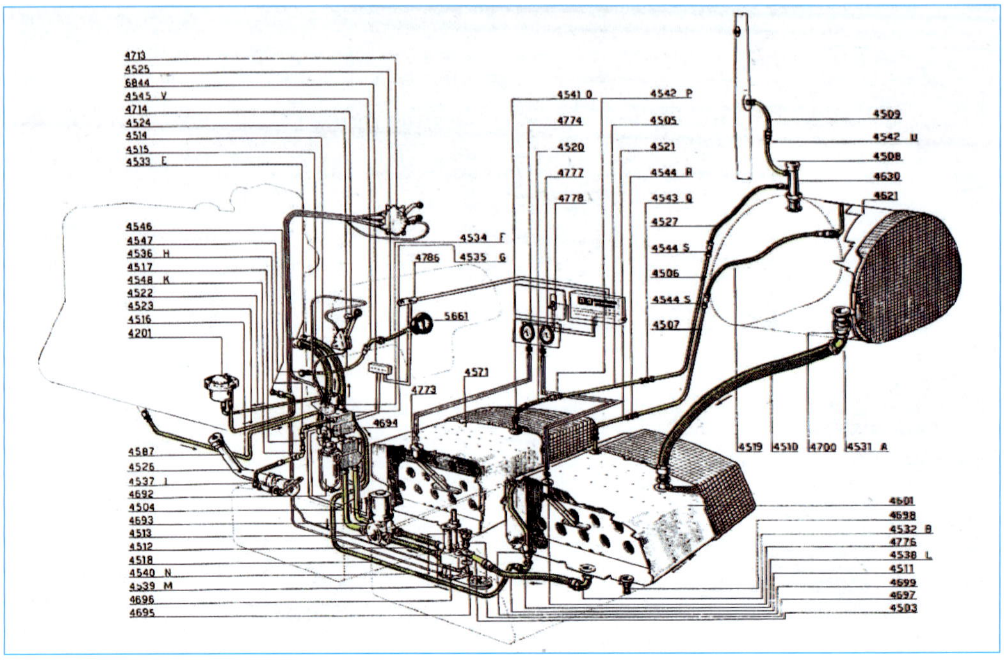

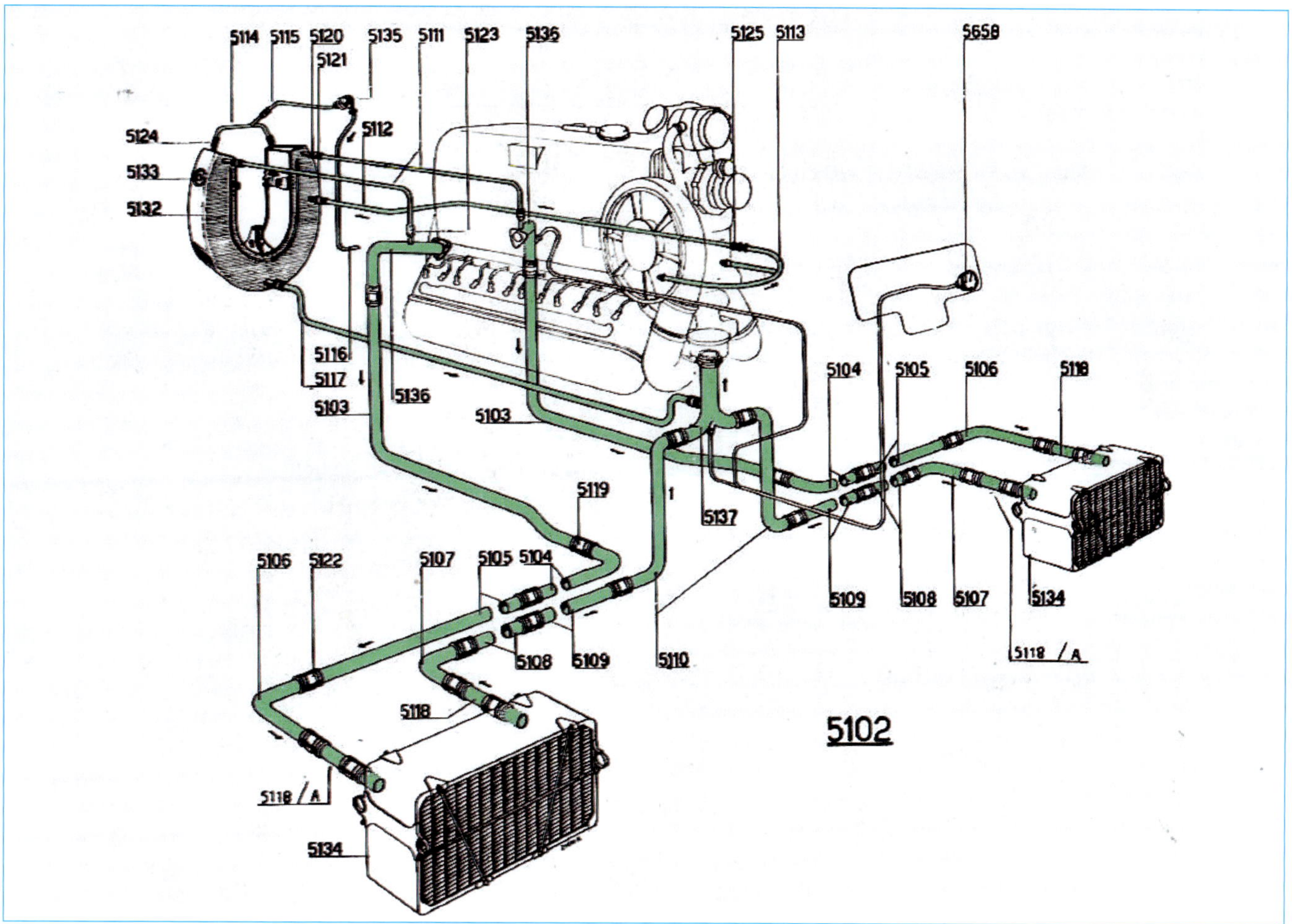

Engine cooling system diagram.
Components of the engine cooling system.

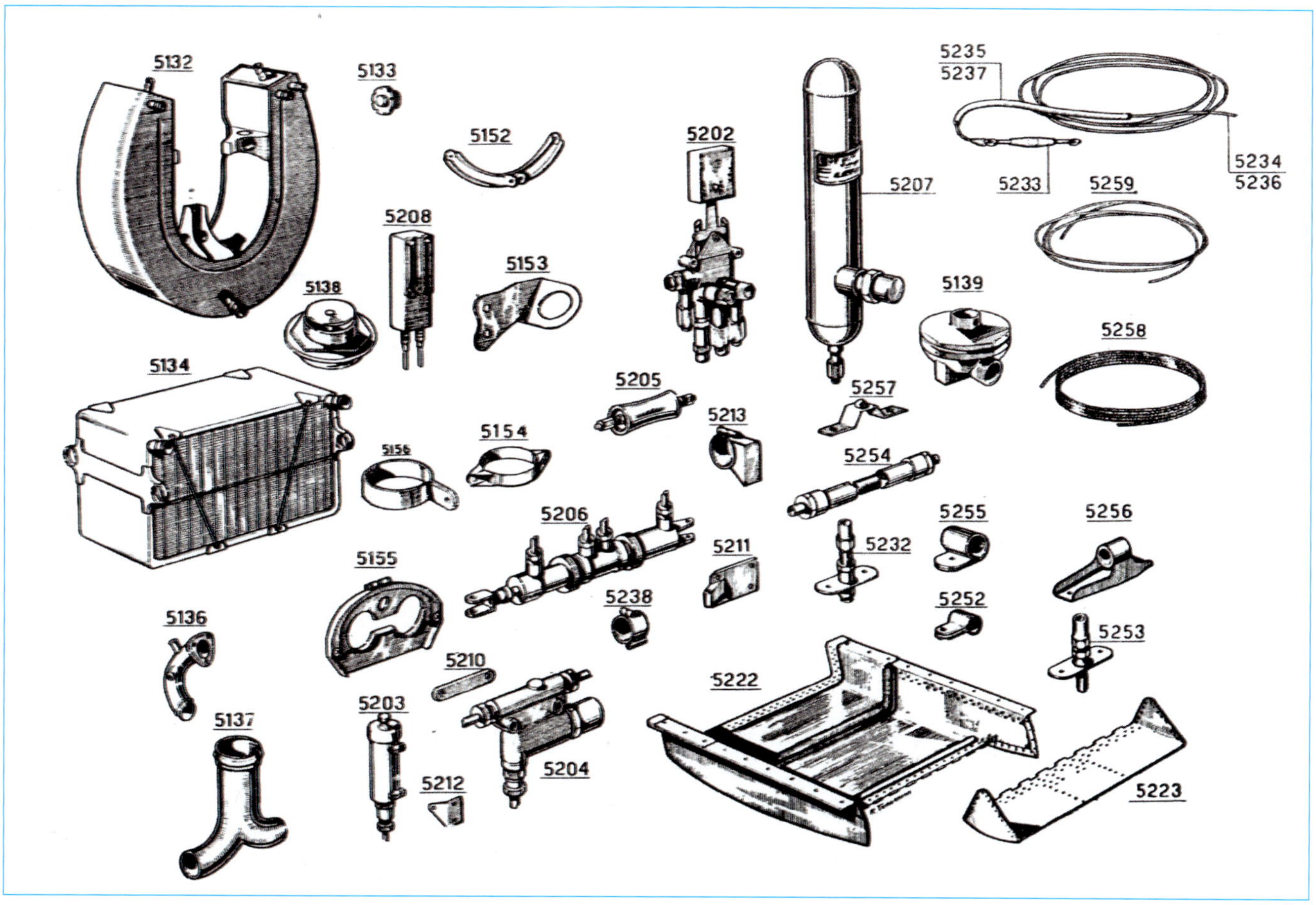

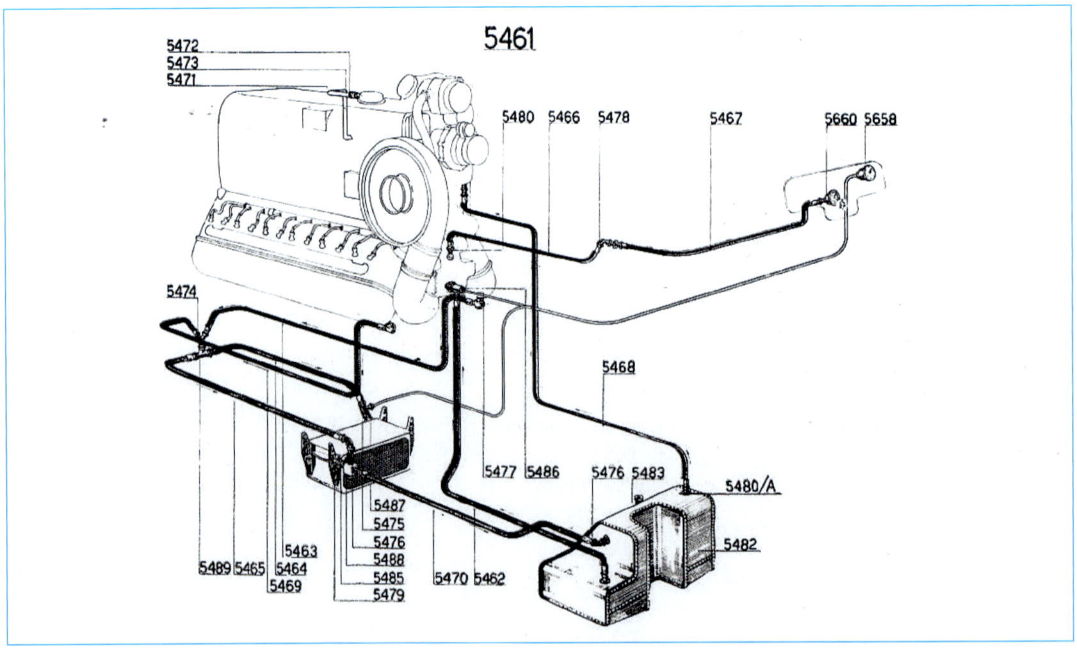

Oil system diagram.

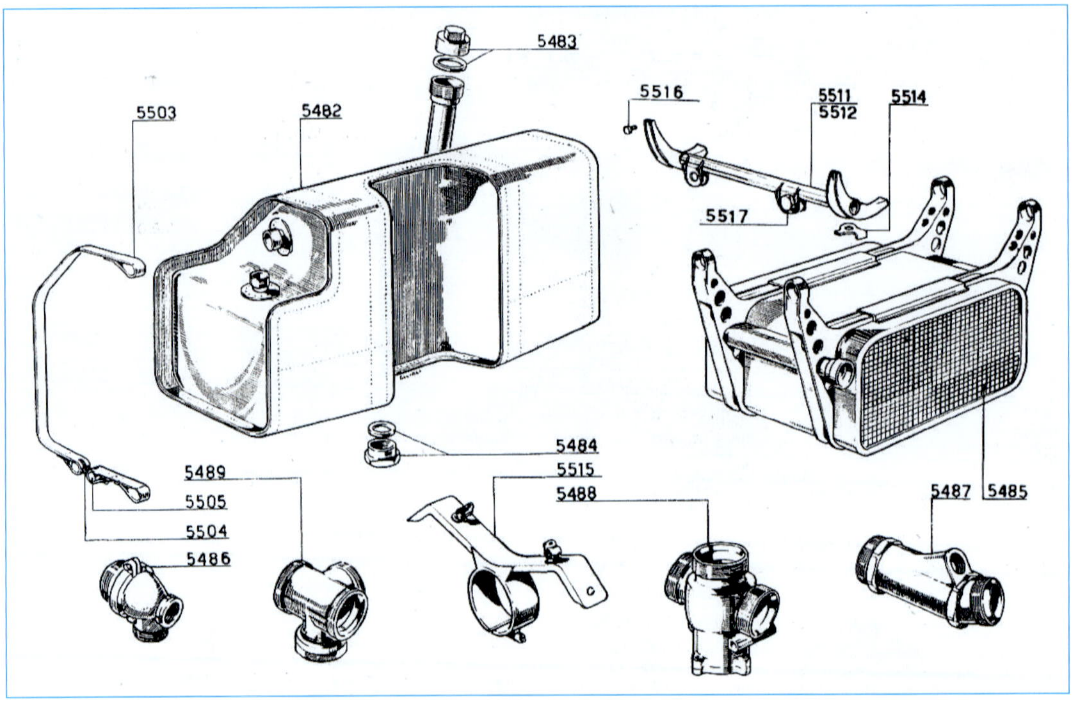

Components of the oil system.

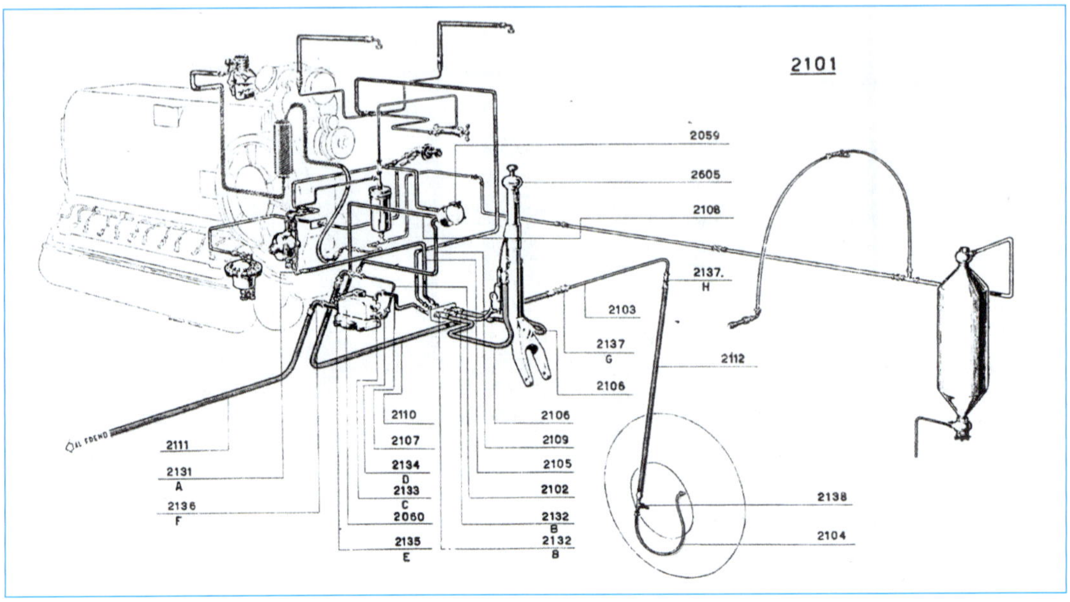

Pneumatic system diagram.

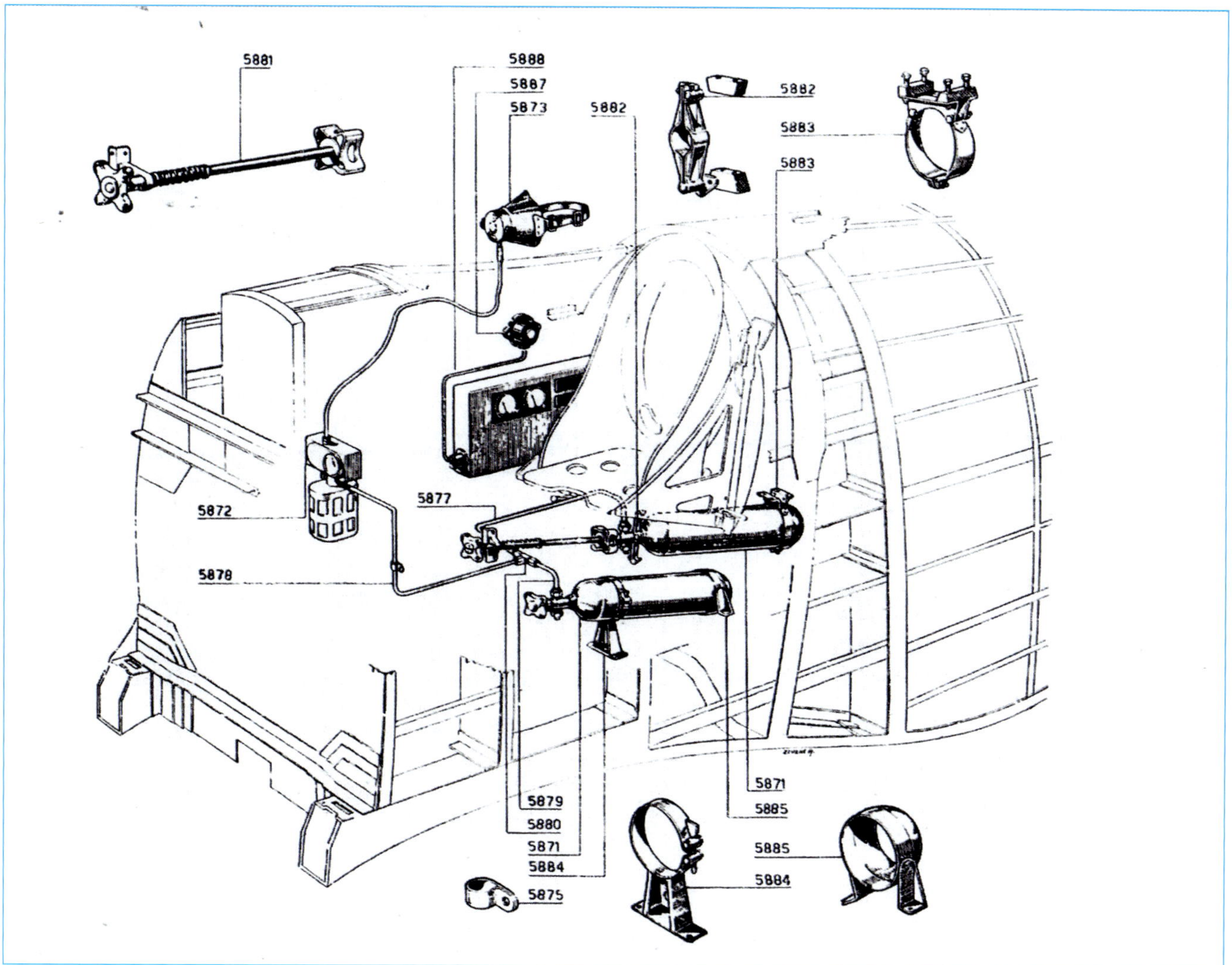

Oxygen system diagram.

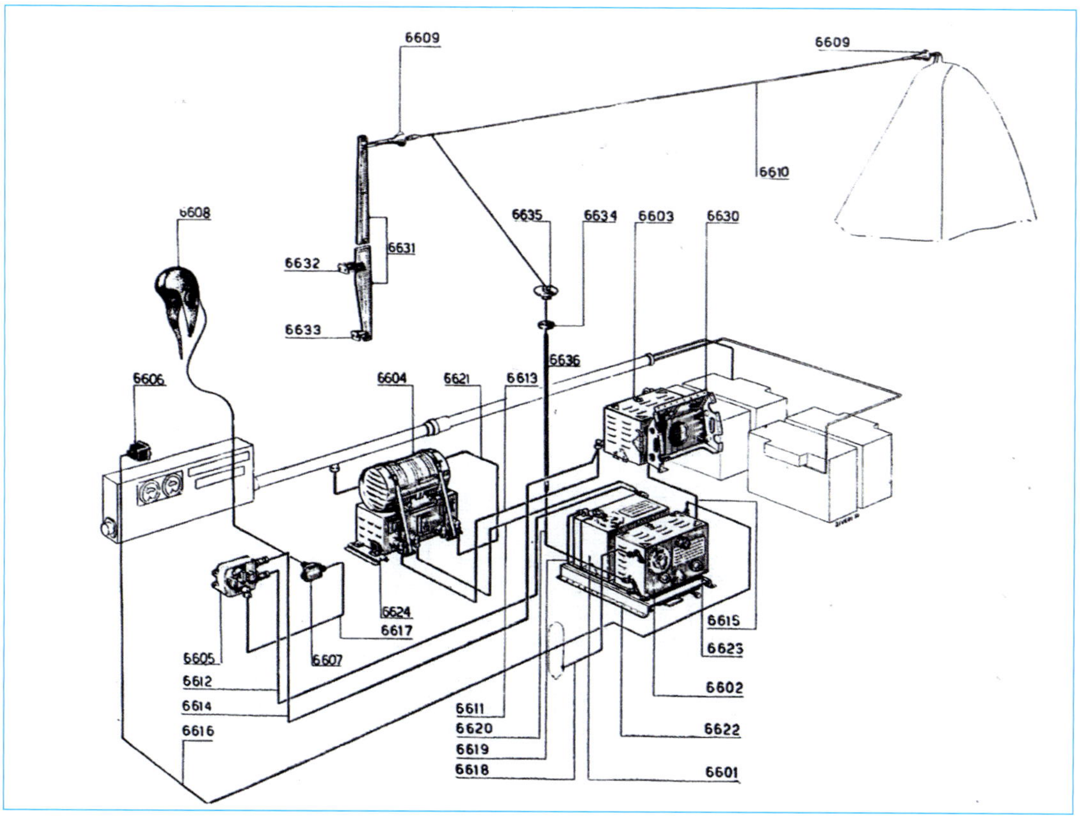

Radio installation with Allocchio Bacchini B.30 radio.

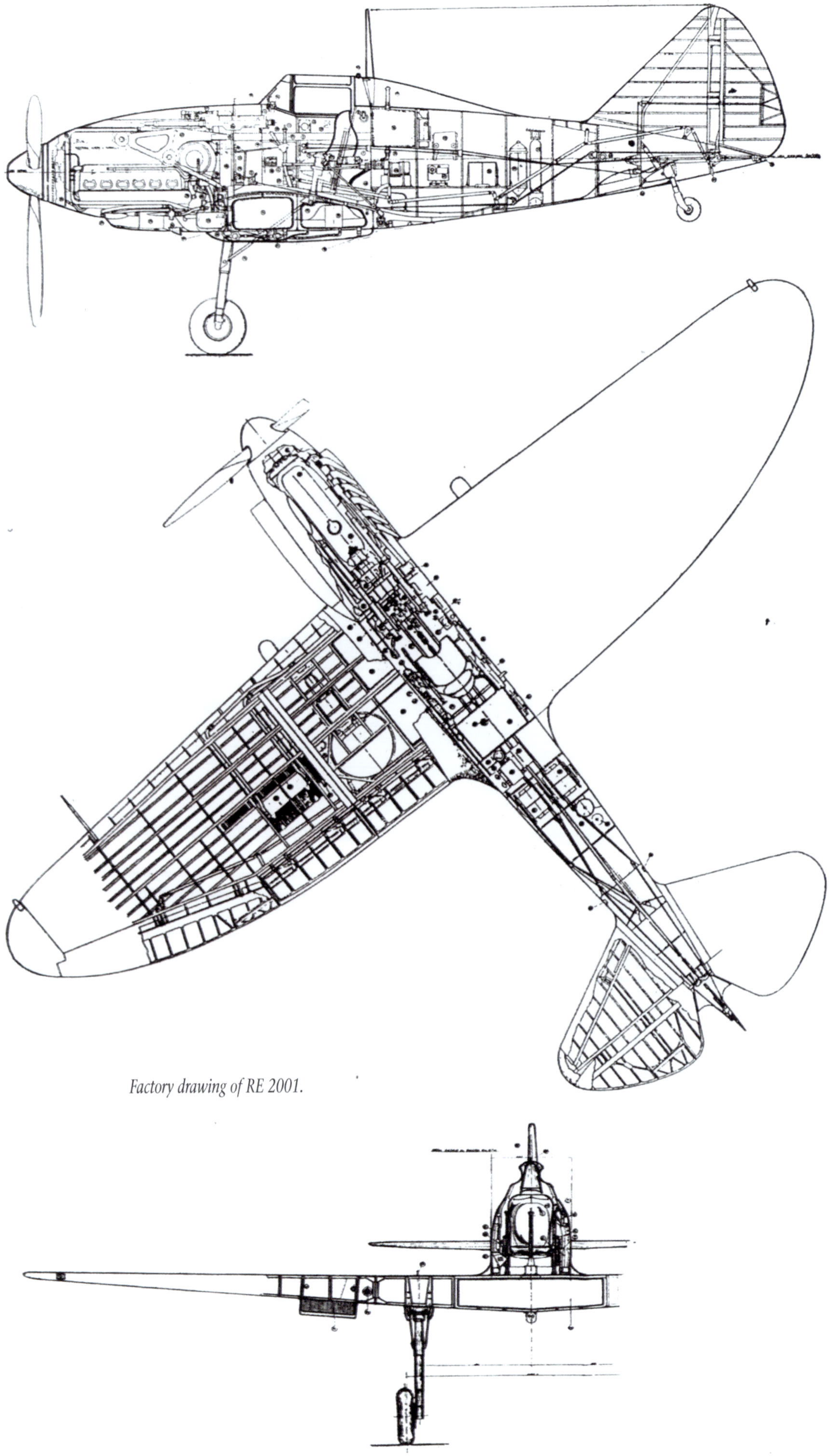

Factory drawing of RE 2001.

Reggiane RE 2001 1st prototype M.M.409.
1/48 scale.

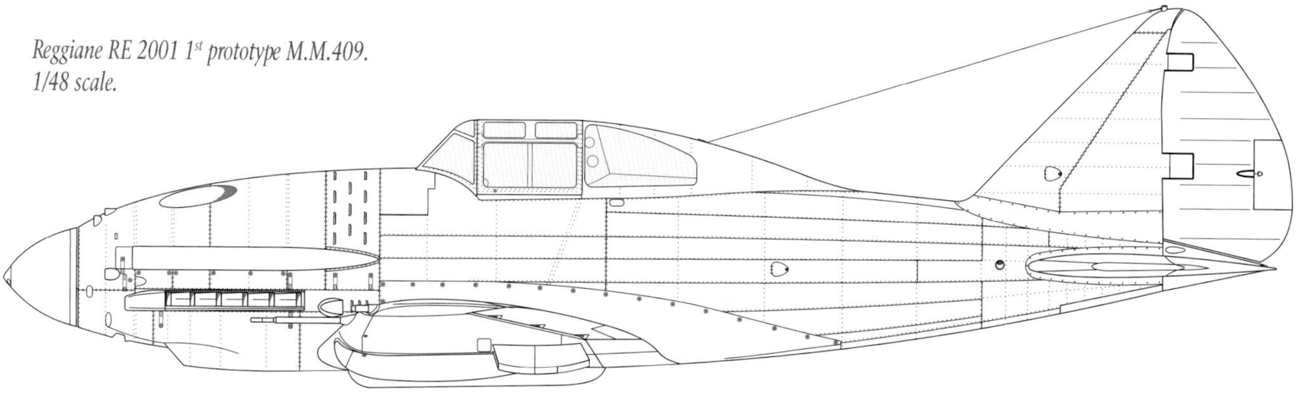

Reggiane RE 2001 2nd prototype M.M.408.
1/48 scale.

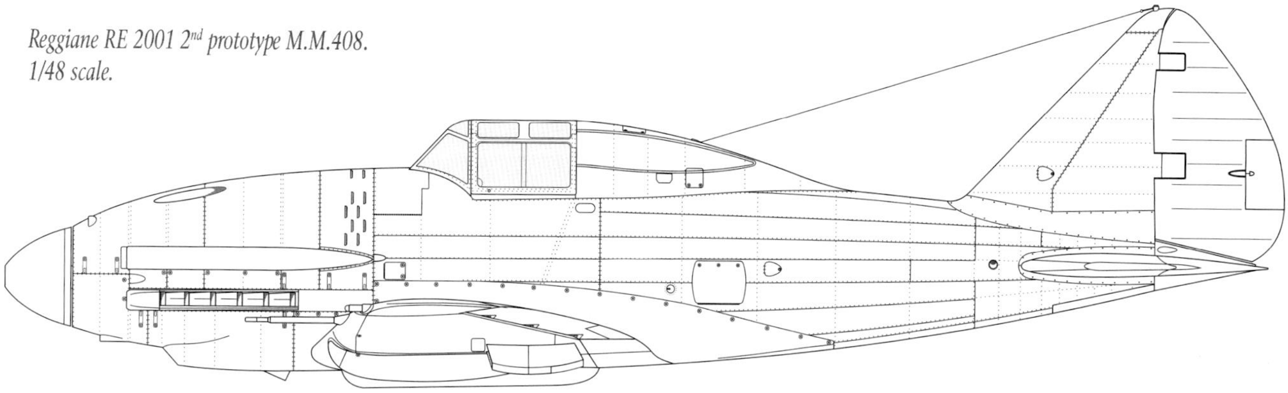

Reggiane RE 2001 Delta.
1/48 scale.

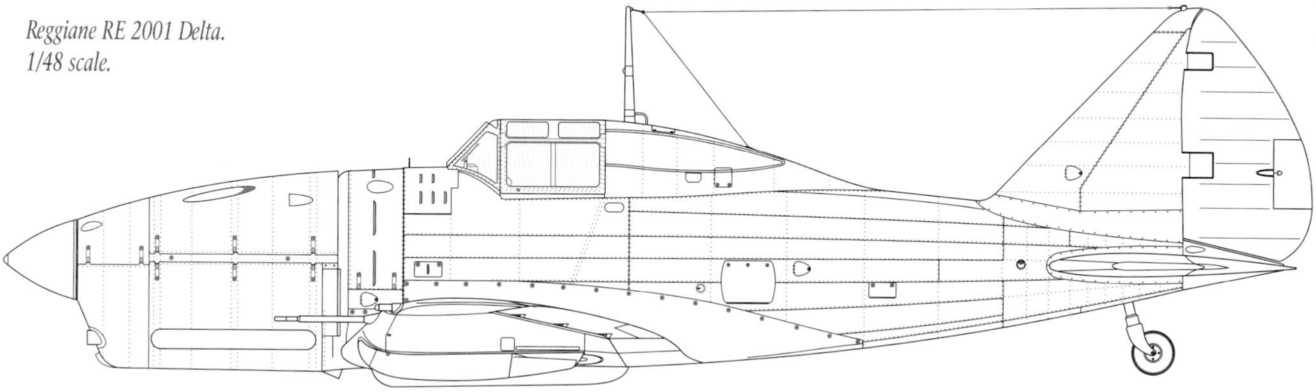

Reggiane RE 2001CN.
1/48 scale.

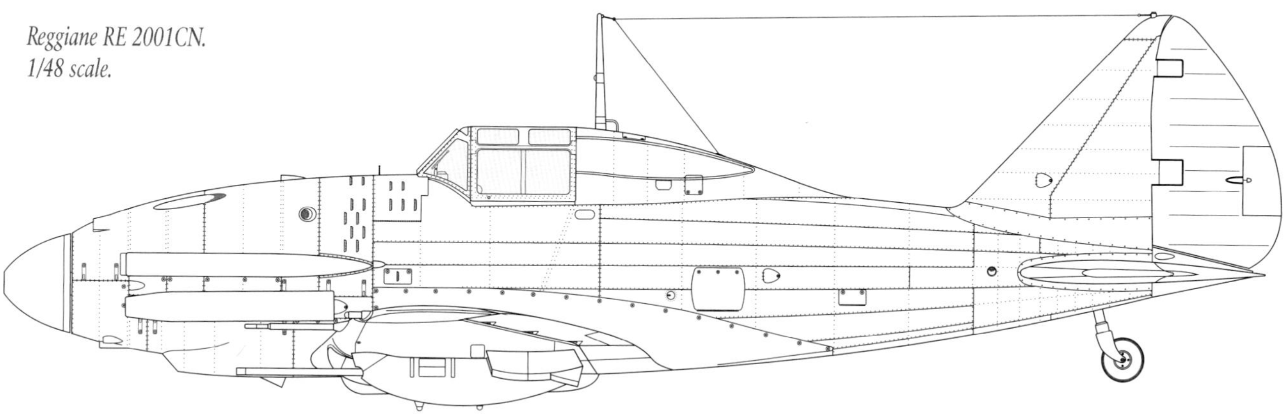

Reggiane RE 2001 photo version (fotografico).
1/48 scale.

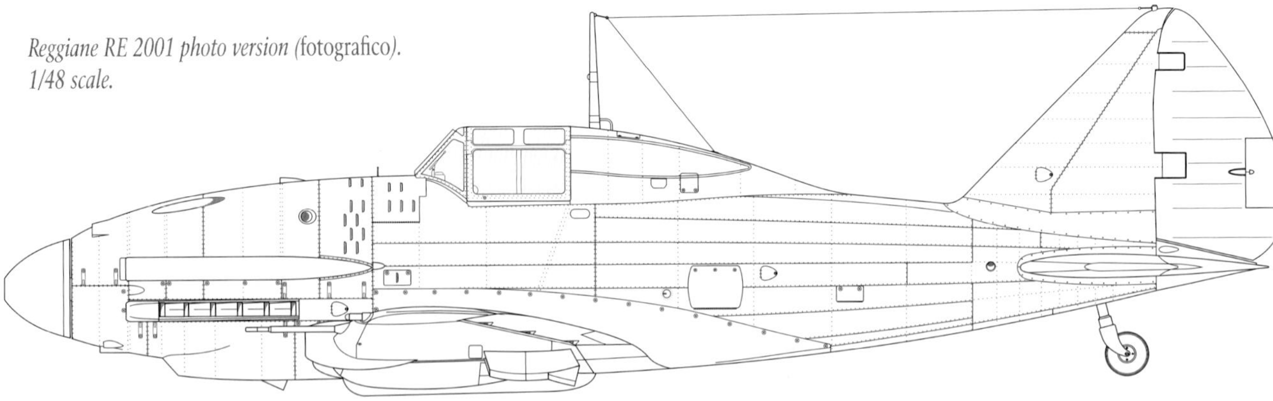

Reggiane RE 2001 OR.
1/48 scale.

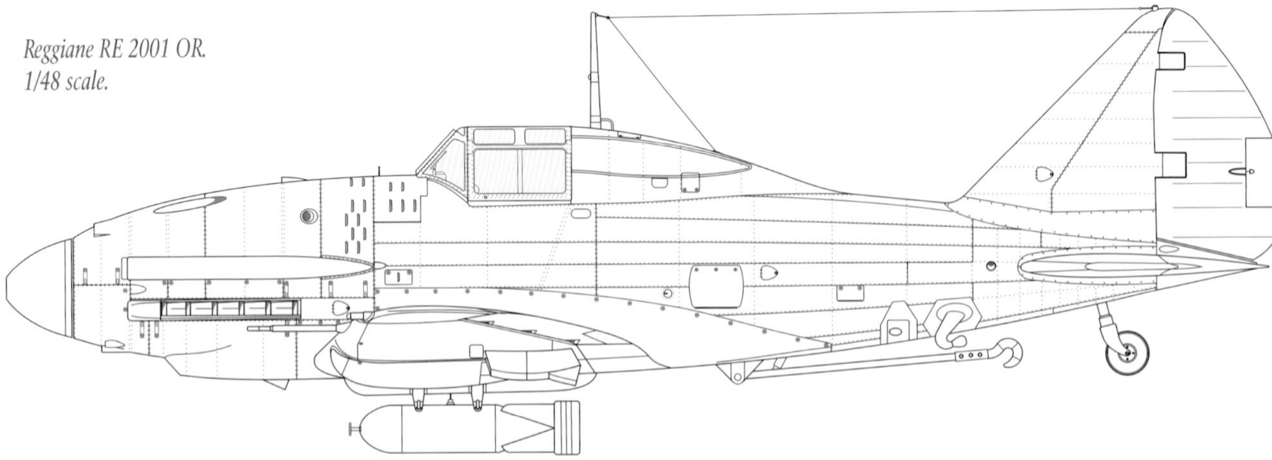

Reggiane RE 2001 OR.
1/48 scale.

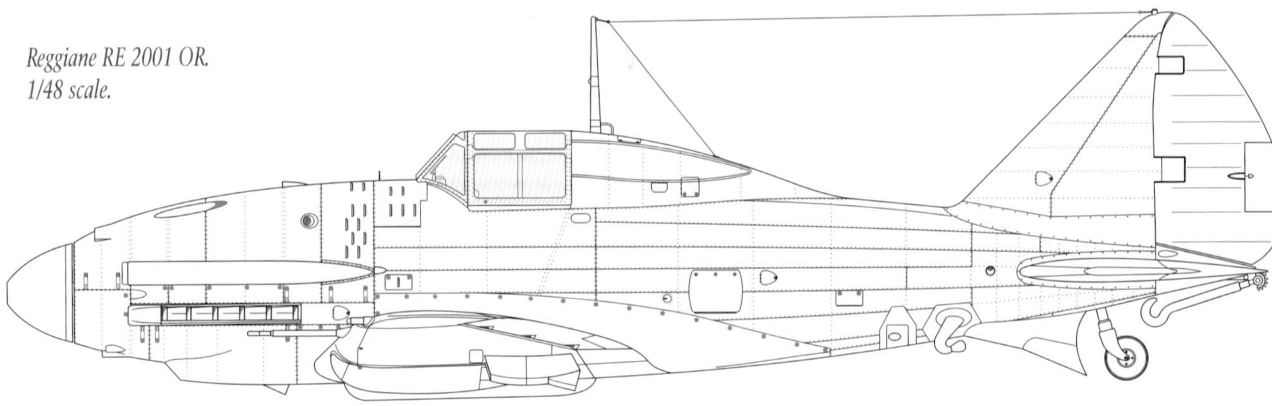

Reggiane RE 2001 GV.
1/48 scale.

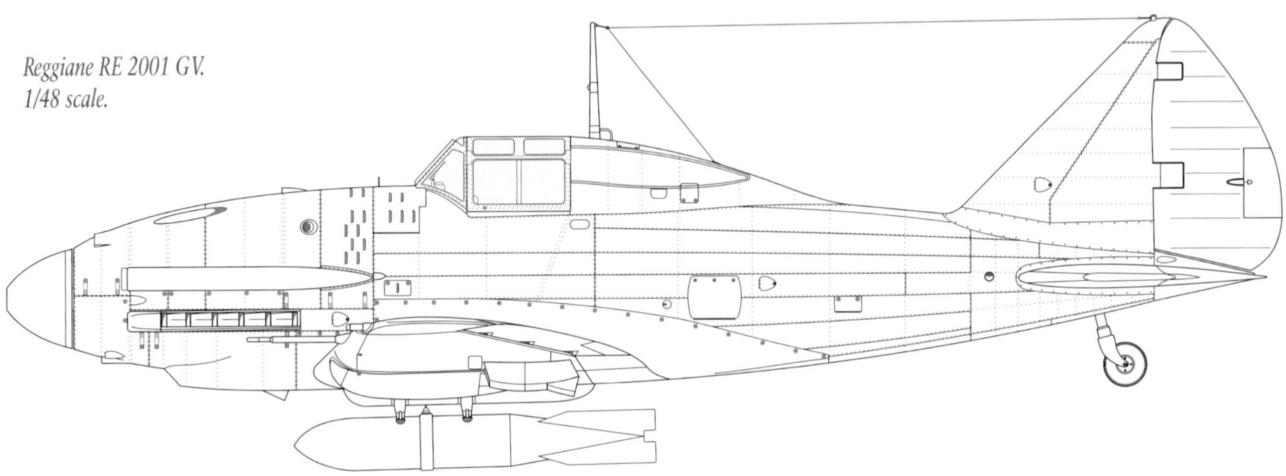

Reggiane RE 2001 CB.
1/48 scale.

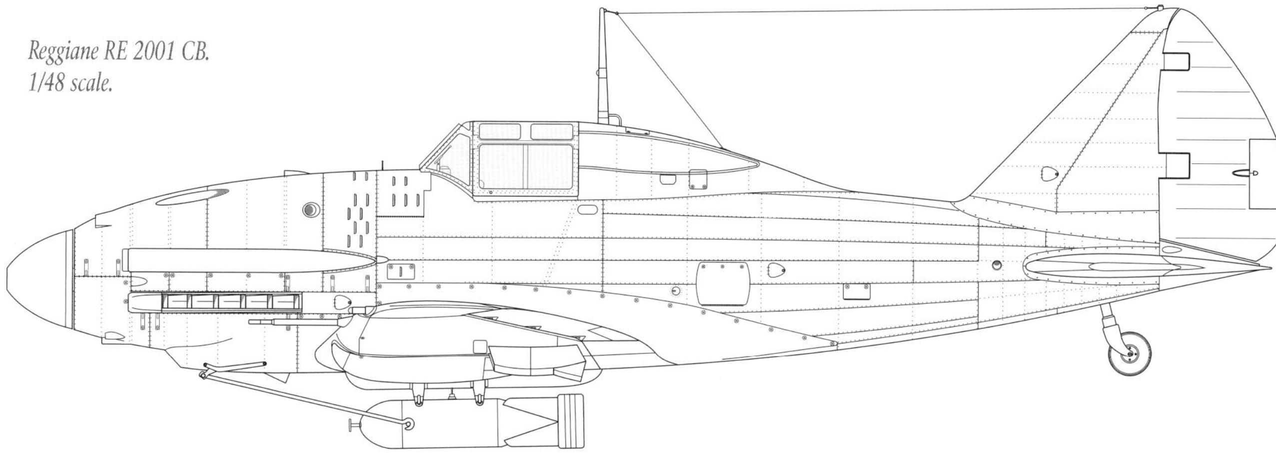

Reggiane RE 2001 MM 90754 with the liquid oxygen bomb.
1/48 scale.

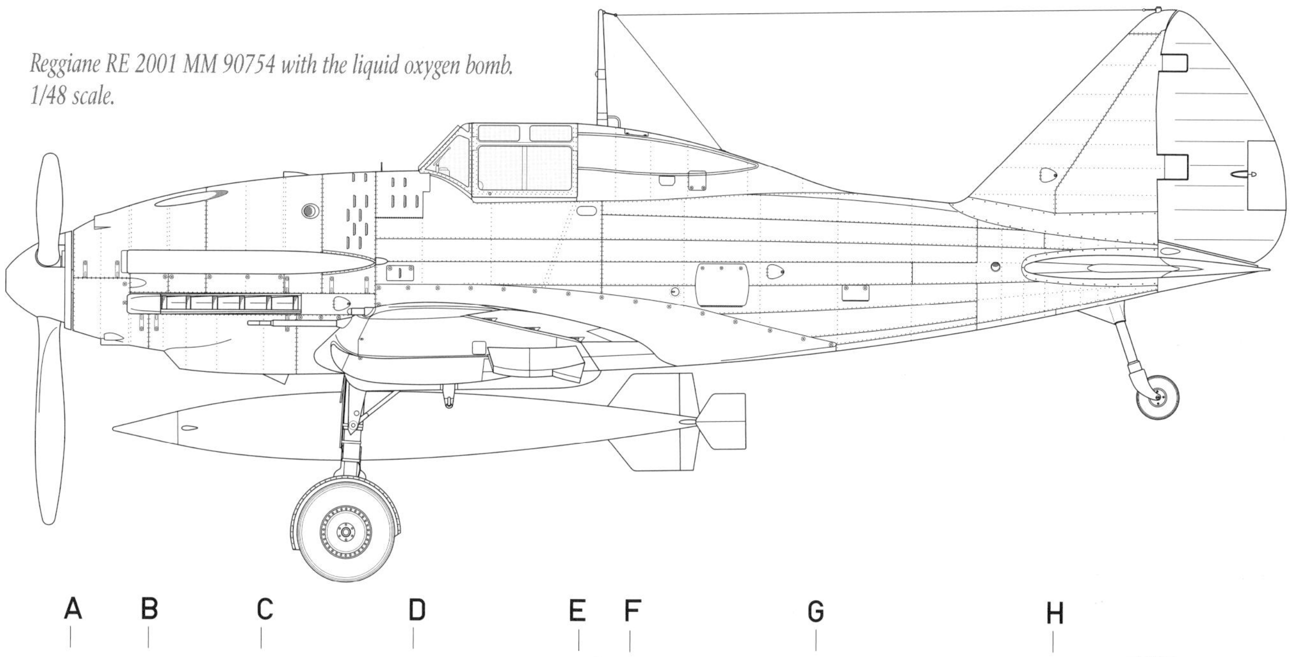

Reggiane RE 2001.
1/48 scale.

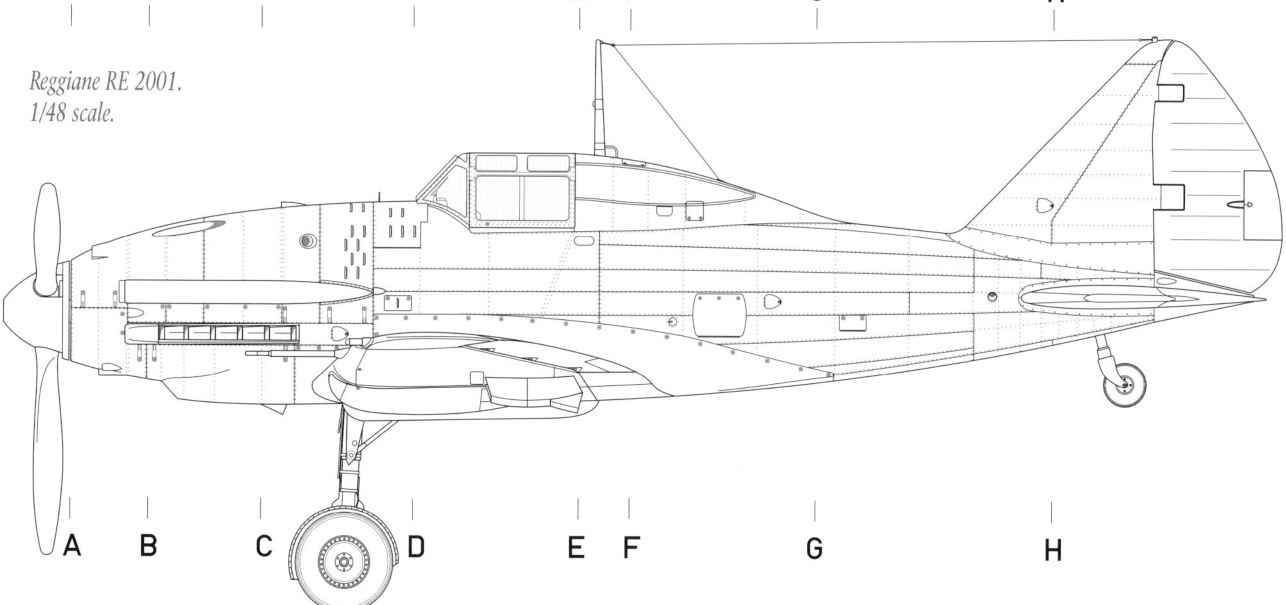

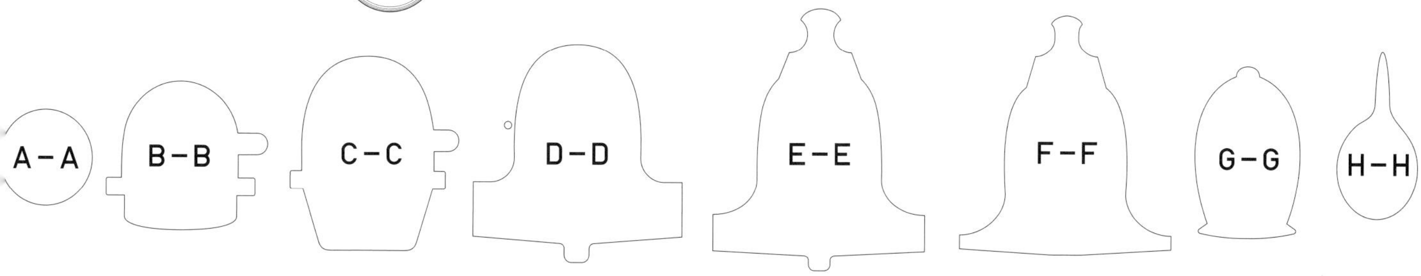

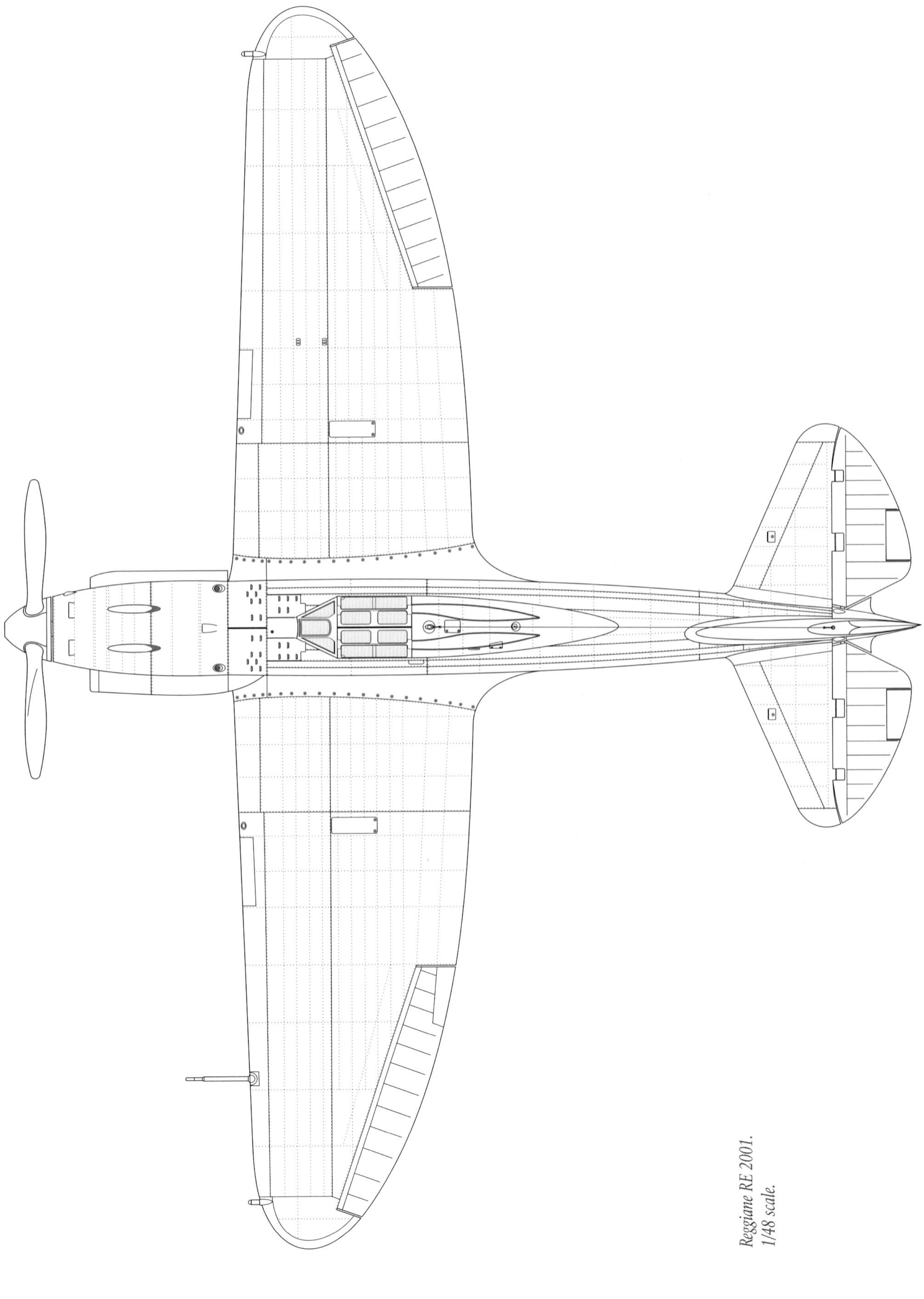

Reggiane RE 2001.
1/48 scale.

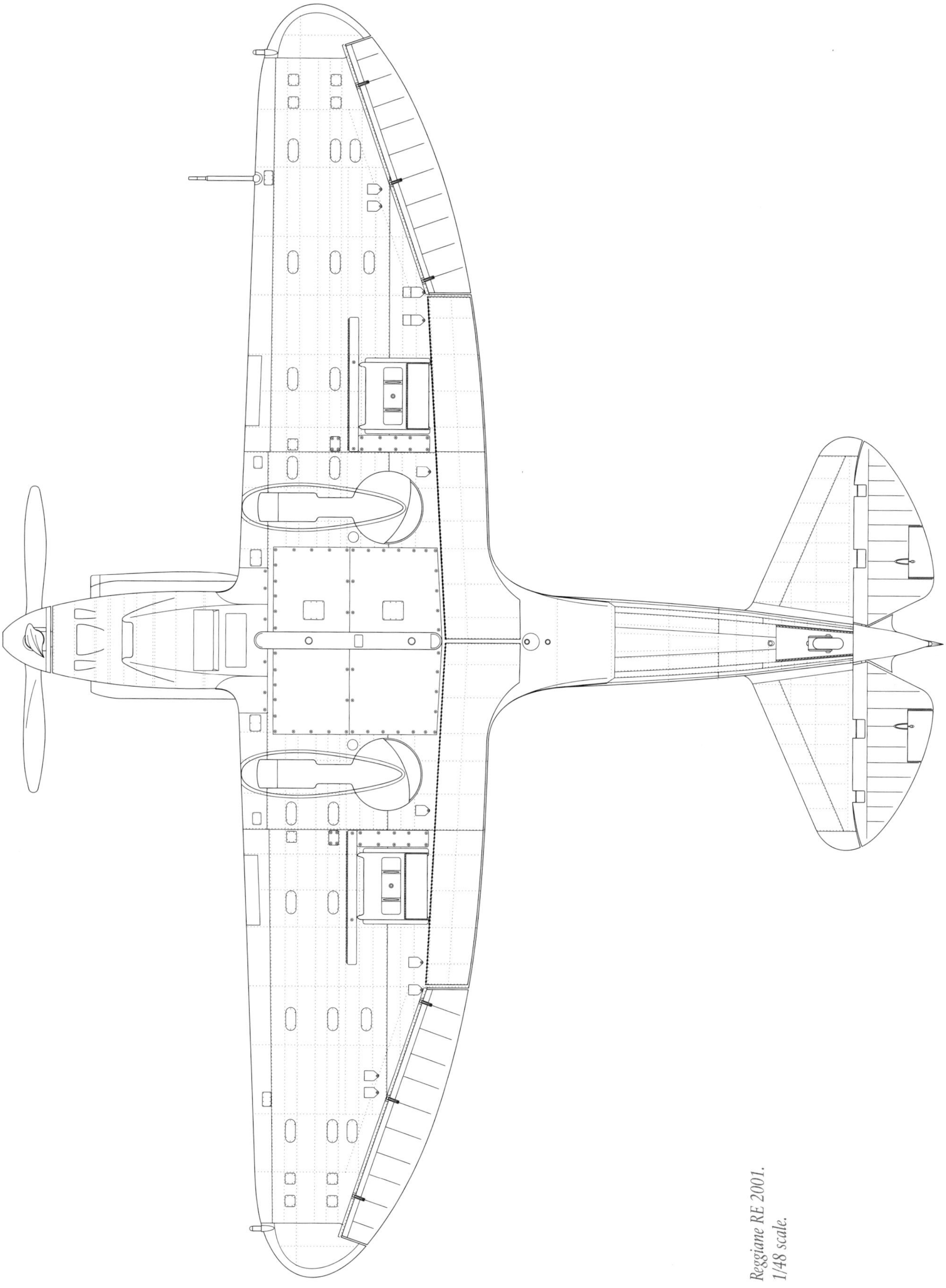

Reggiane RE 2001.
1/48 scale.

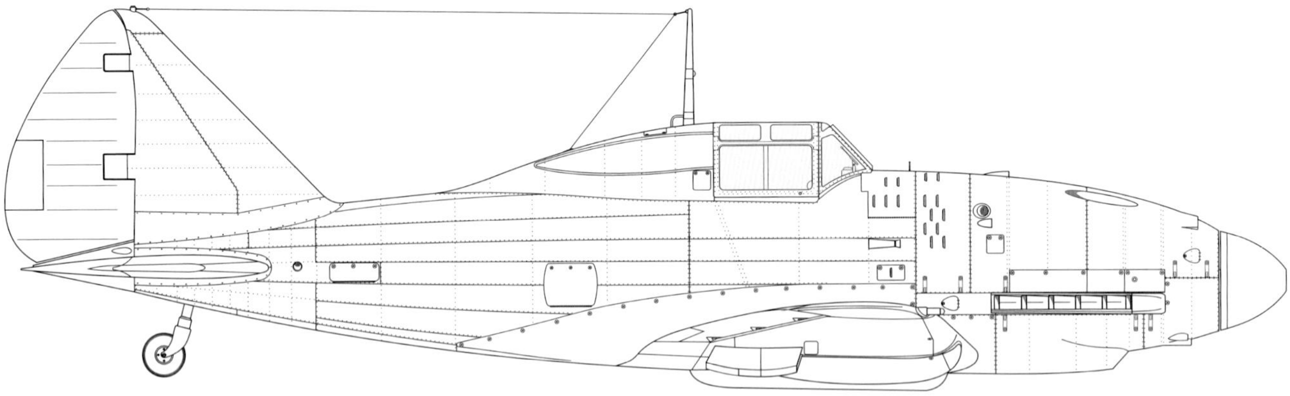

Reggiane RE 2001.
1/48 scale.

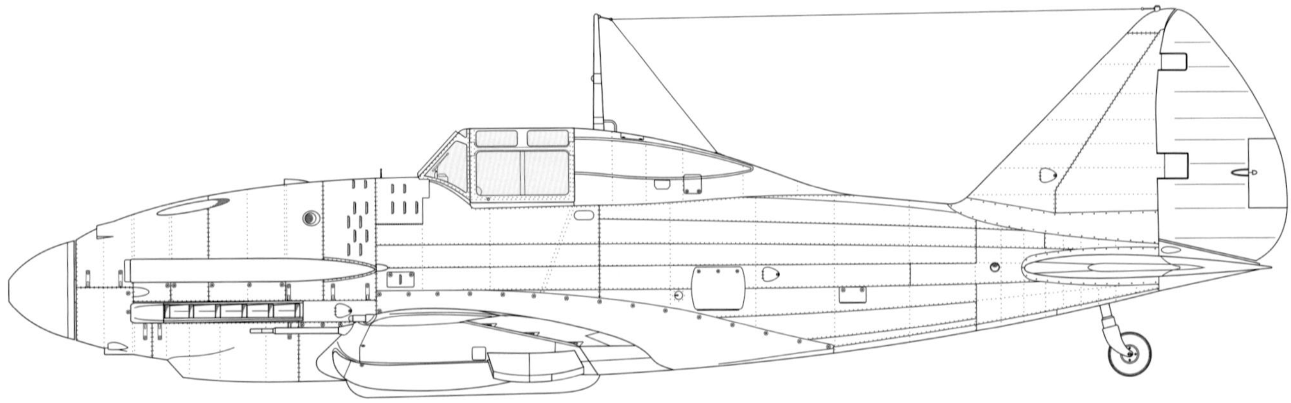

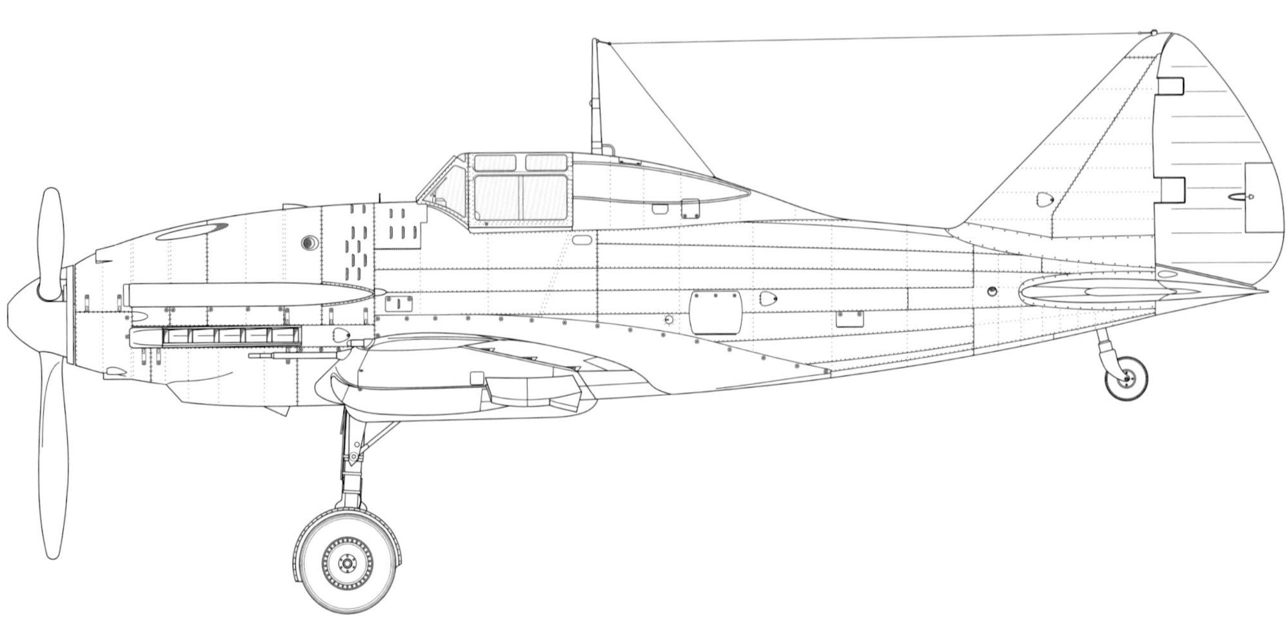

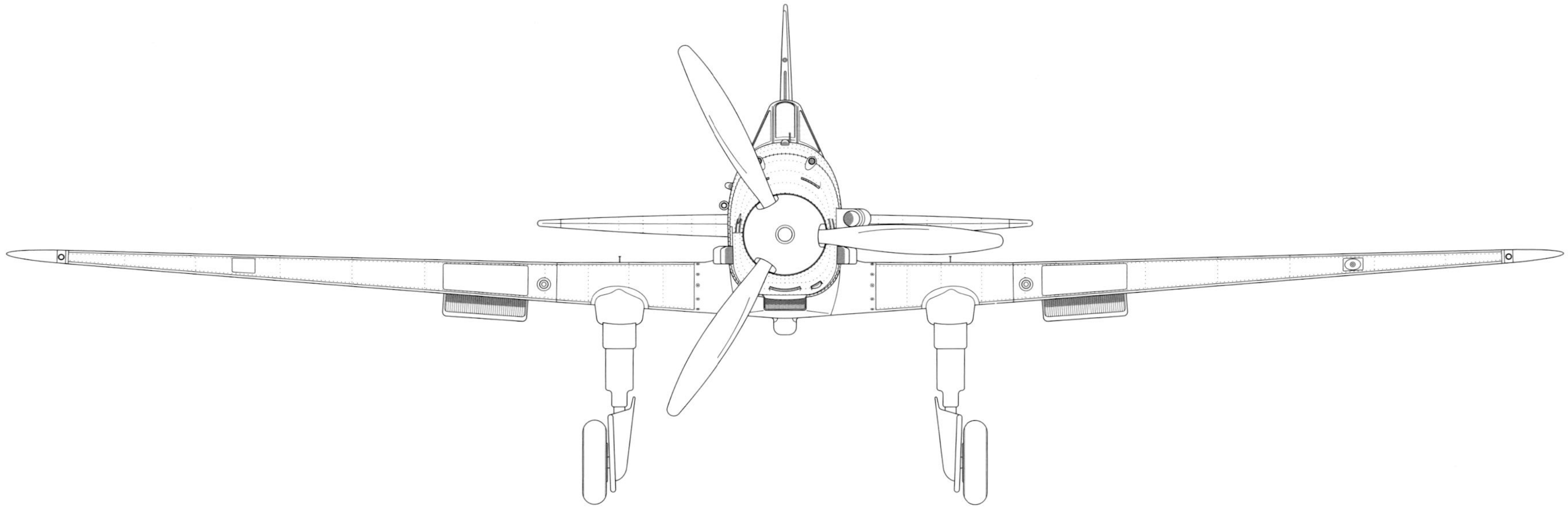

Reggiane RE 2001.
1/48 scale.

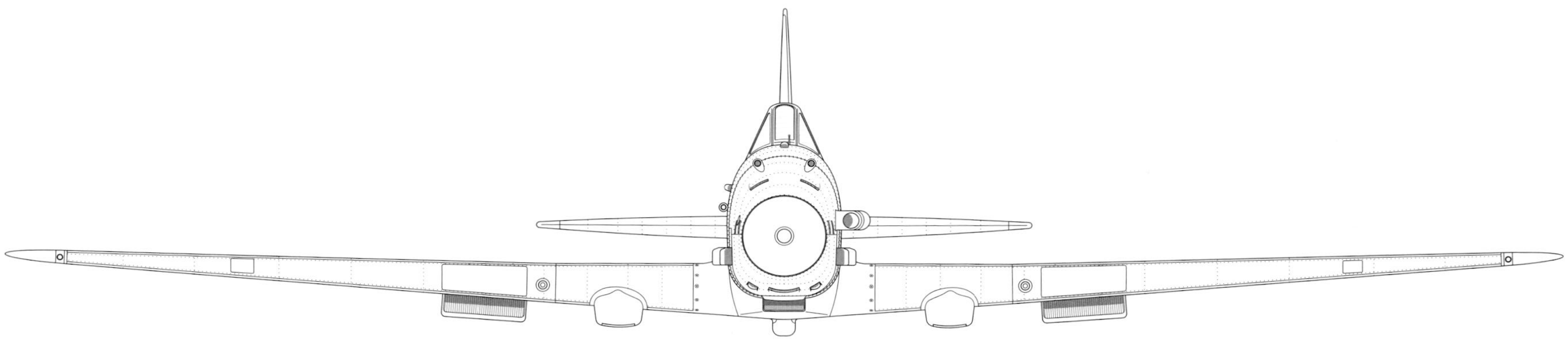

RE 2005 *Serie 0* Technical Description

The Reggiane RE 2005 was an Italian all metal, low-wing monoplane single-seat fighter aircraft.

Fuselage

The fuselage had a completely metal structure and had high structural resistance qualities combined with a relatively low weight. The fuselage structure consisted of 15 oval bulkheads held by stringers. The first bulkhead was also a firewall and the engine mounts were attached to it. The stressed skin fuselage was highly streamlined, save for the protrusions of the hard-riveted finish. The tail had all metal structure with fabric-covered movable surfaces. The cockpit of the RE 2005 was featured with large, open on right side canopy.

Wing and control surfaces

The wing had semi-elliptical plan with the leading edge made rectilinear to simplify production process. The internal structure of which comprised a multi-cell configuration using a total of three spars, stress-skin covering, and four fuel tanks. The ailerons and elevators were fabric-covered.

Landing gear

Landing gear in a classic arrangement with a tail wheel that can be retracted in flight. The main landing gear legs were retracted into the wing bays, towards the wingtip. Landing gear was hydraulically operated and equipped with shock absorbers. The wheels of main undercarriage were produced by Fabbrica Articoli Scientifici e Tecnici (FAST) and had Pirelli Aeroplano tires measured 600x254x170. The steerable tail wheel was retractable and closed by a pair of small doors. The tail wheel (FAST) had Pirelli Aeroplano tire measured 265x100x85.

Fuel, oil and cooling system

The fuel system included four, self-sealing tanks built between the wing spars – two front ones with a capacity of 160 liters each and two rear ones with a capacity of 108 liters each. The total capacity of the tanks was 536 litres. The tanks were covered with SEMAPE lining, which ensured self-sealing in the event of being shot by 12.7 mm bullets. The aircraft was equipped with a cooling system consisting of a liquid cooler and an oil cooler, which were placed together under the fuselage. An oil tank with a capacity of 45 liters was mounted at the root of the left wing. The annular coolant tank was mounted at the front of the engine.

Armament

Armament for aircraft produced in *Serie 0* were two synchronized 12.7 mm Breda-SAFAT machine guns located in the top of the engine cowling with 350 rounds per barrel. The rate of fire was 575 rounds per minute. In addition, the aircraft had a Mauser MG 151/20 20 mm cannon mounted and fired through the propeller shaft with 200 rounds. Another two 20 mm Mauser MG 151/20 cannons were located in the wing, with 200 rounds per barrel. The weapon was cocked and reloaded using the Managhi electro-pneumatic system. The well-proved San Giorgio – Genova Type C reflector gun sight was mounted under the windscreen. Under the fuselage (asymmetrically, to the right of the radiator air intake) was located mount for 100 – 640 kg bomb.

Powerplant

FIAT R.A. 1050 R.C. 58-I “Tifone” (license version of Daimler Benz DB 605A-1) in-line engine, which was capable of generating a maximum of 1475 hp. The weight of dry engine was 700 kg. The engine drives a three-blade Piaggio P. 2001 (according to some sources P. 6001) variable-speed metal propeller of 3100 mm diameter.

Communication and other equipment

HF radio R.T. Allocchio Bacchini B.30 was mounted in the fuselage and Patin radio ranger. RE 2005 was equipped with Leica Motor gun-camera. Another equipment were two Slima type automatic fire-extinguishers located in the engine compartment.

Instrument panel of the first prototype of the RE 2005.

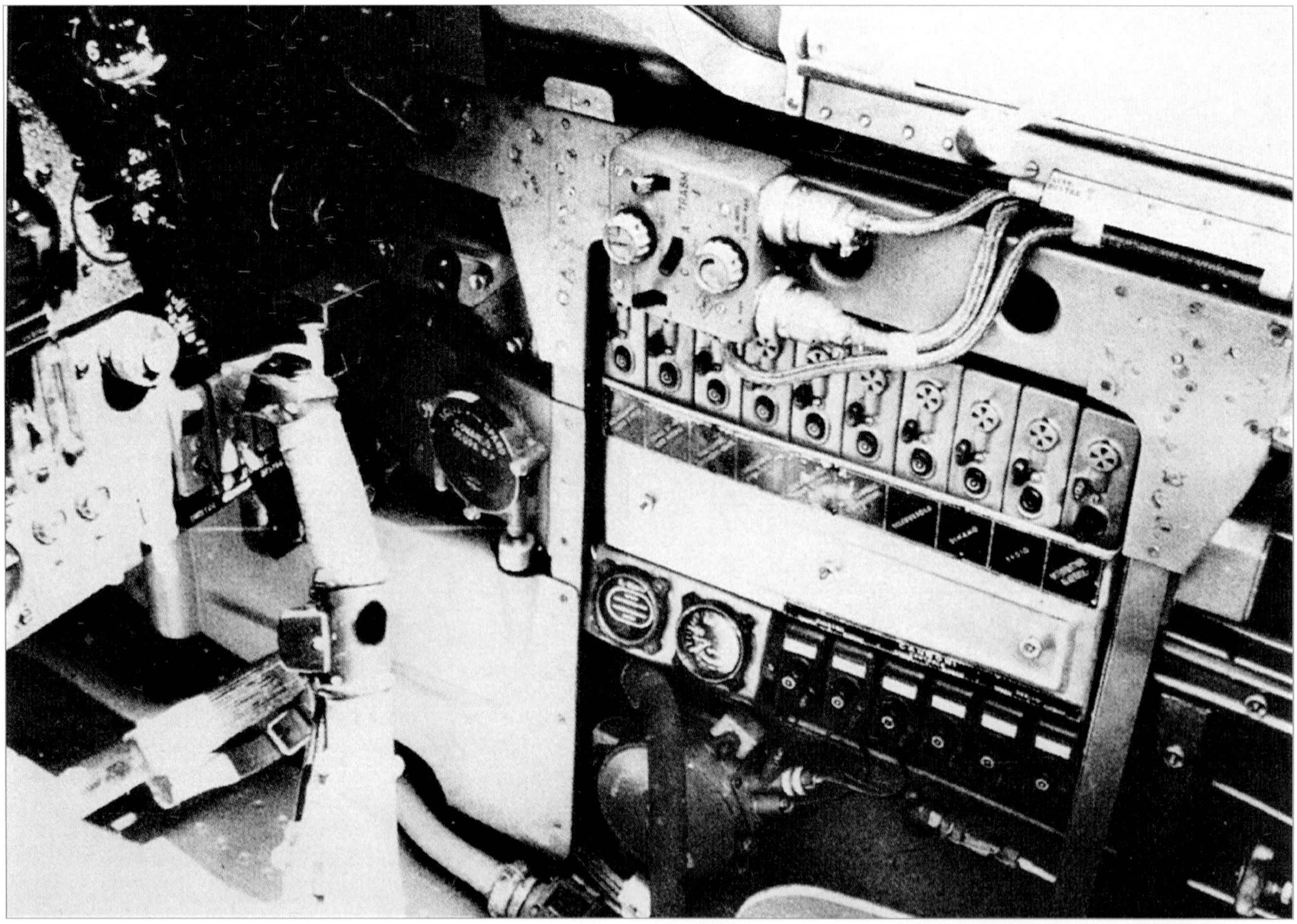

Right side of the cockpit.
Left side of the cockpit.

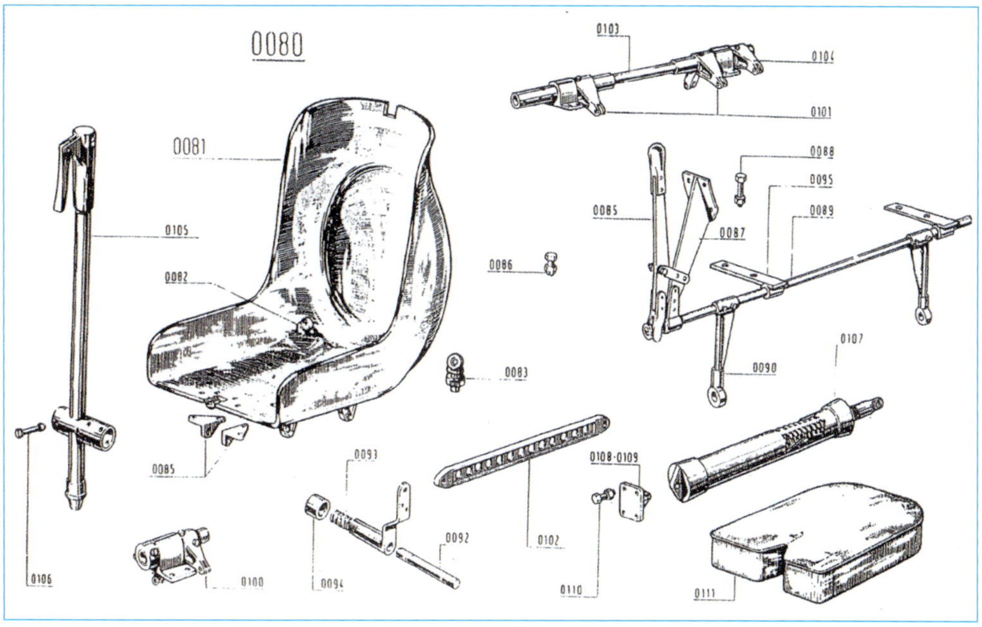

Details of the construction of the control stick and pilot's seat.

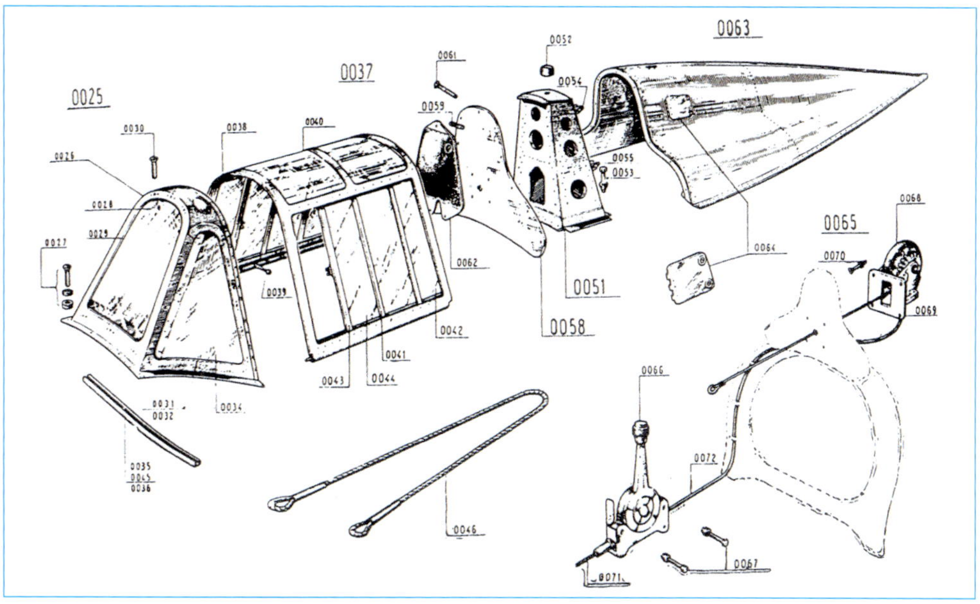

Construction of the cockpit canopy and turnover security bumper.

Pilot's cockpit (without canopy) of the first prototype RE 2005 (M.M.494).

Shortened canopy of the serial RE 2005.

Engine compartment and Breda-SAFAT 12.7 mm machine guns.

Engine compartment – view from below.

Propeller and engine cover of the serial RE 2005.

View of the cooling unit from the rear.

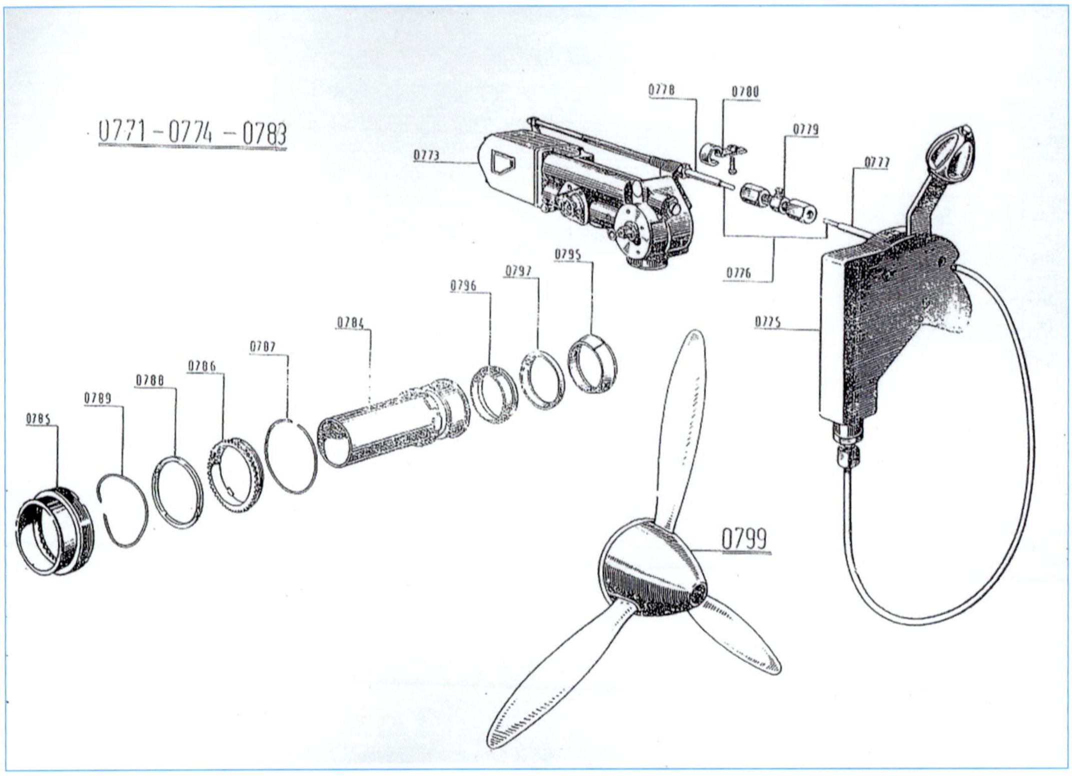

Propeller and propeller pitch control mechanism.

Wing construction (covering removed).

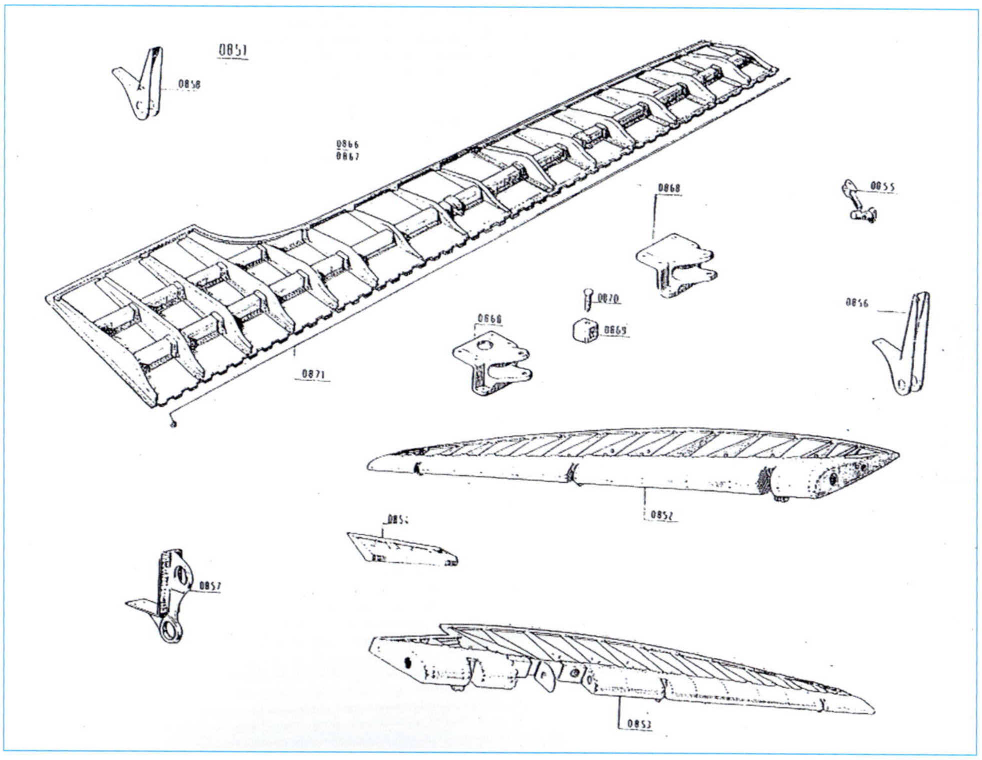

Flap and ailerons.

Flaps in the extended position.

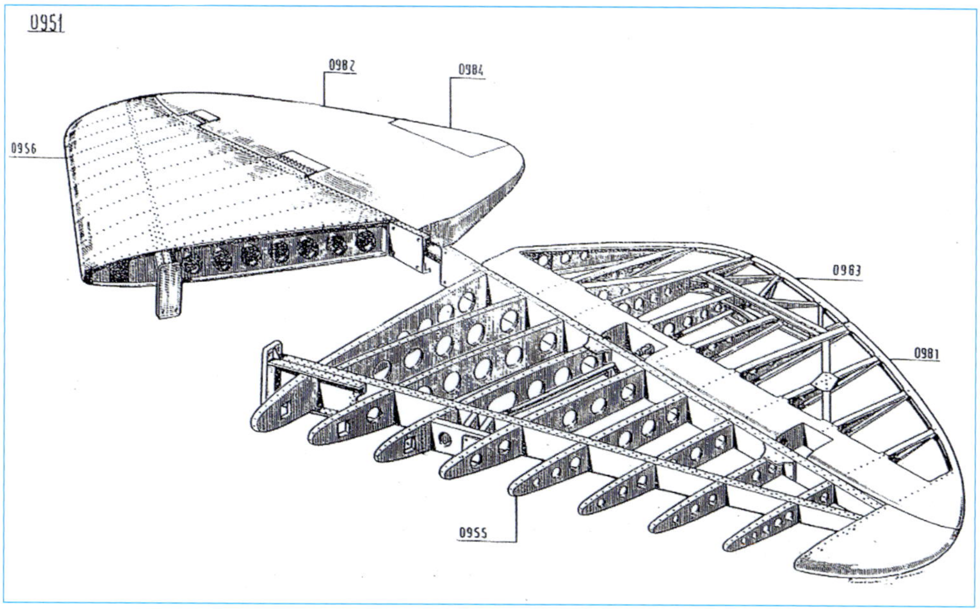

Construction of the horizontal tail.

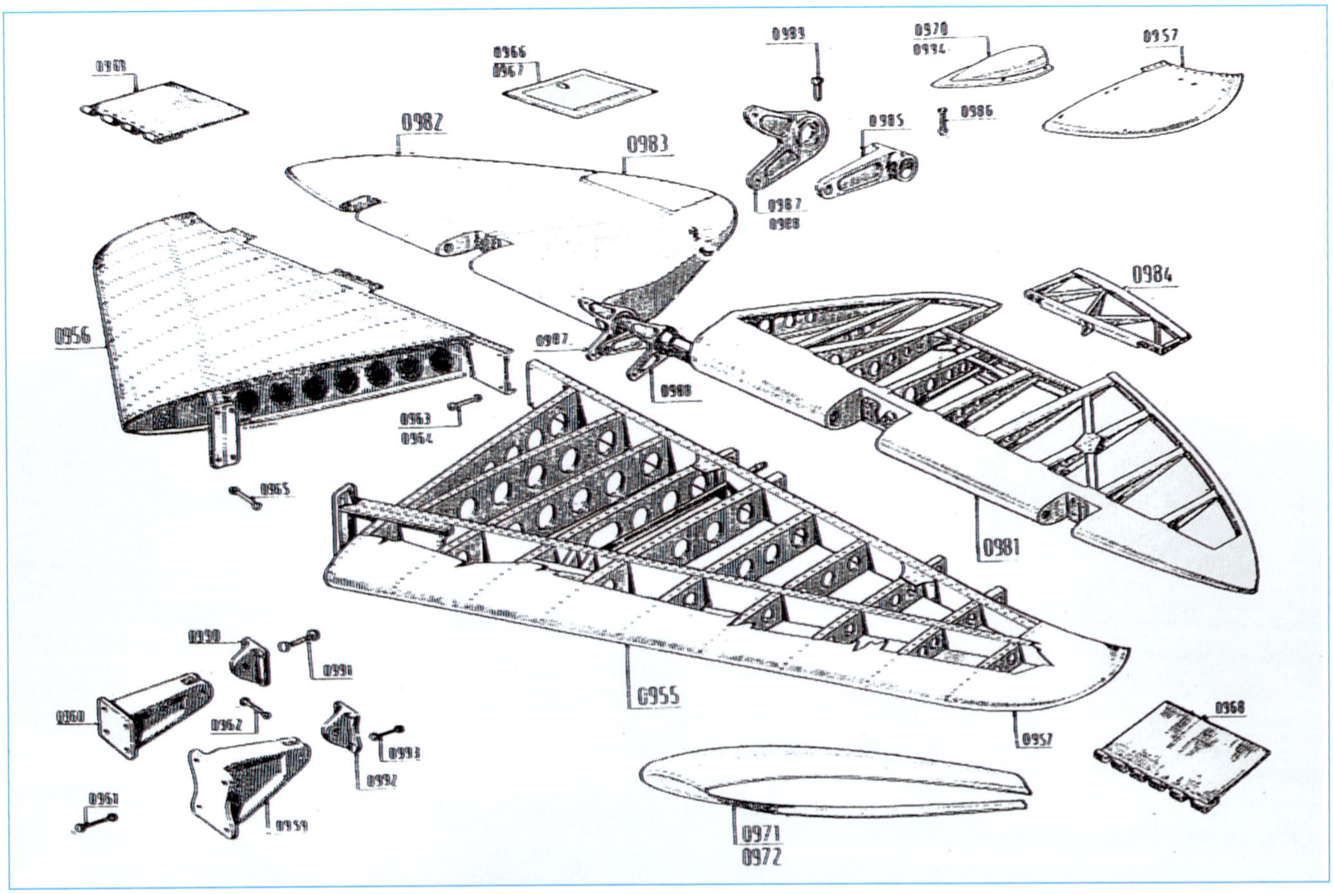

Components of the horizontal tail.
Construction of the vertical tail.

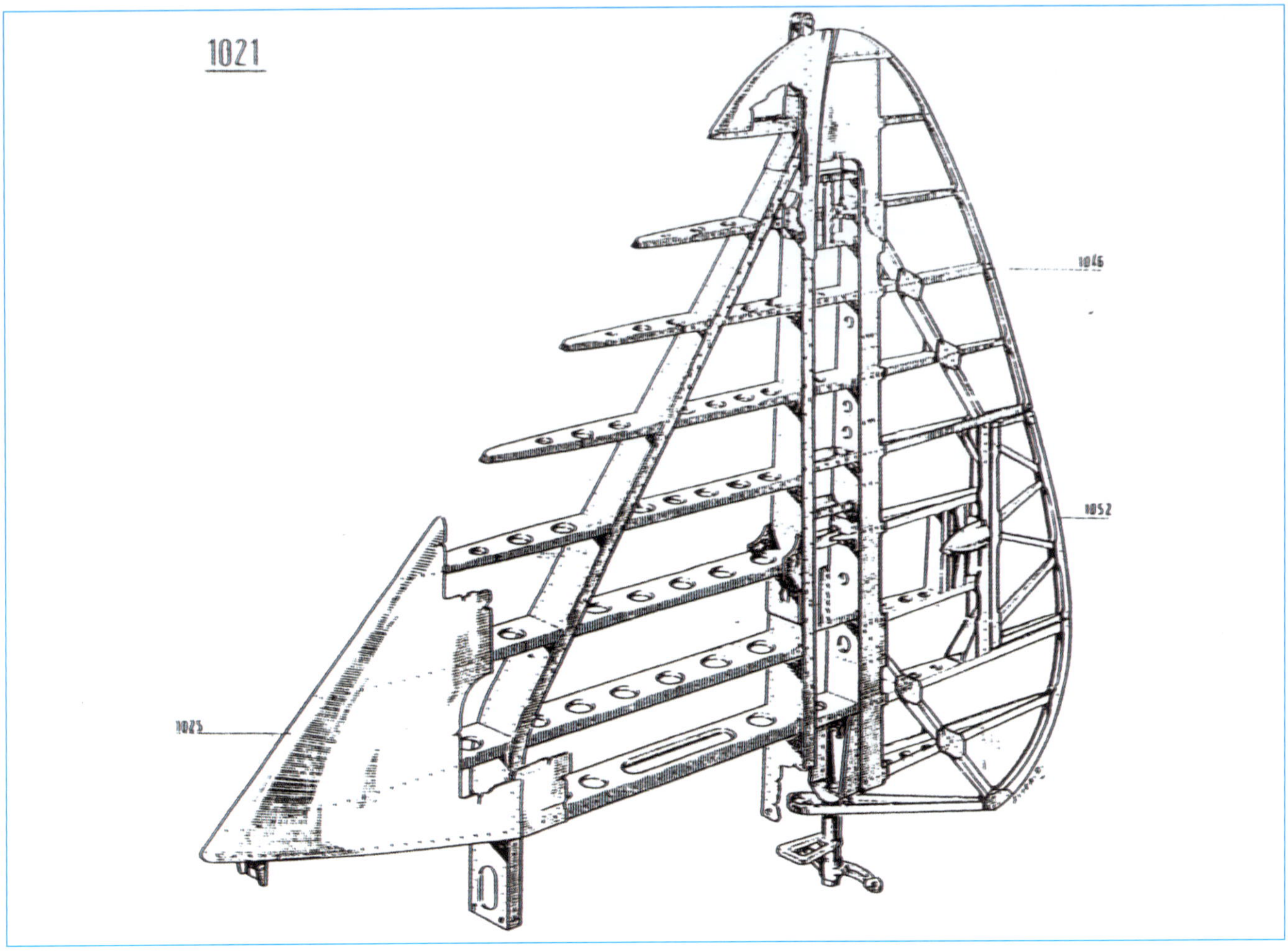

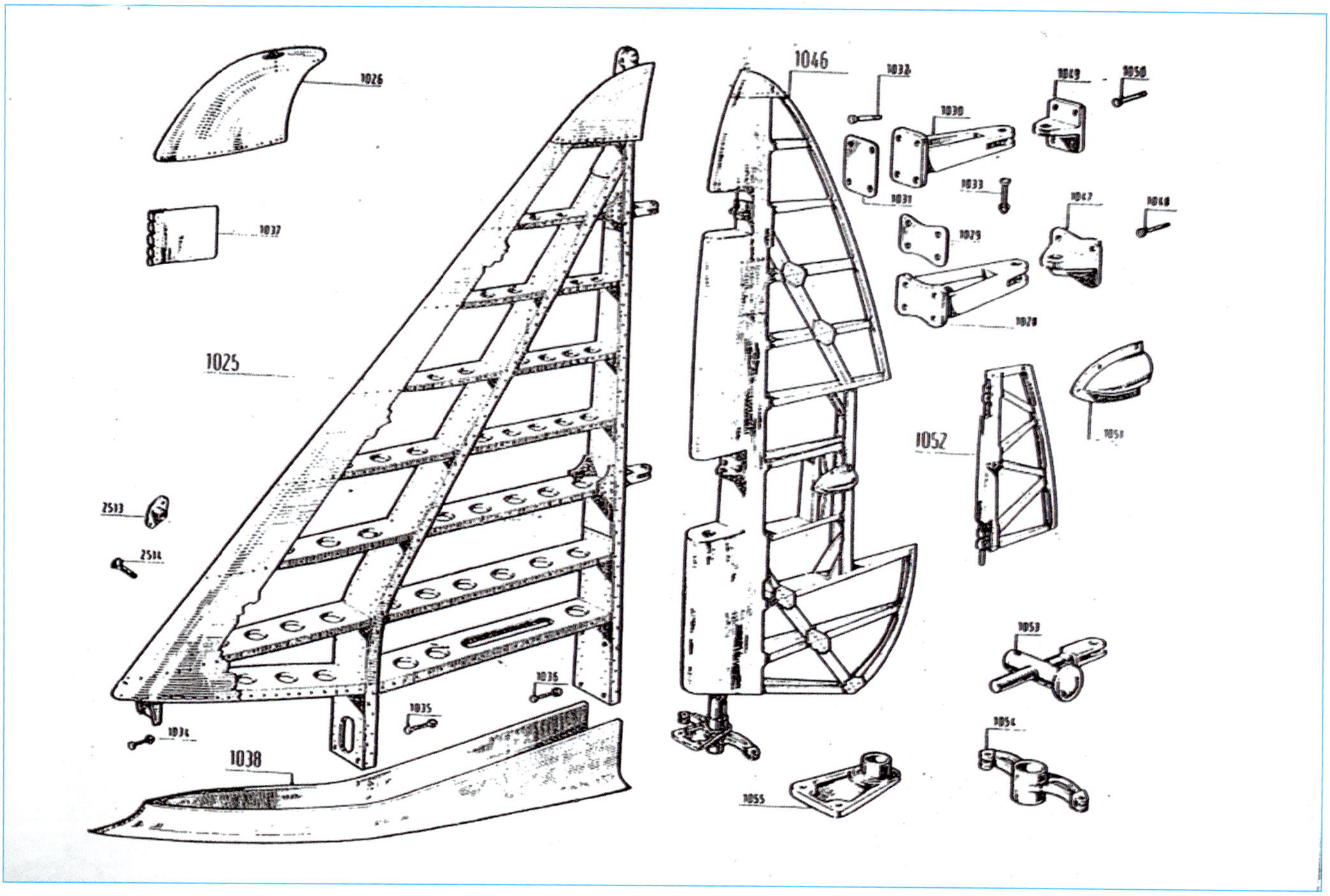

Components of the vertical tail.
Rear part of the fuselage.

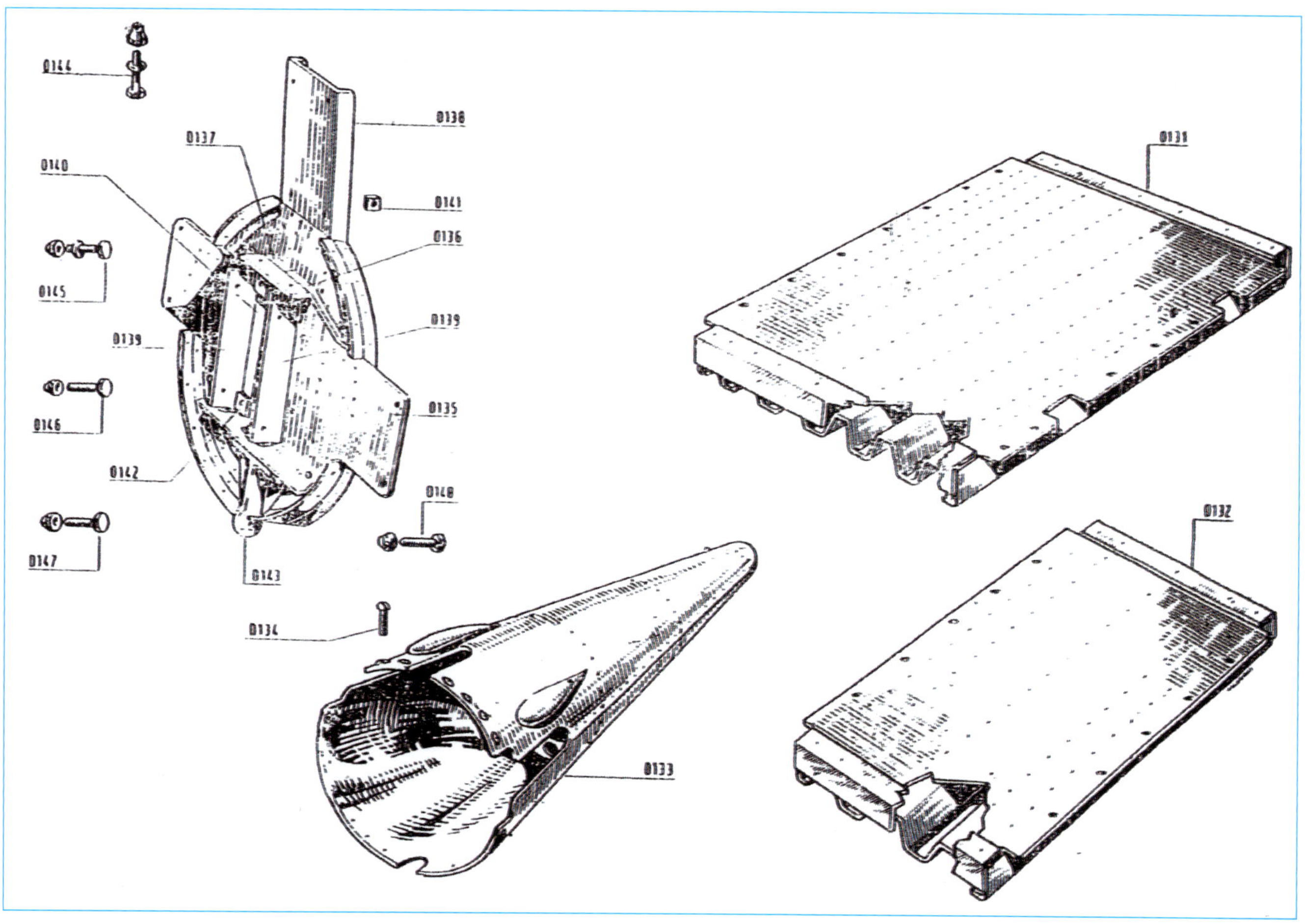

Fuselage armament – Breda-SAFAT 12.7 mm machine guns.

Wing machine gun Breda-SAFAT – the first prototype RE 2005.

Wing machine gun Breda-SAFAT – the second prototype and serial RE 2005.

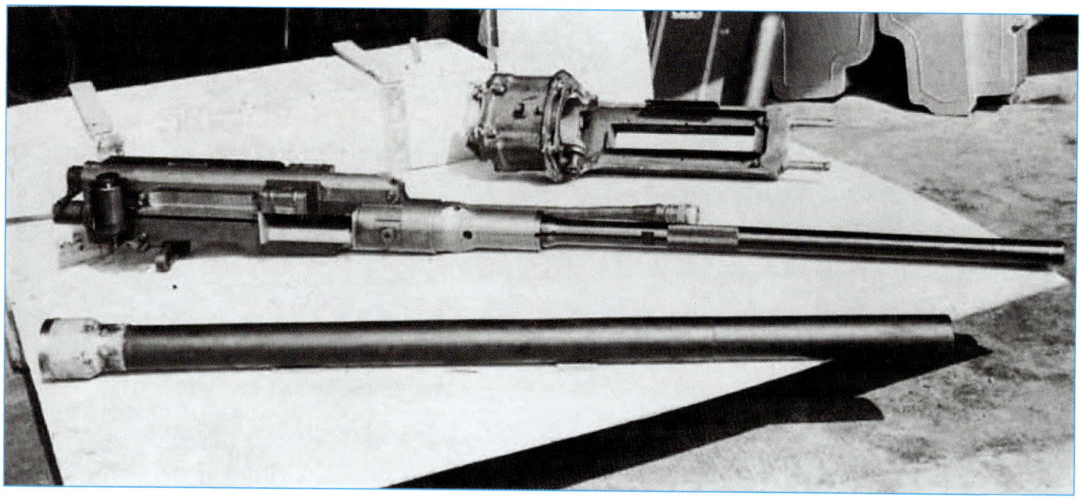

20 mm Mauser MG 151/20 cannon.

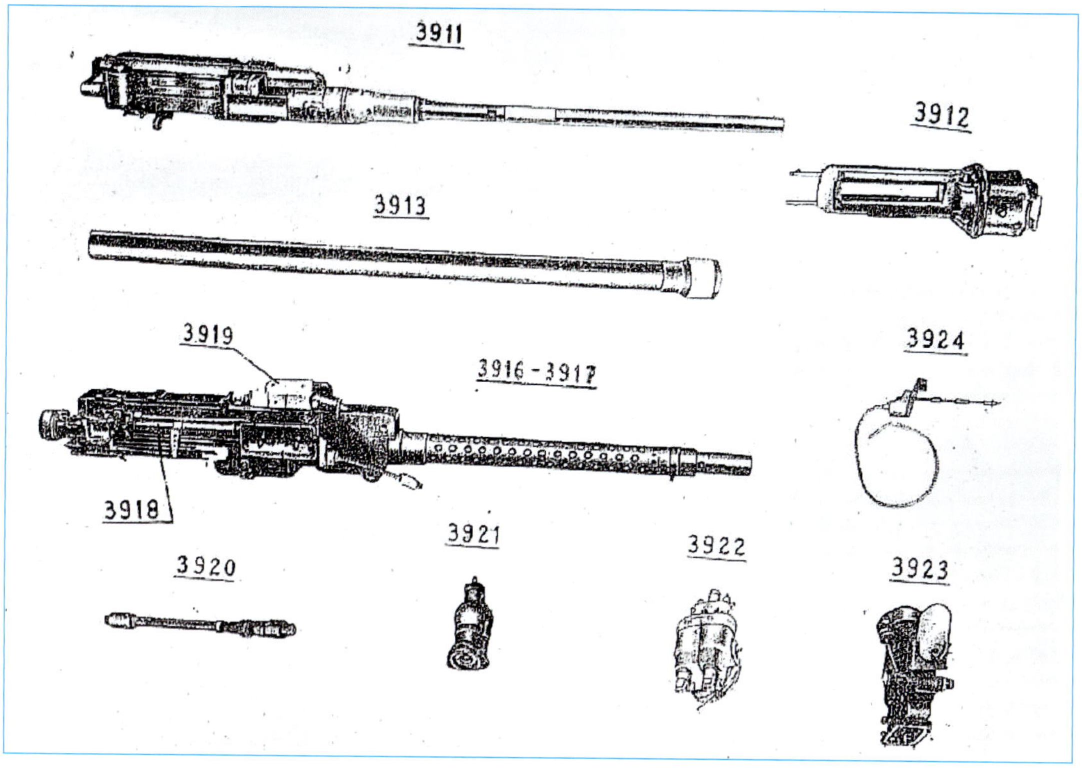

Armament of the RE 2005 – 20 mm Mauser MG 151/20 cannon and Breda-SAFAT 12.7 mm machine gun.

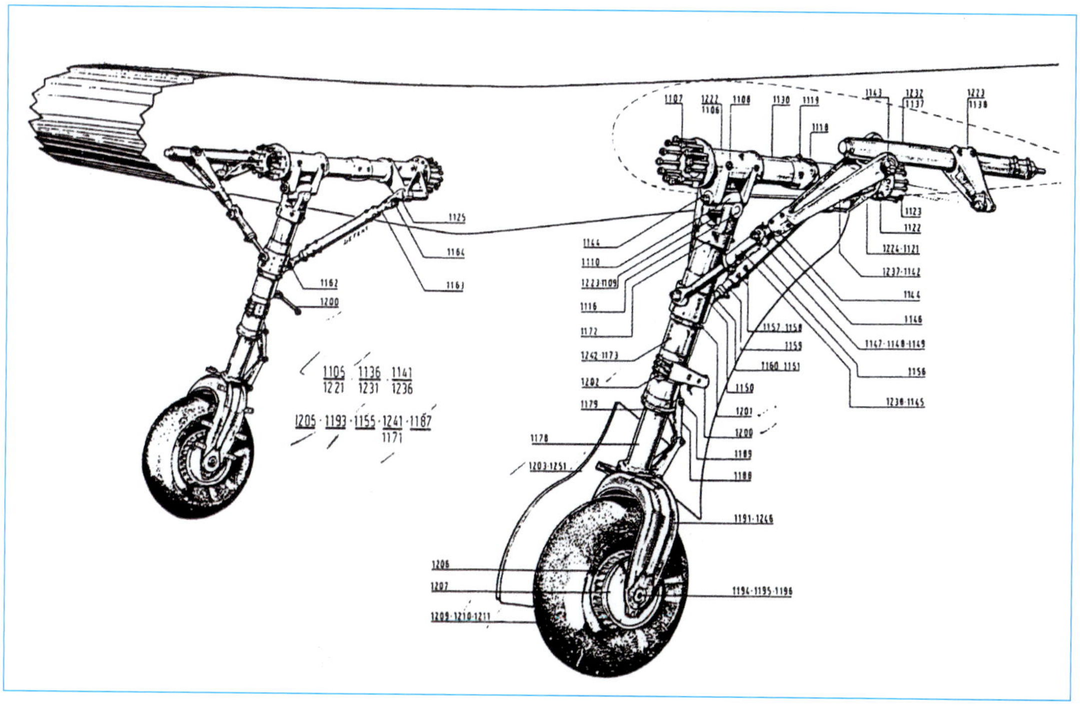

Construction of the main landing gear of the RE 2005.

Main landing gear of the RE 2005.

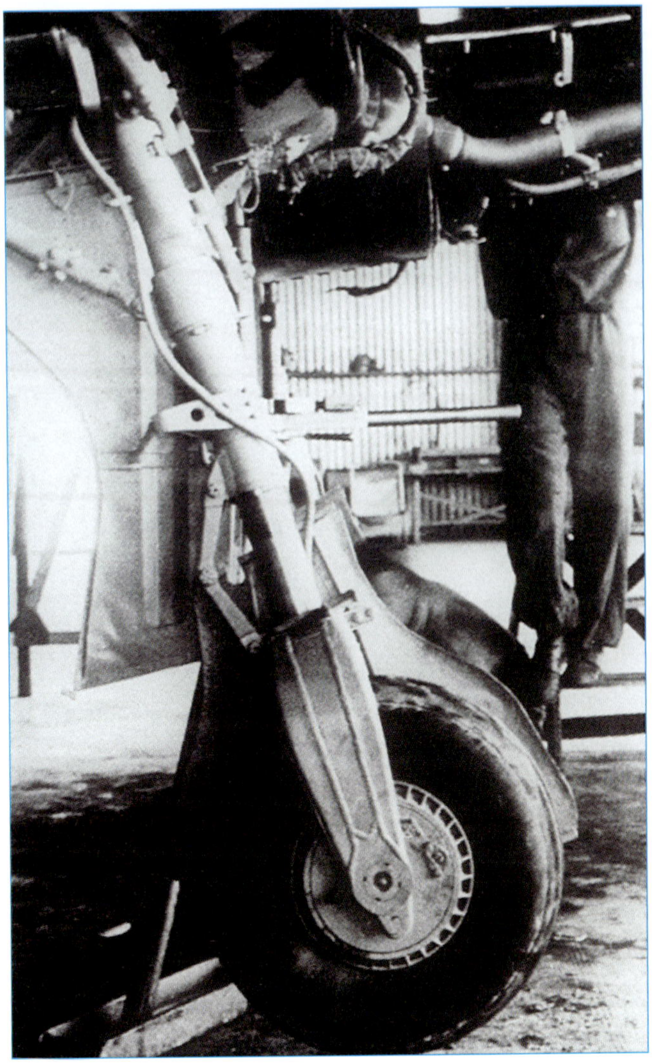

Main landing gear.

Main landing gear covers.

Main landing gear bay.

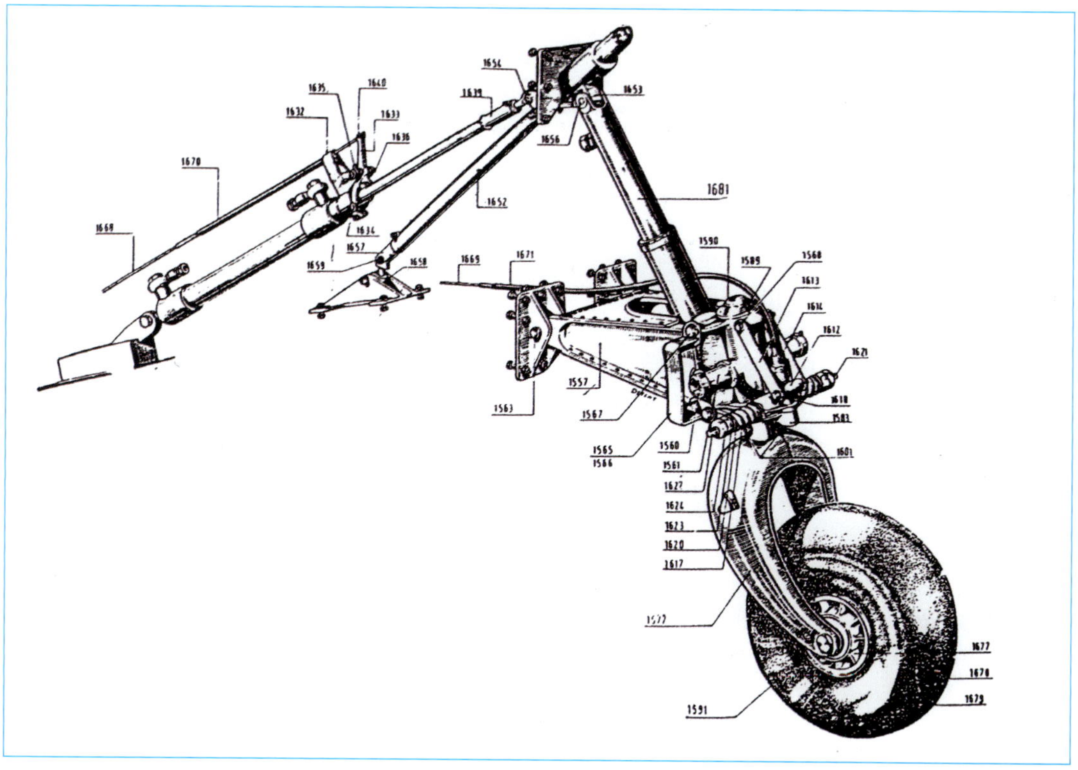

Construction of the tail wheel.

Asymmetrically mounted bomb rack for bombs up to 640 kilograms.
Engine bed.

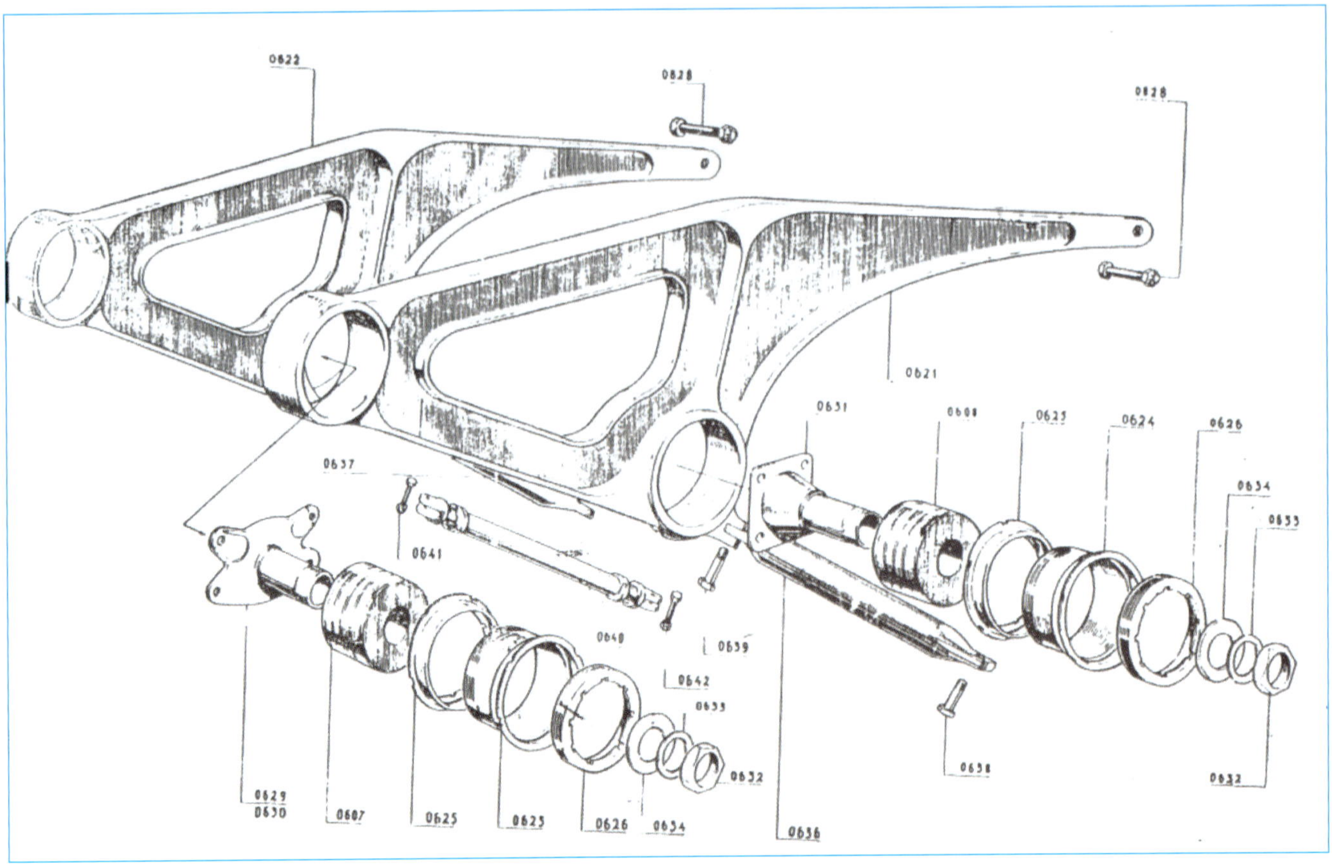

Factory drawings (sections) of the RE 2005.

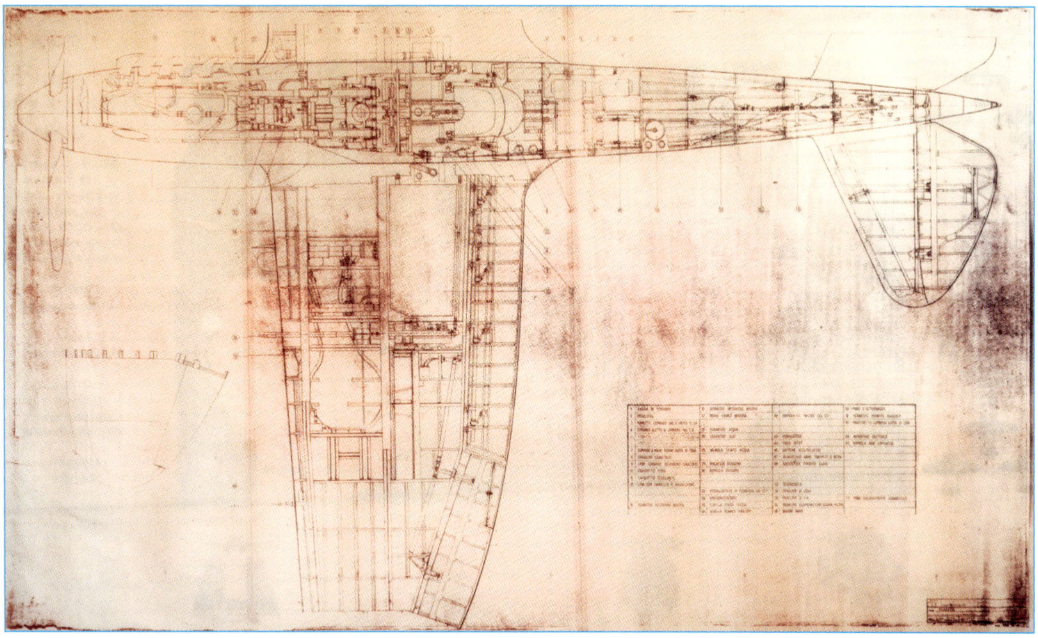

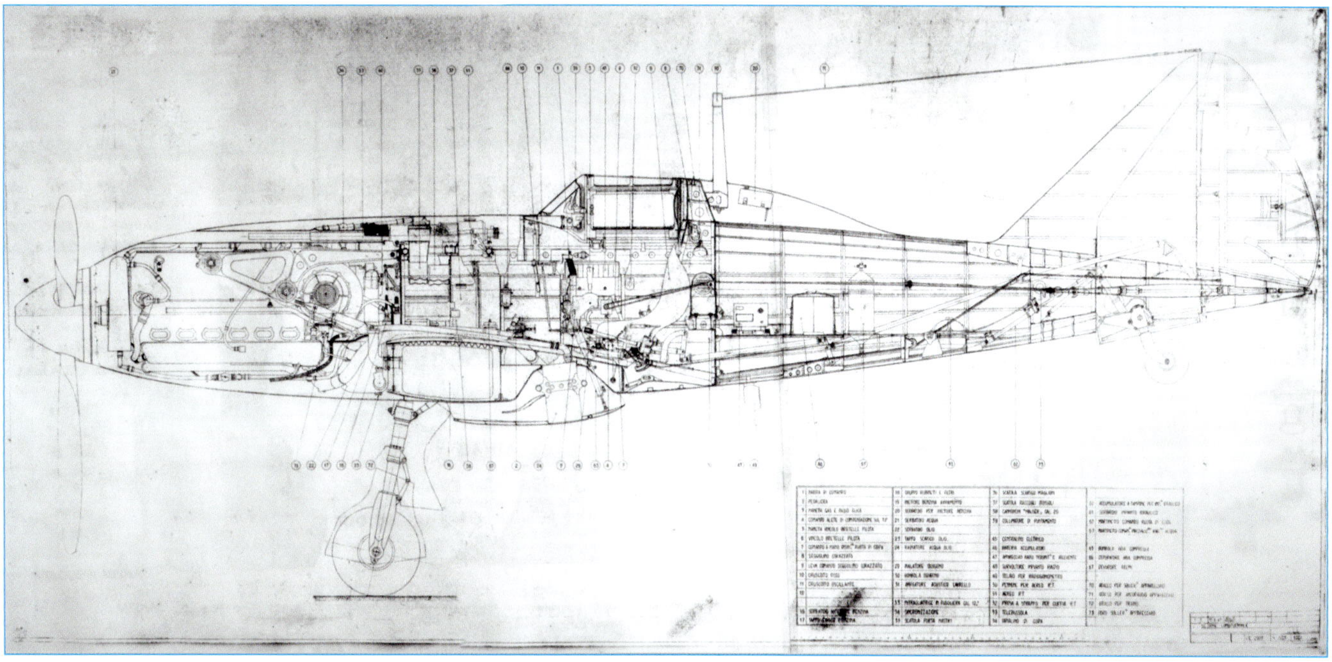

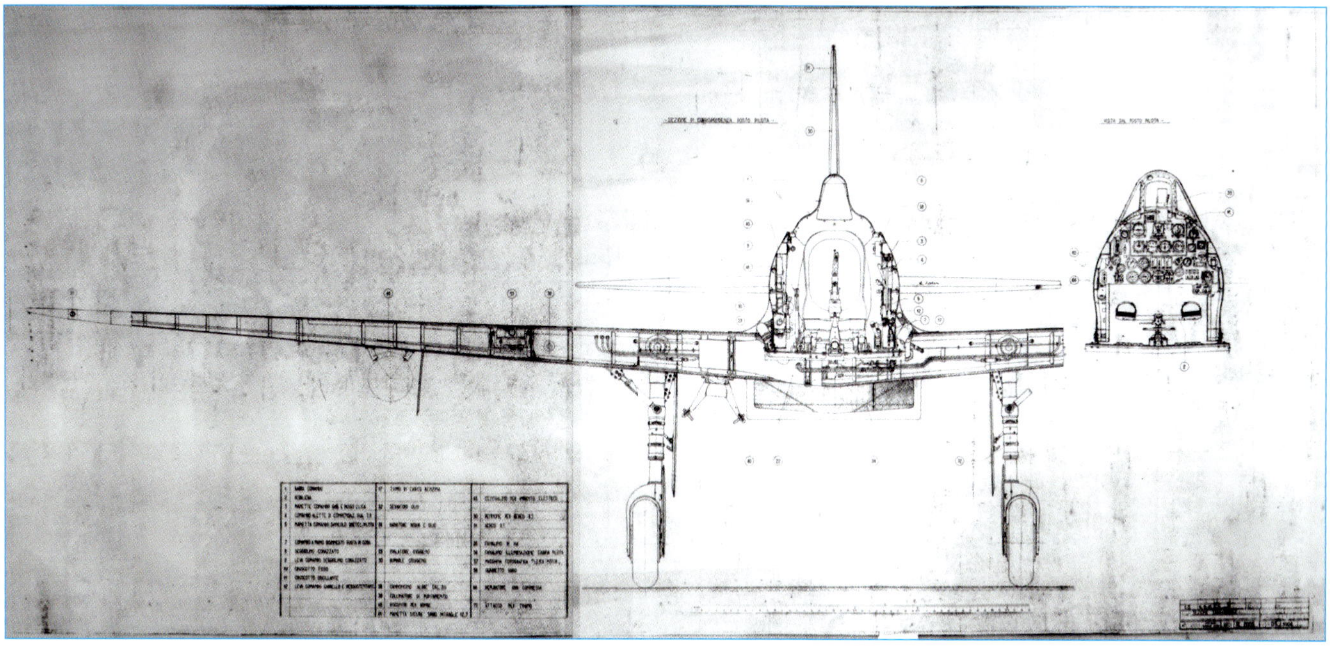

Reggiane RE 2005. The first prototype M.M.494.
1/48 scale.

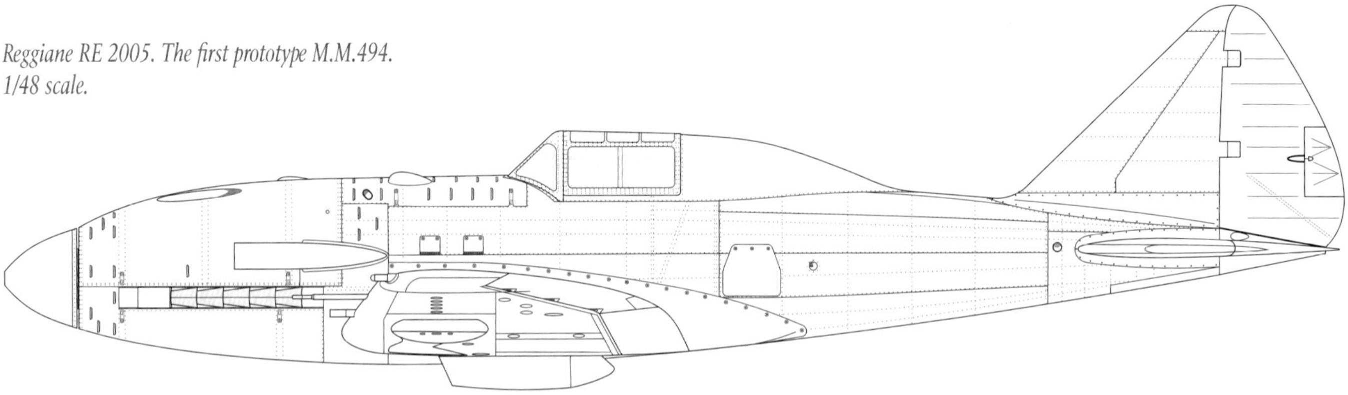

Reggiane RE 2005. The second prototype M.M.495 after modification in June 1943.
1/48 scale.

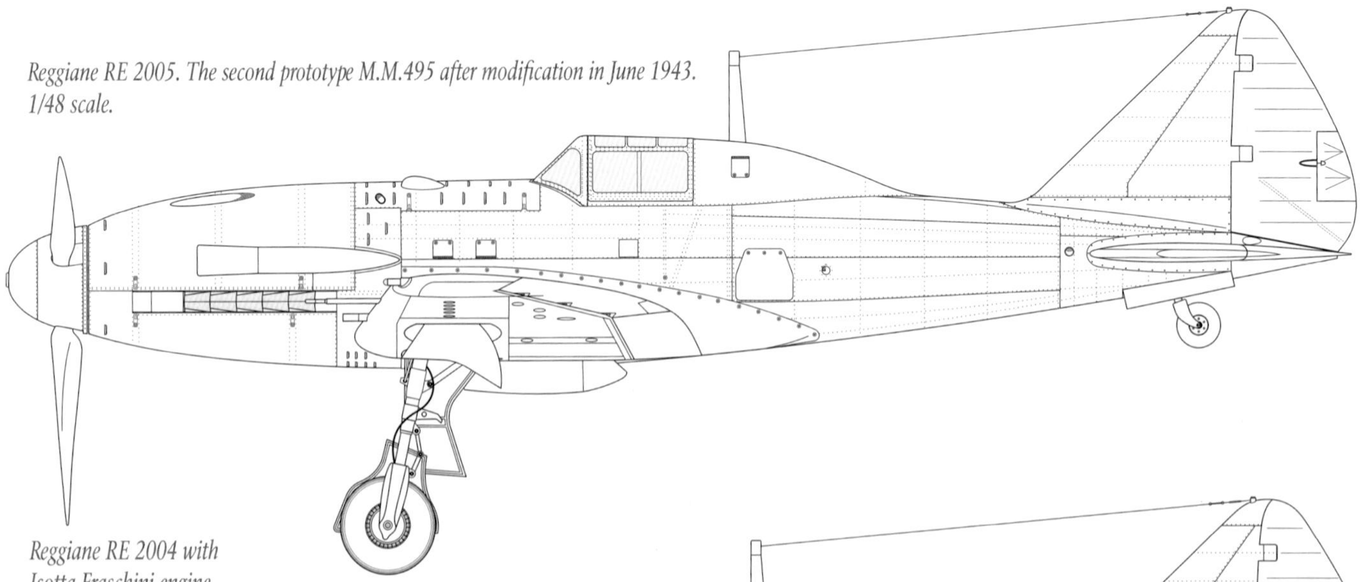

Reggiane RE 2004 with
Isotta Fraschini engine.
1/48 scale.

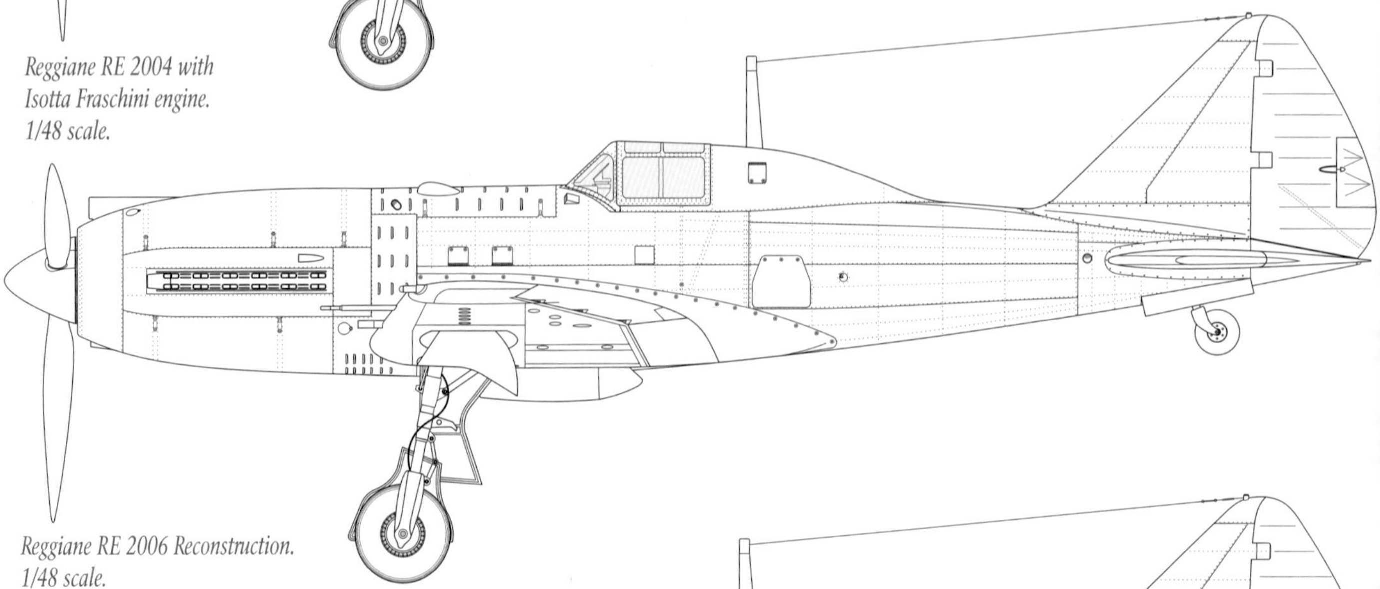

Reggiane RE 2006 Reconstruction.
1/48 scale.

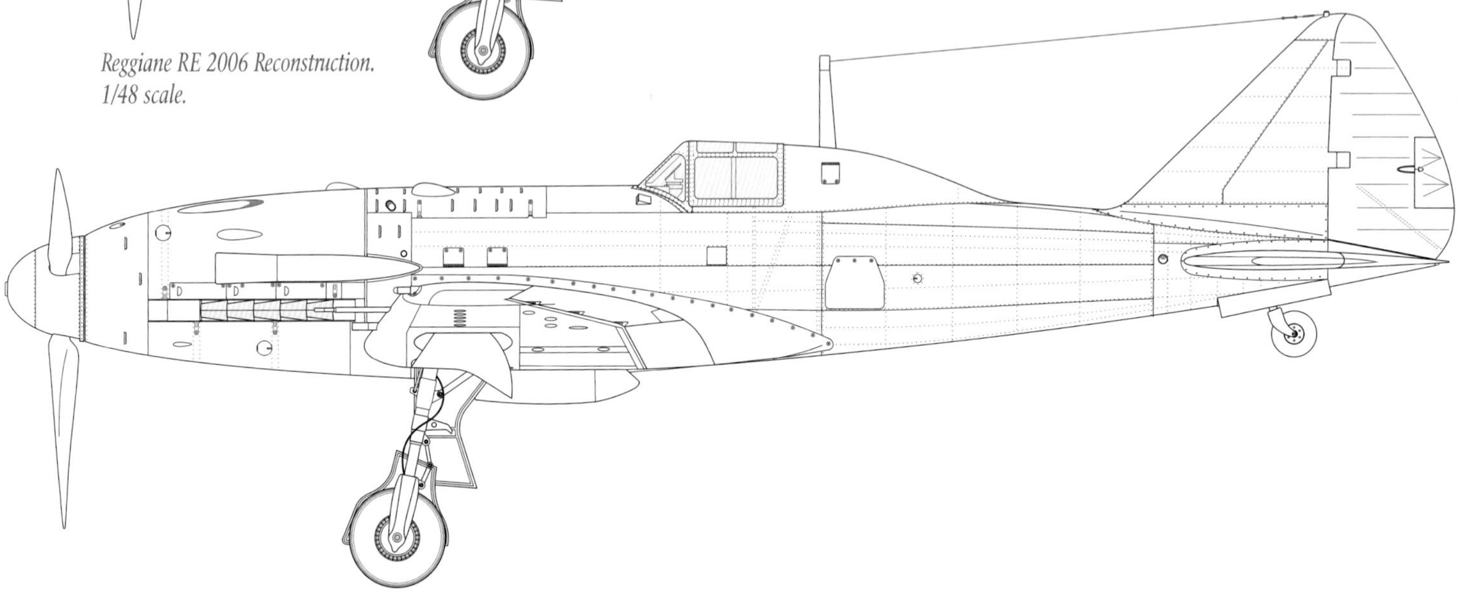

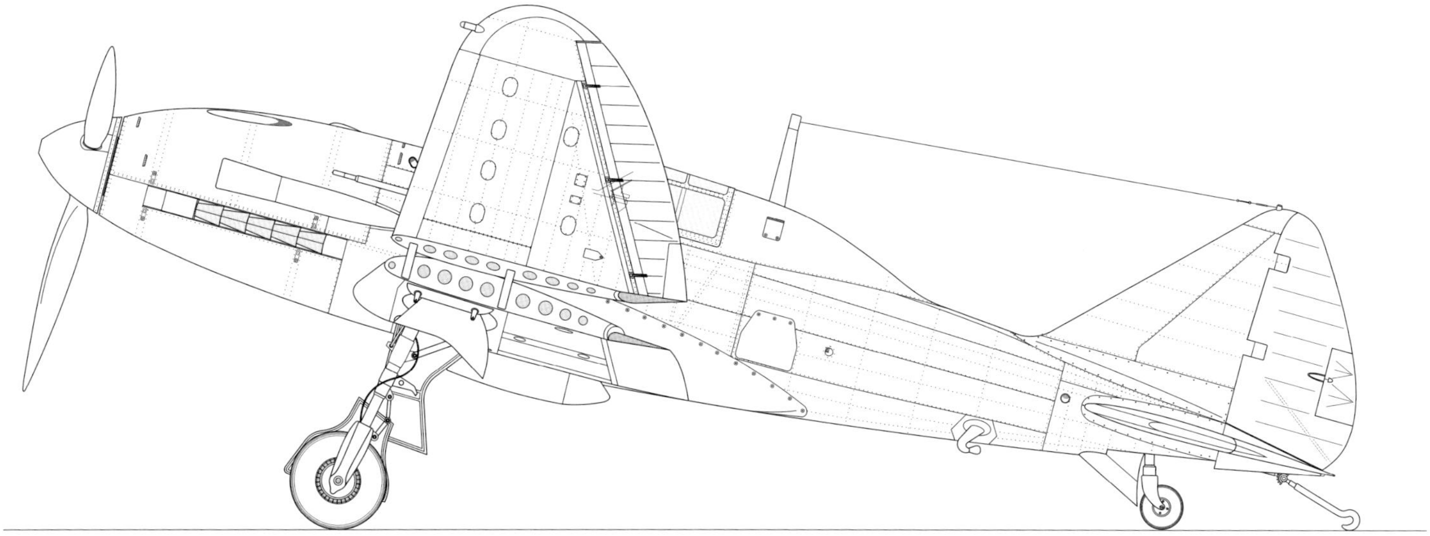

Reggiane RE 2005 marine version.
1/48 scale.

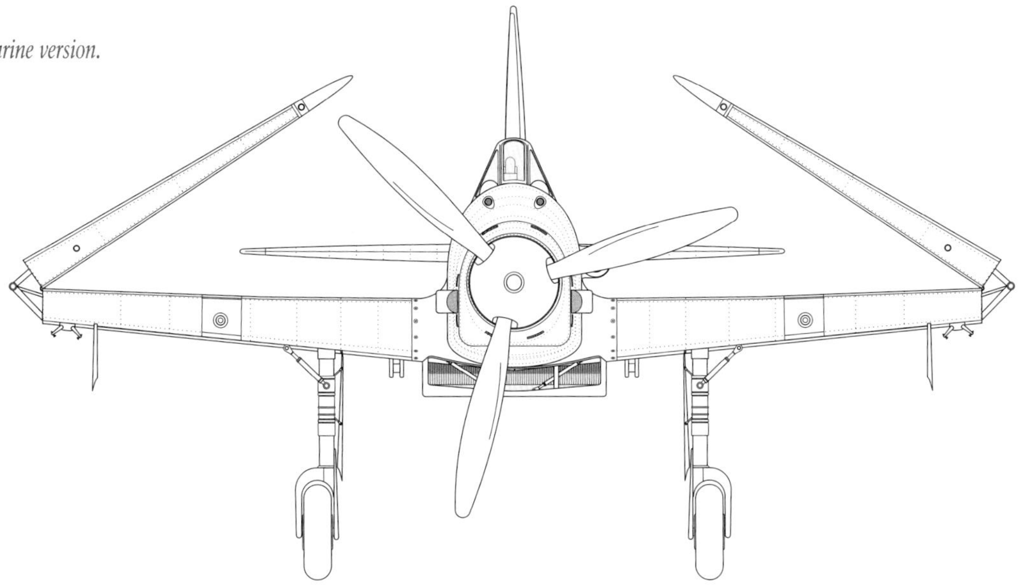

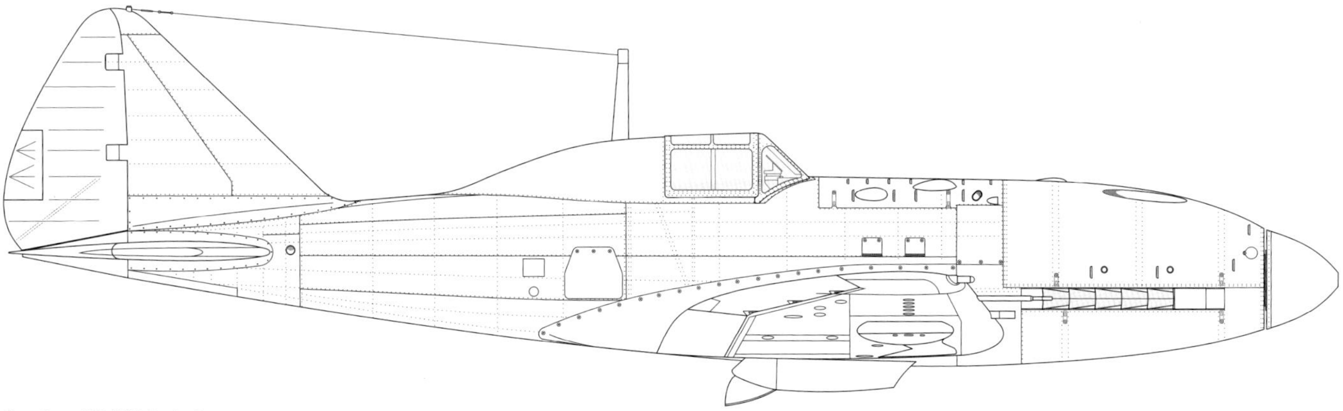

Reggiane RE 005 Serie 0.
1/48 scale.

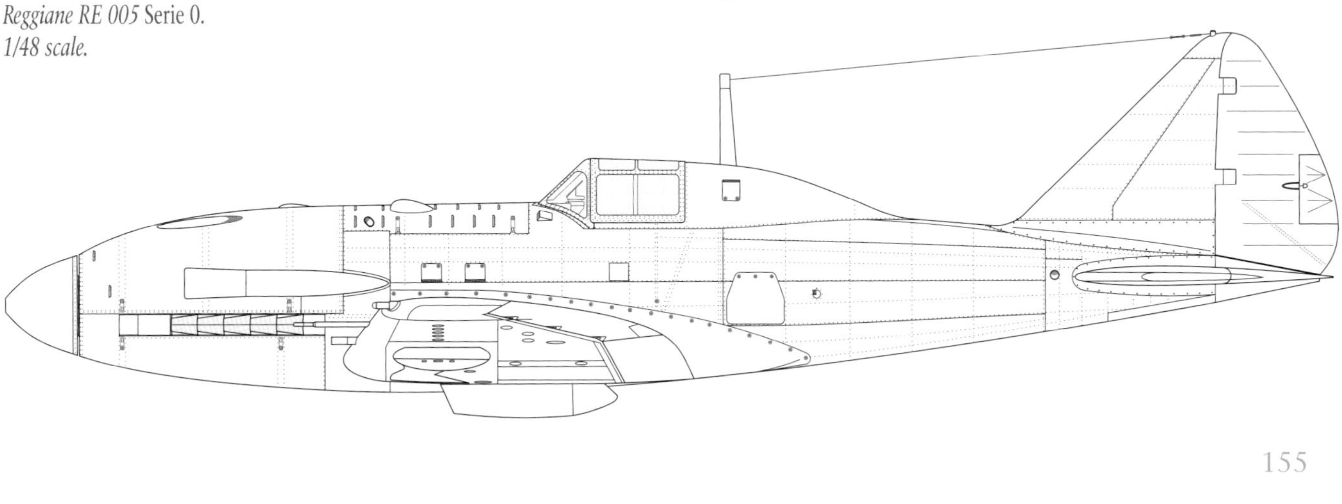

Reggiane RE 2005 Serie 0.
1/48 scale.

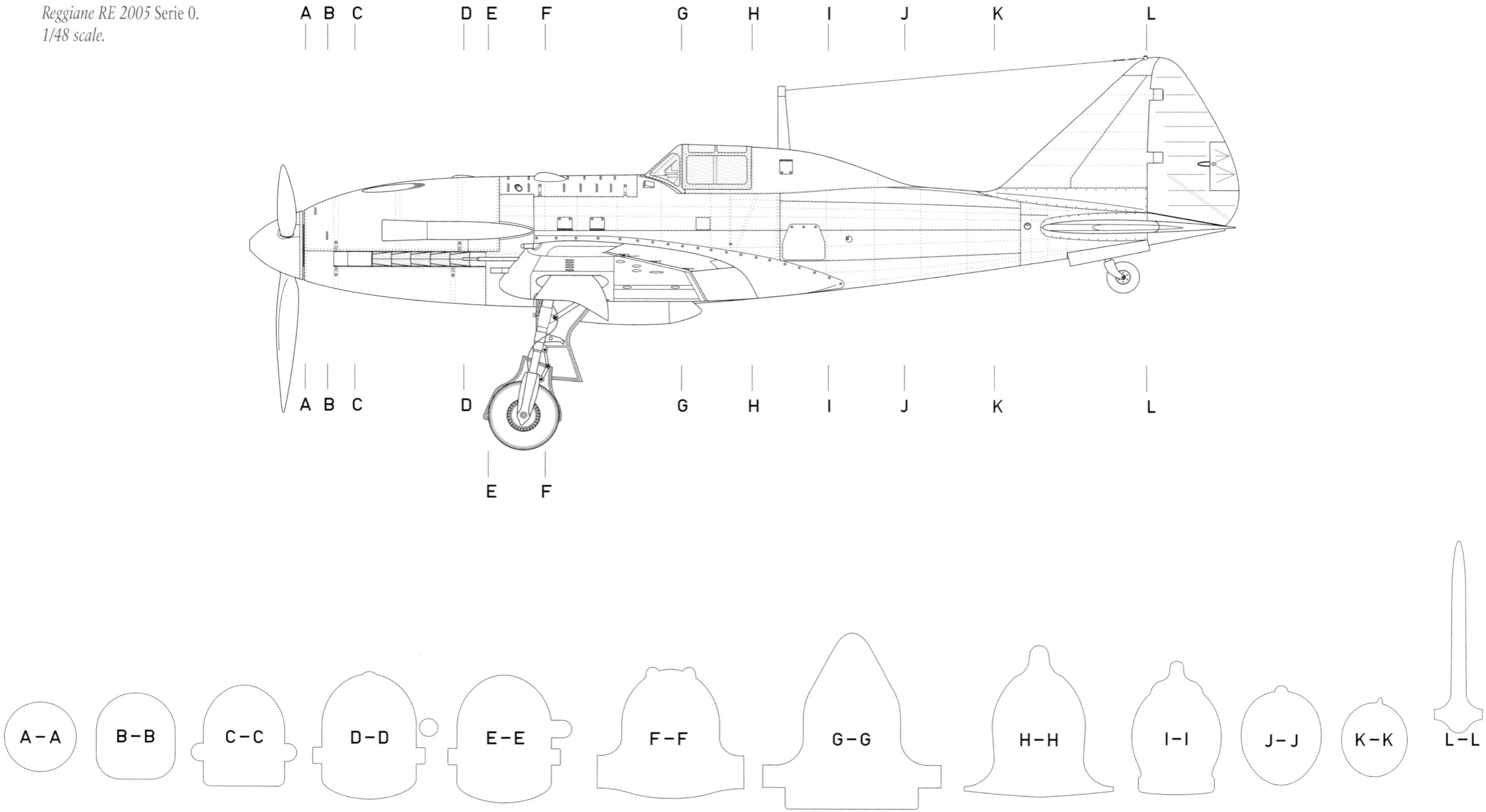

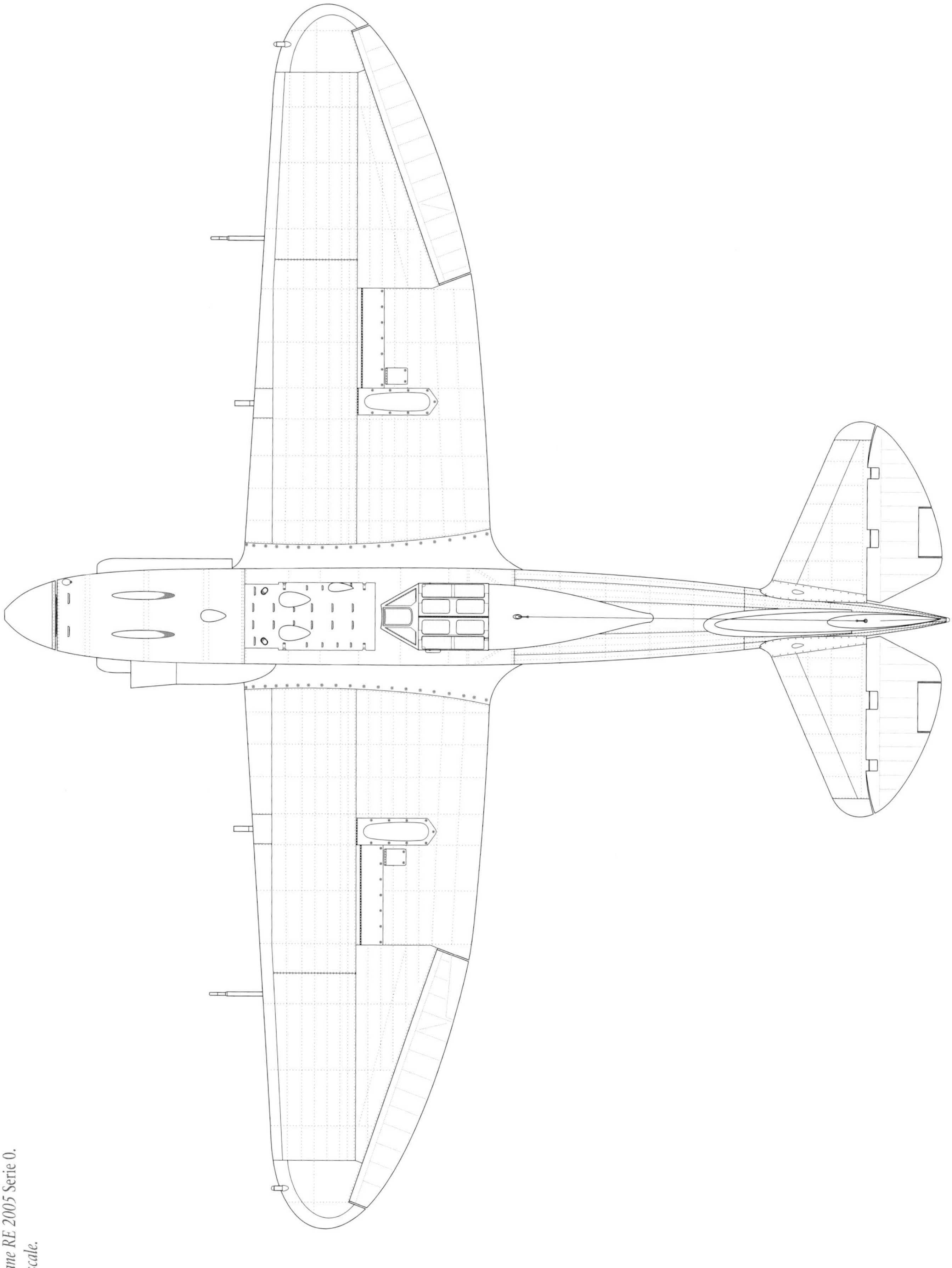

Reggiane RE 2005 Serie 0.
1/48 scale.

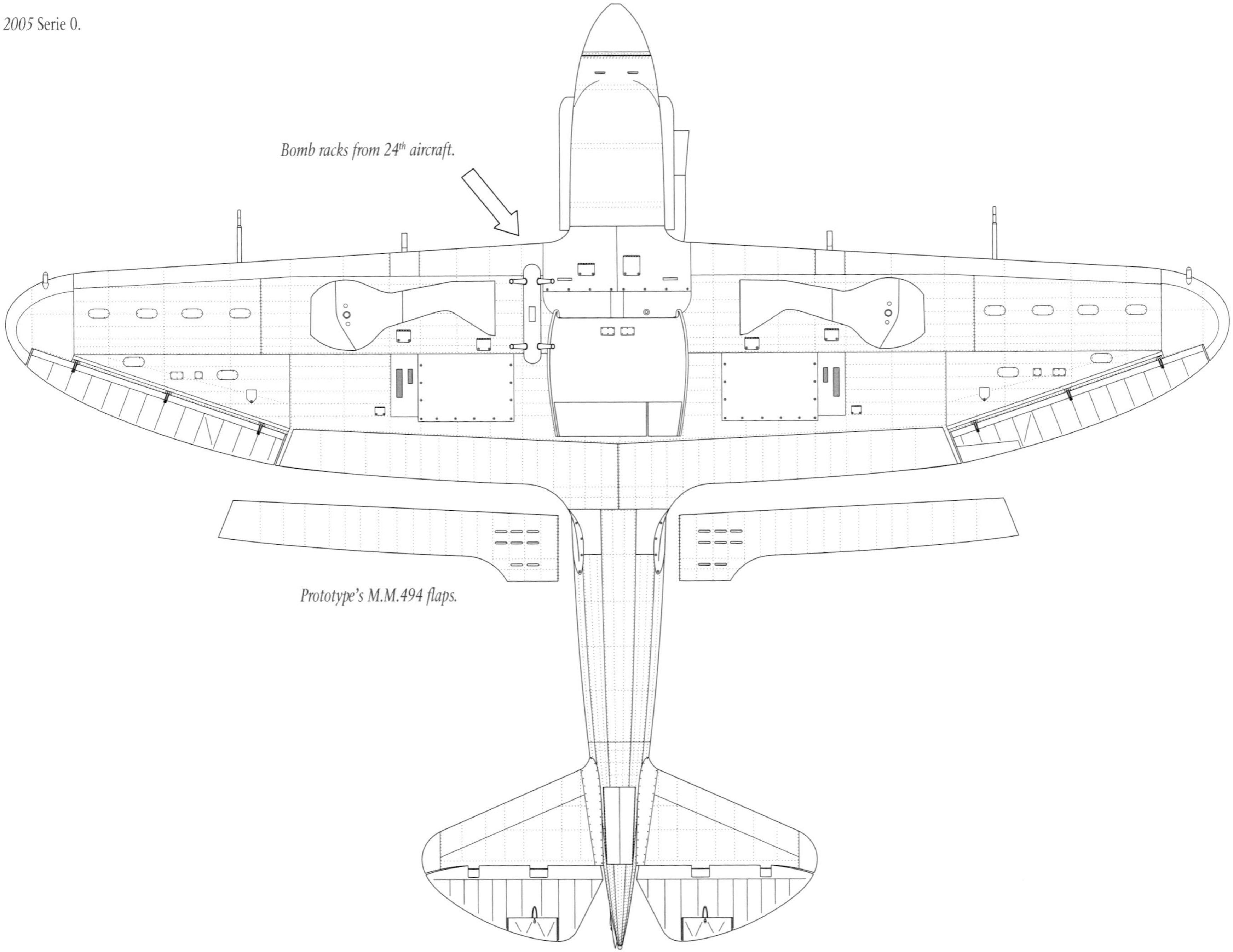

Reggiane RE 2005 Serie 0.
1/48 scale.

Reggiane RE 2005 Serie 0.
1/48 scale.

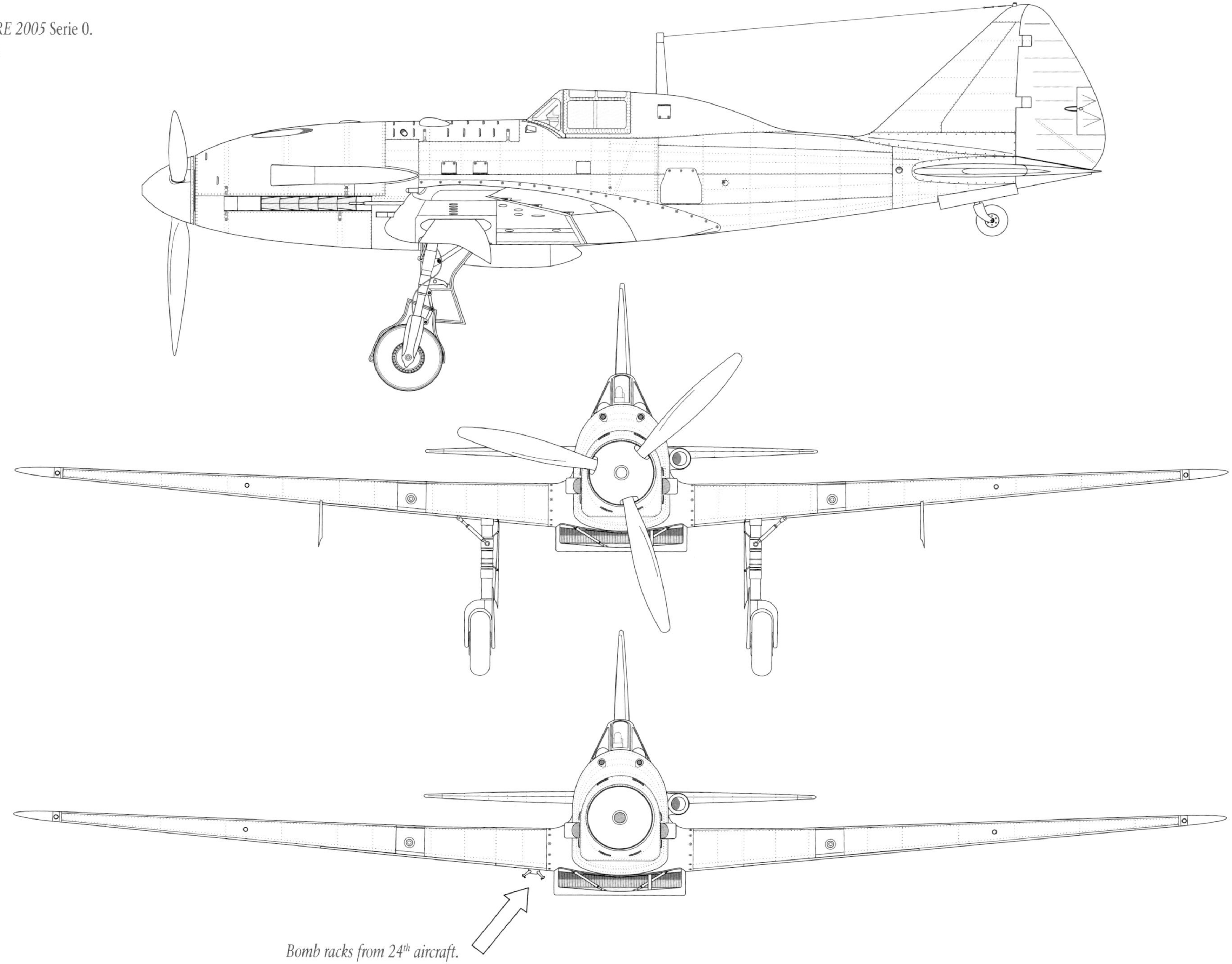

RE 2001 Recovery

Reggiane RE 2001 Serie 0 *serial number MM.08071, which was discovered in the late 1980s near Capo Ferrato (Sardinian Sea) by Giorgio Cao, a member and promoter of the* Gruppo Amici Velivoli Storici *(GAVS). Aircraft was recovered in late 1991 by G. Cao himself (he was tragically missing 2 months after recovery) and by GAVS through private funds and delivered to the Aeronautica Militare Italian (AMI). This aircraft was then entrusted to the Museo Storico Dell'Aeronautica Militare Italiana (Vigna di Valle). Over the years the renovation work was carried out by various institutions including: GAVS (Roma, Torino), Museo Storico Dell'Aeronautica Militare Italiana, 1° RMV Novara, 2° RMV Guidonia, 5° Capodichino, Riva Calzoni Bologna and Alfa Romeo Avio. To this day, the plane has not been included in a museum exhibition.*

This plane has very interesting story. It was tested at Reggio Emilia on 12 May 1941 and was attached to the 2° Gruppo Autonomo C.T. *After landing with retracted landing gear it was returned to Officine Reggiane for repairs. In the first months of 1943 aircraft stayed in Guidonia. It was equipped with two Cineavia cameras and was repainted yellow to participate in the movie "Primo Volo" by Istituto Nazionale Luce. Later in standard fighter configuration was repainted in camouflage and transferred to Sardinia to the 24°* Gruppo. *On 11 April 1943 with* Serg.M. *Giulio Zangheri at the controls aircraft crashed. Pilot was saved thanks to the intervention of a fishing boat.*

View of the plane after being recovered from the bottom of the Mediterranean Sea.

Fuselage with detached wings during washing.

The hull is being transported.

Elements of the plane after being transported to the museum in Vigna do Valle.

Structure of the fuselage.

Centre wing.

Structure of centre wing.

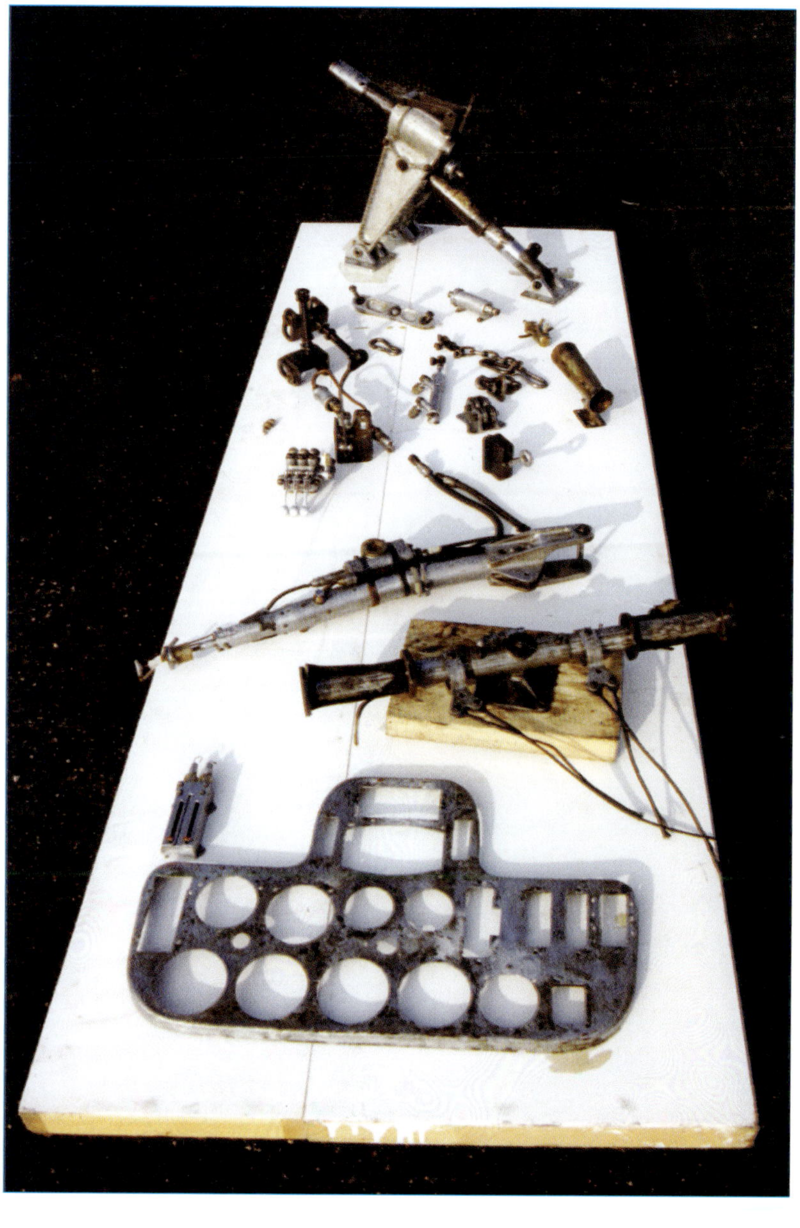

Elements of cockpit equipment. Note the control stick and instrument panel.

7.7 mm Breda-SAFTA machine guns located in the wings.

Ammunition box (12.7 mm machine gun). M.M. number still clear visible.

View of the ventral cover of the fuel tanks.

Exhaust pipe.

Lower part of engine cowling.

RE 2001 (M.M.08071) Restoration

Fragment of the rear section of the fuselage of RE 2001 (M.M.08071) during renovation.

Right and opposite page: *Restored fuselage fragments. Visible is the 12.7 mm Breda-SAFAT machine gun mounted in the fuselage.*

Pilot's seat.

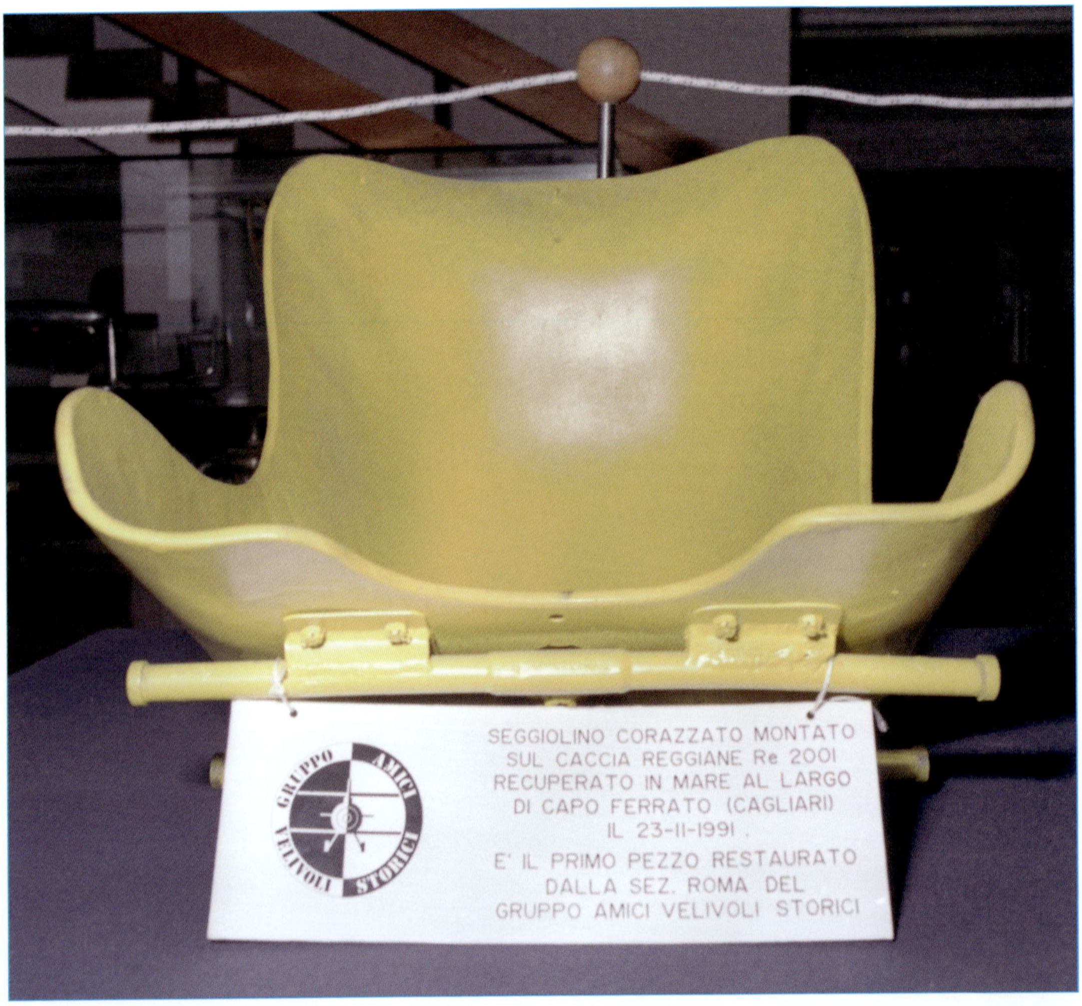

Front part of the fuselage with fire wall.

Fragment of the rear part of the fuselage.

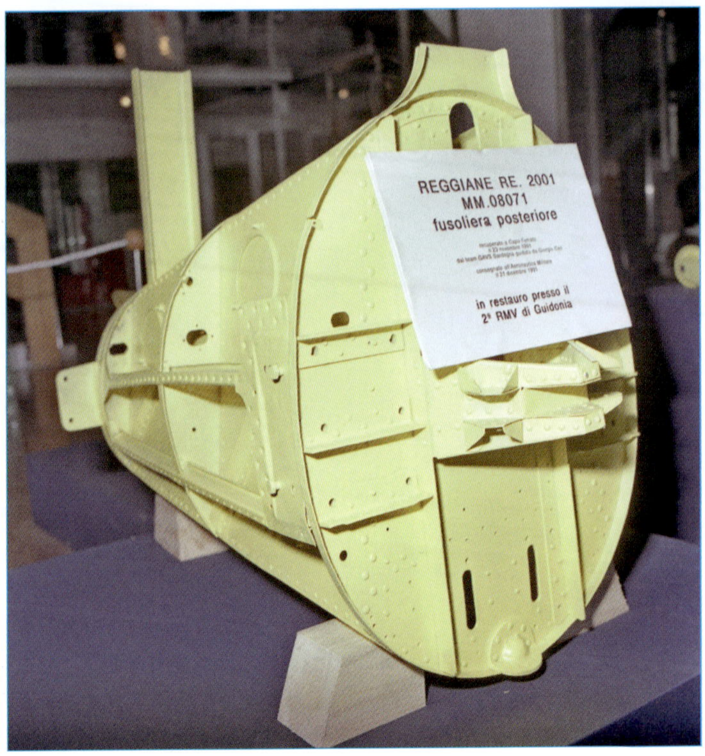

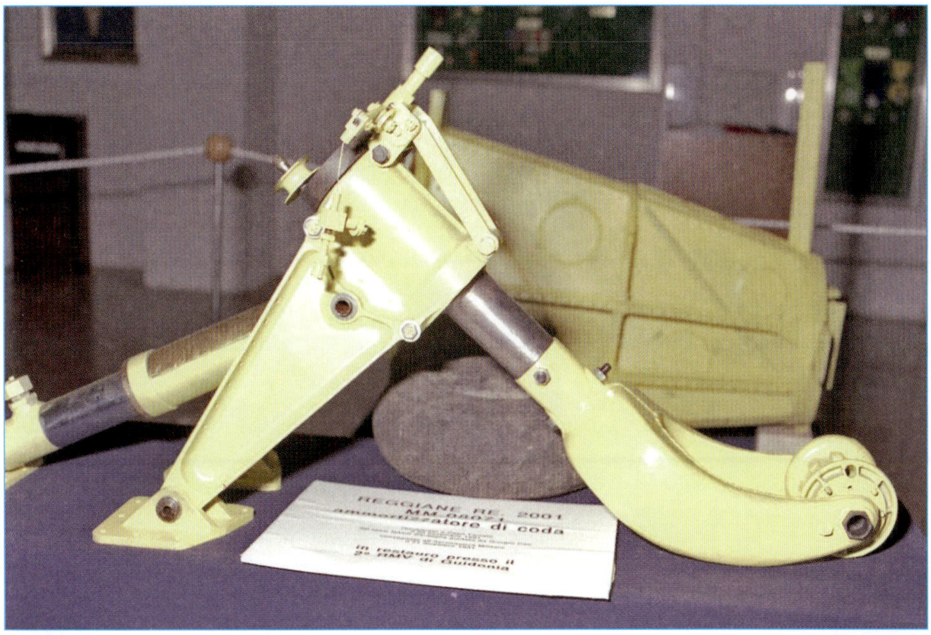

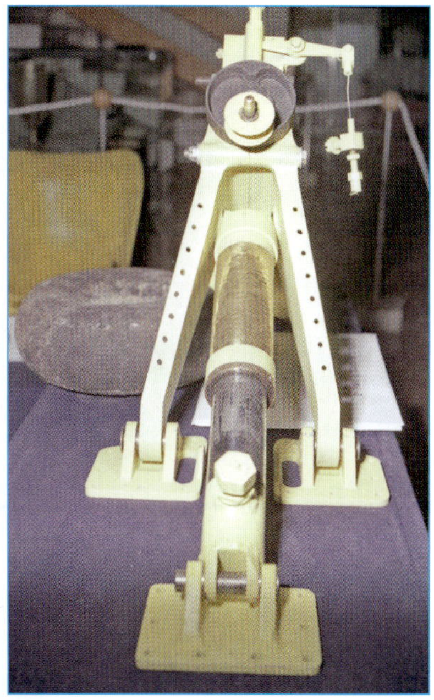

Above left and right: *Leg of the tail wheel.*

Reconstruction work on the fuselage.

Construction of the centre wing.

Alfa Romeo R.A. 1000 propeller and its details.

Leg of the main landing gear.

Rim of the main landing gear wheel.

The DB 601A engine – a power unit used in many RE 2001 Ariete *aircraft.*

DB 605A engine – the power unit of a few RE 2005. Most Sagittarios *had a licensed version of this engine installed, namely FIAT RA 1050 R.C. 58 I "Tifone".*

RE 2005 museum photos

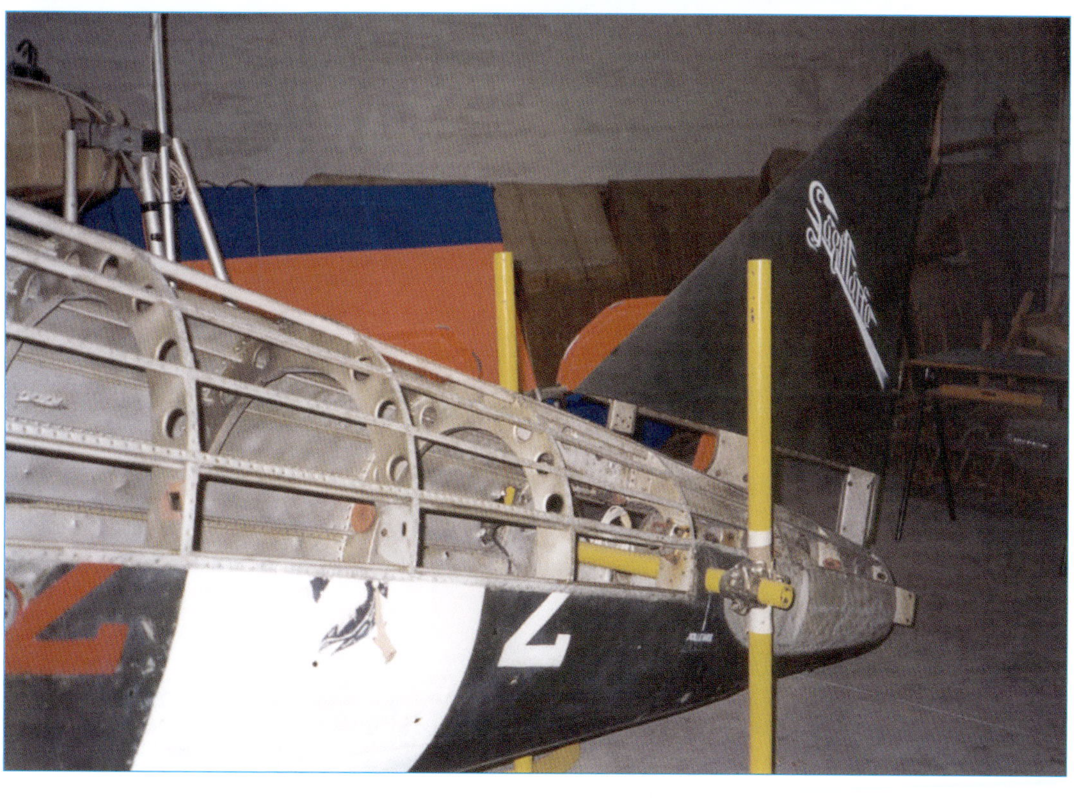

The only surviving fragment of the RE 2005 Sagittario *aircraft. It is the rear fuselage of the Serie I airplane with the number M.M.92351 and the tactical designation 362-2. This exhibit is displayed at the Museo dell'Aeronautica Gianni Caproni in Trento. (Museo Storico Dell'Aeronautica Militare Italiana)*

Details of the rear part of the fuselage - the structure of the construction is visible through the missing elements of the skin.

The rear part and details of the interior of the rear section of the fuselage.

Reggiane RE 2001, 2004, 2005, 2006 – technical data

	RE 2001	RE 2001 Delta	RE 2005 Serie 0	RE 2006*
Wingspan (m)	11.00	11.00	11.00	11.00
Length (m)	8.36	8.75	8.91	9.80
Height (m)	3.15	3.15	3.15	3.65
Wing area (m²)	20.40	20.40	20.40	20.40
Weight (kg)	2,460	2,195	2,600	2,960
Loaded weight (kg)	3,240	3,010	3,610	3,950
Engine	Alfa Romeo R.A. 1000 R.C. 41-I "Monsone"	Isotta Fraschini R.C. 16-48 "Detla"	FIAT R.A. 1050 R.C. 58-I "Tifone"	Daimler Benz DB 603
Output (hp)	1175	840	1475	1700
Propeller	Alfa Romeo R.A. 1000	Piaggio D'Ascanio P.1001	Piaggio P. 2001	VDM
Max speed (km/h)	545	480-490	628	750
Climb to 6000 m	6'30"	10'46"	5'30"	5'50"
Service ceiling (m)	11,000	10,500	12,000	12,000
Range (km)	1,150	1,100	1,250	1,100
Armament	2 x 7.62 mm 2 x 12.7 mm 250 kg bombs	2 x 12.7 mm 2 x 7.7 mm	2 x 12.7 mm 3 x 20 mm 640 kg bombs	2 x 12.7 mm 2 x 20 mm

* technical data for RE 2006 are estimated

Reggiane RE 2001, 2004, 2005, 2006 – production data

Version	Manufacturer	M.M. numbers	Quantity, notes
		RE 2001	
Reggiane RE 2001 first prototype	Reggiane	409	1, initially built as RE 2000 second prototype
Reggiane RE 2001 second prototype	Reggiane	408	1
Reggiane RE 2001 Serie 0	Reggiane	08071–08080	10, M.M.08071 transformed into photographic version, M.M.08075 became prototype of C.N version
Reggiane RE 2001 Serie I	Caproni Predappio	6547–6646	Planed 100, only 10 built as C.N. version (6547–6556)
Reggiane RE 2001 Serie II	Reggiane	7209–7408	Planned 200, only 100 built (7209–7308)
Reggiane 2001 Serie III	Reggiane	9921–9952	32, one aircraft (M.M.9921) built as RE 2001G prototype. According other data 30 aircraft only (M.M.9921–9950)
Reggiane 2001 Serie IV	Reggiane	90000–90049	50
Reggiane RE 2001 Serie V/VI	Reggiane	90751–90800	50 built, possibly initially 550 was planned
Reggiane RE 2001	Reggiane	92459–92518	60 in version O.R., not built
Reggiane RE 2001	Reggiane	98718–98777	60 in version O.R., not built
Reggiane RE 2001 Delta prototype	Caproni Taliedo	9920	1
RE 2001 Delta	Caproni Taliedo	90650–90749	100, order cancelled in December 1942
Reggiane RE 2001bis	Reggiane	538	1, possibly ex M.M.08072
		RE 2004	
RE 2004 first prototype	Reggiane	505	1
RE 2004 second prototype	Reggiane	506	1
RE 2004 Serie 0	Reggiane	09953-09964	Initially 12 aircraft ordered, later reduced to 4, finally order cancelled in December 1942
		RE 2005	
RE 2005 first prototype	Reggiane	494	1
RE 2005 second prototype	Reggiane	495	1
RE 2005 Serie 0	Reggiane	092343–092358	16, first order
RE 2005 Serie 0	Reggiane	096100–096117	18/13, second order
RE 2005 Serie I	Reggiane	092359–092458	Planned 100, no one built, according some sources one aircraft built (M.M.092359)
RE 2005 Serie II	Reggiane/CAB	095419–095918	Planned 500 aircraft – 300 built by Reggiane and 200 by Caproni Aeronautica Bergamasca (CAB), no one built
		RE 2006	
RE 2006 first prototype	Reggiane	540	1 built, but not tested in flight
RE 2006 second prototype	Reggiane	541	1 not built